Step by Step
Web Design

Alan Dillon

Gill & Macmillan

Gill & Macmillan Ltd
Hume Avenue
Park West
Dublin 12
with associated companies throughout the world
www.gillmacmillan.ie

© 2004 Alan Dillon

0 7171 3738 4

Print origination by Replika Press Pvt. Ltd., India.

The paper used in this book is made from the wood pulp of
managed forests. For every tree felled, at least one tree is
planted, thereby renewing natural resources.

LECTURERS!
SUPPORT MATERIAL

For your support material check our website at:

www.gillmacmillan.ie

Support material is available to lecturers only within a secure area of this website.
Support material for this book consists of solutions to assignments or tasks.
To access support material for *Step by Step Web Design:*

1. Go to www.gillmacmillan.ie
2. Click on the 'logon' button and enter your username and password.
   (If you do not already have a username and password you must register. To do
   this click the 'register' button and complete the online registration form. Your
   username and password will then be sent to you by email.)
3. Click on the link 'Support Material'.
4. Select the title *Step by Step Web Design*.

Contents

Section 1: Beginners Web Design Projects

Section 2: More Advanced Web Design Projects

Section 3: Web Design Project Guidelines

About This Book

The projects in this book were written for PCs using the Microsoft Windows operating system. You can do the projects using any version of Windows from Windows 95 on, although it is best if you are using Windows 2000 or Windows XP.

In this book you do not have to know about web design before you start because the projects begin at a very basic level. You learn through practice, with lots of practical web design projects. The book has three sections:

Section 1: Beginners Web Design Projects
Section 2: More Advanced Web Design Projects
Section 3: Web Design Project Guidelines

There are five practical web design projects, starting with simple ones. There is also a handy reference list of the HTML tags and toolbar buttons at the end of each web project. By working through all the projects in *Step by Step Web Design*, you learn how to create web sites by using a range of software tools. You also learn about adding multi-media content to web sites using a digital camera, scanner and microphone. The projects cover all the course material for the FETAC Level 2 Web Authoring Module.

In Section 1 of *Step by Step Web Design*, you learn how to create web pages using HyperText Markup Language (HTML). You write all the HTML code using Notepad, a program included in the Microsoft Windows operating system. When web designers are creating web pages, they often use Dreamweaver, a web design software package, to create most of the HTML code and then make any adjustments to the HTML code afterwards. You may be thinking 'What's the point of writing all the HTML code when Dreamweaver can do it for me?' Creating web pages by writing all the HTML code yourself is a very good way of learning HTML. If you do not go through this process, it is very difficult to edit HTML code or to understand someone else's HTML code.

In Section 2 of *Step by Step Web Design*, you learn how to create web pages using Dreamweaver but you will still write some HTML code. You find out how to format web pages using Cascading Style Sheets (CSS). Cascading Style Sheets offer great control over how elements in a web page are formatted. In Section 2 you also learn how to edit images and create basic web graphics using Paint Shop Pro. Section 3 contains guidelines for planning and completing your own web site.

The way that web pages are created is changing. A new language, XHTML, is gradually replacing HTML. Both languages are very similar, but XHTML is much more precise and has more powerful formatting capabilities. As there are millions of web pages already written in HTML and the change from HTML to XHTML will take time, it is important to learn and understand HTML. Often there is no difference between the HTML and XHTML code for the projects in this book. If there are any differences, this will be clearly explained.

Step by Step Web Design is not a definitive guide to HTML, but many of the commonly used HTML tags are included. You will learn about some of the powerful features of Dreamweaver and Paintshop Pro. After working on the projects in this book, you can experiment with other specialist web software to create and enhance a web site, such as like Macromedia Flash and Fireworks, Microsoft Frontpage and Adobe Photoshop.

The CD that comes with this book has content for creating web sites. For Web Projects 3, 4 and 5, there are completed web pages to copy. This will allow you to develop larger and more complex web sites, without spending a lot of time entering data yourself. There are also digital photographs and graphics to download, so you can practice putting them in web sites. For later projects you create your own digital photographs and graphics.

When you have completed the web projects in the book, you can check your work by logging onto www.gillmacmillan.ie.

Designing and creating a web site calls for many skills: programming, an eye for design and page layout as well as an understanding of colour, graphics, photography and sound. The aim of this book is introduce you to each of these skills.

In specialist web design companies, a team of experts with at least one programmer and one graphic designer works on each project. In smaller companies, often one person does all the work – from page layout and formatting to image creation and coding web pages with HTML. By completing all the projects in *Step by Step Web Design*, you will learn the skills to design a web site for a club, society or small company.

Getting Ready for Web Site Design

What Web Sites Can Do For You

A web site is a low-cost way of getting a message across to potentially millions of people. They all can view the web site, even though only one copy of it is stored on a server. This is much cheaper than printing huge quantities of books, magazines and newspapers and distributing them to customers.

It is hard to find a business that does not to have a web site. Most companies use web sites to advertise their products and services. E-commerce web sites, where products and services can be ordered online, are becoming more and more popular. Many larger companies have intranets, their own internal web sites, as a way of giving employees information.

Clubs and societies now have their own web sites, making information available to their members. More and more colleges use their web sites to attract new students. College web sites often include a student bulletin board where students can leave messages for each other. Lecture notes can also be downloaded. Distance learning has become much easier using web sites as a means of communication. In some cases, lectures may be broadcast by web cam live over the World Wide Web.

As technology improves, accessing web sites will become easier and faster. The broadband network will improve access time and revolutionise Internet access. Services available online will continue to grow in the future. The World Wide Web is changing the way we live and work.

The Software You Need

If you work with spreadsheets or databases, the chances are that you are using one software package exclusively. For example, when you design a spreadsheet with Excel, all the tools for that spreadsheet are included in the Excel software package. If you design a database application using Access, it is rare that you would have to use other software to add more features to your database.

A web site project is different because a well-designed web site requires a number of different skills. You will find yourself using more than one software package as you create a web site. There are many web-design software packages available, the most popular being Dreamweaver.

On its own, Dreamweaver is not enough to create a good web site. You will also need graphics software, such as Paint Shop Pro, to create and edit backgrounds and images as well as editing digital photographs. If your web site has sounds or music, you will need sound editing software. Most PC operating systems include basic sound recording software. Finally, to test your web site, you will need web browser software. The most popular web browsers are Internet Explorer and Netscape Navigator.

Software			
Browser software	Macromedia Dreamweaver	Jasc Paint Shop Pro	Windows 95, 98, 2000 or XP
Internet Explorer Netscape	Dreamweaver	Paint Shop Pro	

Fig. 1

The Hardware You Need

The great thing about web pages is that they allow you to get your message across to your audience using a combination of different media: text, graphics, photographs, video and audio. Creating and putting digital photographs and audio files in a web site requires specialist hardware: a digital camera and a microphone. More expensive digital cameras have a facility for creating digital video files.

A scanner is also a useful item to add to your collection of hardware. Scanners convert images that exist on paper into digital format so that these can be stored and displayed on a PC. If you do not have a digital camera but have access to a scanner, you can scan photographs to put on web pages.

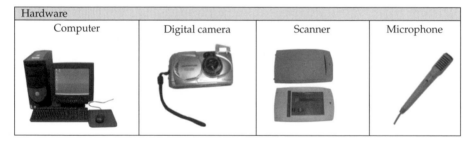

Hardware			
Computer	Digital camera	Scanner	Microphone

Fig. 2

About The Internet

The Internet is a network of computer networks – millions of computers that communicate with each other through telecommunications systems. Developed almost by accident, the Internet's roots lie in the Advanced Research Projects Agency Network (ARPANET), set up in the 1960s by the United States Department of Defense.

The Department of Defense was looking for a way to facilitate university research by linking computers from different universities in a network. What they developed was a system of networks that could work independently but which could also join together to form a bigger network. As this was the time of the Cold War, the idea was that the US could have a system that could keep lines of communication open even if part of it was destroyed.

As ARPANET grew, people began to see the potential of electronic communication. The number of computer networks greatly increased, and at the same time changes were taking place in computing. In 1981, IBM developed the first personal computer (PC). For the first time, computers were not used only by scientists and engineers. During the 1980s and the 1990s, the PC gradually developed from being a business tool to a household item. Today, most homes have a PC, and ARPANET has become the Internet.

Set up in 1992 as part of the Internet, the World Wide Web provides access to a collection of interlinked web pages stored on computers all over the world. Technically, it is called a graphical user interface (GUI). The World Wide Web sits on top of the Internet, something like the way that the Windows operating system on a PC is a GUI on top of the DOS operating system.

Because the World Wide Web has graphics, it is very easy to learn, understand and use. The World Wide Web makes it possible for millions of people to access the power of the Internet. Fig. 3 shows how the Internet is made up of communications hardware, communications protocols and services including email, WWW, File Transfer Protocol (FTP).

Web sites were able to develop quickly because the protocol that computers use to communicate over the Internet – the TCP/IP (Transmission Control Protocol/ Internet Protocol) – is freely available. Anyone can connect to the Internet and develop a web site as long as they have a computer, a modem and an Internet connection.

More and more companies have web sites to advertise their products and services. As the number of people buying PCs and having an Internet connection has grown, more of us 'shop' by viewing products on web sites and paying by credit card.

Not only has the Internet changed the way we do business, it has also changed the way we work. Teleworking, or working from home using a computer and a modem, is becoming more popular. With the increase in traffic congestion and commuting distances, it seems even more attractive.

Email has become almost essential for communications. Companies like Yahoo, Hotmail, and Eircom provide free email to attract people to their web site. Users access and send emails by logging onto the web site of the company providing the email service. If a lot of people log on, the email service provider can sell advertising space to other companies.

Since the development of the World Wide Web, the number of computers connected to the Internet has increased year by year. In 2002, there were approximately 604 million Internet users. Today, you can go online to do your grocery shopping, pay your bills or do your banking. Computers have become such a part of everyday life that not knowing how to use one is a major disadvantage.

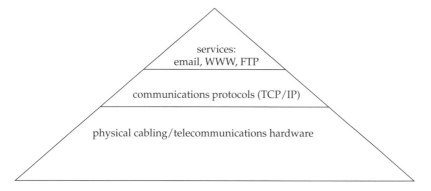

Fig. 3 The structure of the Internet

In the same way, as the Internet becomes more and more a part of the way we do business, the ability to access and use the Internet will become increasingly important.

What is a Web Page?

A web page is not like a printed page. Web pages are designed to appear on computer screens. They can contain a mixture of text, images, animated graphics, sound and video. A web page, unlike an A4 page, does not have a set length. A web page might be very short or you might have to do a lot of vertical scrolling to the end of the page.

Fig. 4   The Google home page viewed on a computer monitor

The web page for the search engine Google is displayed in Fig. 4. This web page does not have a lot of text and images, so the whole web page fits on one computer screen. The next example is the Yahoo web page, shown in Fig. 5.

This web page in Fig. 5 has lot more text and graphics, so you cannot see the whole web page on one computer screen. You would have to scroll down, using the vertical scroll bar, to get to the bottom of the web page.

This illustrates a very important point about web pages. Unlike a printed page, a web page does not have a fixed length. The more information put on the web page by the web page designer, the longer that web page is. Technically speaking, a web page can be as long as you want it to be. In practice, the longest web pages are no more than three or four screens long.

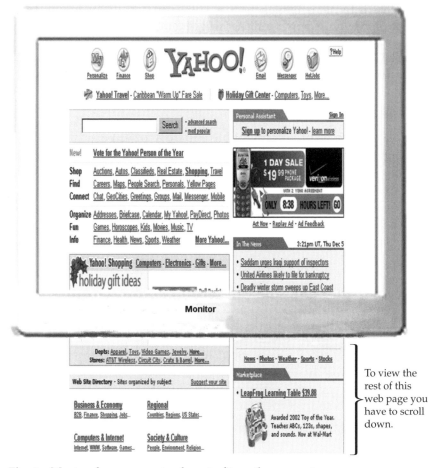

To view the rest of this web page you have to scroll down.

Fig. 5   Most web pages are too long to fit on the computer screen

Web pages are created using a language called HTML (HyperText Markup Language). HTML is a page-positioning language. Using HTML, the web page designer can specify where text and graphics are to be positioned on the web page. Most web pages are designed for viewing on a computer screen. The text and static image content of web pages can be printed. Obviously, animated graphics, sound and video cannot be re-created on a printed page.

The idea of a web page is to communicate information to someone. Companies all over the world advertise their products and services using web pages. Not all web pages are commercial. Web pages can be educational, with information about schools and colleges. Web pages can also be recreational, giving information for local clubs and sports. The list of subjects covered is endless. If you can think of a topic, the chances are there is a web page out there somewhere about it.

What is a Web Site?

A web site is a collection of web pages, all related to the same topic. For example, the Gill & Macmillan web site contains lots of web pages, all about books or publishing. Each web page in a web site is stored as a separate file. Moving from one web page to another is different from turning the pages in a book. A special type of link, called a hyperlink, is needed to move from one web page to another. Web pages are not necessarily viewed in the same order as the pages in a book. It is up to the person viewing the web site to choose the web page they want to see next.

Fig. 6 The pages in a book are normally read in sequential order, starting at the beginning.

Information in a book is normally read in sequential order, by starting at page 1, then reading page 2, followed by page 3 and so on until you reach the end of the book. Information in a web site can be read in any order. Five web pages from the Southern Estate Agents web site, which you will create in Project 3 of *Step by Step Web Design*, are shown Fig. 7.

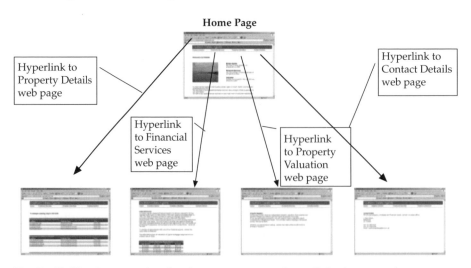

Fig. 7 Unlike the pages in a book, you can access hyperlinks in any order.

The home page is the page that appears first when someone accesses your web site. The home page of the Southern Estates web site has four hyperlinks. The person viewing a web page can access additional web pages in the site by clicking on the hyperlinks. The order of accessing the hyperlinks is completely up to the web page viewer.

The hyperlinks in Fig. 7 are called internal hyperlinks because each hyperlink brings you to another web page in the same web site. Hyperlinks can also be external. An external hyperlink is a link to a web page, normally the home page, in a different web site.

Fig. 8 Internal and external hyperlinks on the Yahoo home page

The Yahoo home page has lots of hyperlinks. Each item of underlined text is a hyperlink to another web page stored in the Yahoo web site.

Viewing Web Sites on the World Wide Web

We often take many electronic inventions for granted because we use them so often. Internet and web page technology has become so advanced that you can now create a web page on your own PC and make it available to millions of people around the world in less than an hour. Just think about that for a moment. It is a pretty mind-blowing fact!

With the advances in hardware and software, viewing web sites on the World Wide Web has become very easy. Most PCs are sold 'internet ready', meaning that they are already set up to view web pages on the World Wide Web.

To access web pages on the World Wide Web, you need:
- a PC with a modem and web browser software (e.g. Internet Explorer)
- a telephone connection
- an Internet service provider (ISP).

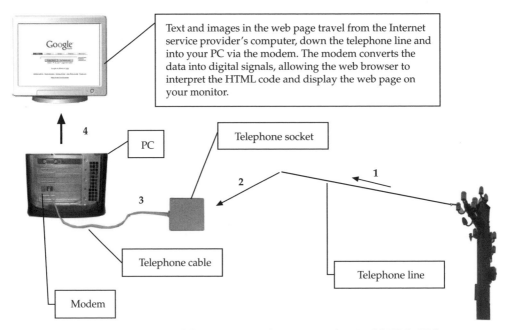

Text and images in the web page travel from the Internet service provider's computer, down the telephone line and into your PC via the modem. The modem converts the data into digital signals, allowing the web browser to interpret the HTML code and display the web page on your monitor.

Fig. 9 The technology you need for viewing web pages on the World Wide Web

When you connect to the Internet and view a web page, the web page that you see is not stored on your computer. It is either stored on a very powerful computer owned by an Internet service provider (ISP) or, in the case of many company web sites, on a company web server. When you view a web page on your home PC, it has been transmitted down the telephone line and converted into a digital image by your PC's modem. Web pages viewed on the World Wide Web can be downloaded from Internet service providers from almost every country in the world.

Perhaps you are asking what is an Internet service provider. ISPs provide a service that allows you to access web pages on the Internet by connecting your PC to their computer through the telephone system. If you develop your own web pages, you can pay an ISP an annual fee to store these web pages for you and to provide a web site address so that your web pages can be accessed on the World Wide Web.

Once the web page data has been sent down the phone line from the ISP and converted into digital signals by the modem, special web-browser software interprets the instructions that it finds in the HTML code and displays the web page on your PC's monitor. The two main web-browser software products on the market are Internet Explorer and Netscape Navigator. If you do not have a web browser installed on your PC, you will not be able to view web pages.

There has been fierce competition betweeen Internet Explorer and Netscape Navigator. In the early days of the World Wide Web, Netscape Navigator was the leading web browser. Just like any other software, you had to buy it. This changed when Microsoft included a web browser, Internet Explorer, in the Windows 95 operating system. Because nearly every new PC had Windows 95 installed when it was sold, Internet Explorer was free. From this point on, Netscape Navigator's share of the market fell drastically. Over 90 per cent of PCs accessing the Internet now use Internet Explorer.

Developing Your Own Web Site

Web sites are developed by creating individual web pages and storing them on your own PC. As individual web pages are created and linked together with hyperlinks, a web site is formed. At this point, only the web site developer can view the web pages. To make the web site accessible to others you need the services of a web hosting company. Your site goes 'live' on the World Wide Web once it is given a web site address and is stored on the web hosting company's server.

You would be forgiven for thinking that millions of euros worth of hardware and software is needed to do all of this. The good news is that surprisingly little investment is needed to create a working web site.

- **Hardware**
  As a minimum you will need a relatively fast PC with a modem. The more you work with graphics, the faster and more powerful your PC needs to be. To include digital images in a web site you will need a digital camera and/or scanner. If you want to include sound files on your web site, you will need a sound card, a microphone and speakers.

- **Software**
  Web pages can be created without buying any special software. However, you will save yourself a lot of time by having Dreamweaver MX, the most popular web design software package. To create your own graphics, you will need a graphics package such as Paint Shop Pro.

  You will also need Internet Explorer and Netscape Navigator to test your web pages. Internet Explorer is installed on most PCs but can also be downloaded from the Microsoft web site (www.microsoft.com). Netscape Navigator can be downloaded from the Netscape web site (www.netscape.com). Both of these web browsers are also widely available on CDs that are free with magazines such as *PC Live*.

  Finally, to make your web site 'live' on the World Wide Web, you will need File Transfer Protocol (FTP) software. FTP software allows you to copy web pages from your PC onto a remote server. FTP is included as part of Dreamweaver. Specialised FTP packages, such as FTP Pro and Cute FTP are also available.

- **Domain Name**
  Just as the address of your flat, apartment or house identifies the location of your home, a domain name identifies the location of your web site on the World Wide Web. Most people talk about a web site address, when referring to the domain name. For example, www.gillmacmillan.ie is the domain name of the Gill & McMillan web site. Expect to pay an annual fee of around €20 to €25 for a .com domain name. Domain names that end with .ie are more expensive. Once a domain name has been 'rented out', no one else can use that domain name as long as the rental period lasts.

- **Web Hosting Company**
  To make your web site live on the World Wide Web, the web pages must be stored on a server that is continuously connected to the Internet.

There are two types of web hosts:
- Web sites offering a 'free' hosting service
- Web sites that charge an annual fee.

If you choose a 'free' hosting service, your web site address will also include a reference to the hosting company. Advertisements will also appear on your web pages if you choose this method. For an annual fee of less than €100, you can have your own web site address with complete control over what appears on your web pages.

In the early days of the Internet, only people with technical training created web pages. At that time very few people owned PCs, and the software and hardware for making web page available on the Internet was very technical and complicated. Today, anyone with a little computing knowledge and the correct hardware and software can put a web page up on the World Wide Web.

These symbols are used in the book. In Section 2 of *Step by Step Web Design* you will be using a digital camera, microphone and scanner.

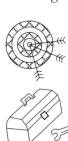 Project objectives

 Software and hardware to be used for the project

 Web design theory

 Use a PC

 Rule

 Tips and shortcuts

 Important points

 Use a digital camera

 Use a microphone

 Use a scanner

 Copy a file from the CD

 Completed web site model available on the Gill & Macmillan web site

Beginners Web Design Projects

Main Objective: Learn how to create basic HTML tags using Notepad

Web Project 1: Personal Web Site

Learning Objectives
- Create a web page
- Store web pages in a folder
- Write HTML code using Notepad
- Add text to a web page
- Add a title to a web page
- Centre text on a web page
- Display text in bold, italics and underline
- Create hyperlinks between web pages

Revision Exercises
- Wicklow Whitewater web site
- Progress Test 1

New in Web Project 1: <html>, <head>, <body>, <br/>, <title>, <b>, <u>, <i>, <a> and <p> HTML tags and mouse pointer

Web Project 2: Mike's Motors Web Site

Learning Objectives
- Plan the structure of a web site
- Develop a menu system using hyperlinks
- Create a horizontal rule
- Format text using heading styles
- Create a basic table
- Create a marquee
- Create a Return to Top bookmark

Revision Exercises
- Rugby World Cup web site
- Progress Test 2

New in Web Project 2: <hr/>, <h1>, <table>, <tr>, <td> and <marquee> HTML tags

Web Project 3: Southern Estate Agents

Learning Objectives
- Plan the structure of individual web pages
- Merge table cells
- Display text using a variety of font styles and colours
- Change the background colour of table cells
- Add comments to your HTML code
- Display images on a web page
- Display text in a bulleted list
- Create a mailto hyperlink

Revision Exercises
- Update Personal web site
- Update Mike's Motors web site
- Progress Test 3

New in Web Project 3: <img>, <font>, <ul> and <li> HTML tags

Web Project 1

Personal Web Site

Scenario

John Murphy lives in Achill, Co. Mayo, and is studying at University College Galway. He has just started to study Web Design and would like to set up his own web site. In Web Project 1 you will create a web site that describes where John lives and studies.

Project Objectives

By completing this web project, you will learn how to:
- Create a web page.
- Store web pages in a folder.
- Write HTML code using Notepad.
- Add text to a web page.
- Add a title to a web page.
- Centre text on a web page.
- Display web page text in bold, italics and underline.
- Create hyperlinks between web pages.

To complete John Murphy's personal web site, you need these software tools:

 Notepad

 Internet Explorer

What is a Folder?

 The first step in a web site project is to set up a folder with sub-folders to store all the files that will be used in the web site.

In the same way that a filing cabinet can be divided into drawers to make storing and retrieving files more efficient, folders can be created on a floppy disk, zip disk, hard disk or USB storage device. A folder is simply a part of the disk that has been named by the computer user.

Fig. 1.1 shows that creating four separate folders on disk is like a filing cabinet with four drawers.

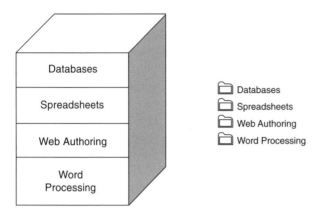

Fig. 1.1 Organising your files into folders is like using drawers in a filing cabinet

Just as a drawer can be divided into sections, a folder can be divided into sub-folders, see Fig. 1.2.

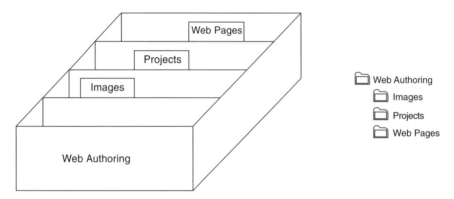

Fig. 1.2 Sub-folders are like individual sections inside each drawer

Creating Web Pages

A computer language called HTML, or HyperText Markup Language, controls the way in which text and graphics are arranged on a web page. The structure of every web page that can be accessed through the Internet is created with HTML. Even though every web page is created with HTML, you don't necessarily have to know HTML to design a web page. Web pages can also be created using specialist web authoring packages such as Macromedia Dreamweaver and Microsoft Frontpage. They look like a word processing package. As the web designer puts text and graphics on the page, the web-authoring package 'writes' the HTML in the background.

To summarise, there are two main methods of creating a web page with HTML.

- Write all the HTML code yourself, using a script editor such as Notepad.
- Use a web-authoring package, such as Macromedia Dreamweaver or Microsoft Frontpage, to generate the HTML code.

An experienced web designer will often use a combination of these two methods when creating web pages. Dreamweaver is used to quickly set up the basic layout of a web page. Direct HTML coding is used for adjustments and fine-tuning.

Starting with HTML

The main function of HTML is to position text and graphics on a web page. It does this using a series of commands, which are called tags. Each tag is enclosed in angular brackets < >.

Most HTML commands require an opening tag and a closing tag:

```
<html>
</html>
```

Every web page that can be viewed on the World Wide Web begins and ends with the HTML tag. Notice that the tag is written twice but the closing tag has a forward slash in front of it.

HTML can be written using a program called Notepad, which is part of the Windows operating system.

Structure of a Web Page

All web pages have the same structure. They are divided into two sections, called the head and the body. The body contains HTML code, which places text and graphics on a web page. The results of HTML code entered in the body can be seen by the web page viewer. The main function of HTML code entered in the Head section of a web page is to allow search engines, such as Google or Yahoo to find a web page. The results of HTML code in the Head section cannot be seen by the web page viewer. (There is one exception to this rule that will be introduced in this project.)

In each project in *Step by Step Web Design*, you will learn to create web pages by entering HTML code in the Body section of a web page. In Web Project 4, you will learn about the HTML code that is entered in the Head section.

Creating the Head section requires opening and closing head tags:

```
<head>
</head>
```

Similarly, the Body section must have opening and closing body tags:

```
<body>
</body>
```

HTML, head and body tags are combined to form the structure of a web page:

```
<html>

<head>
</head>

<body>
</body>

</html>
```

Every web page on the World Wide Web has this structure.

Create Your First Web Site

We will now create a folder to store John Murphy's web site. We will then create a web page and store it in the folder. Once the web page has been saved, it can be viewed in Internet Explorer

Create a Folder

1. Double click the My Computer icon on the Desktop.
My Computer
(If you have a special Windows theme installed, My Computer will be represented by a different icon to the one shown here.)

2. Select the drive where the folder will be created. You can create your folder on your computer's hard disk or on a removable storage device such as a floppy disk, zip disk or USB storage device. In Fig. 1.3, the USB storage device has been listed as a removable disk. If your computer is relatively new, it may not have a floppy disk drive.

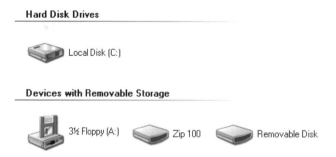

Fig. 1.3 Storage devices where web pages can be saved

3. johnmurphy   Create a new folder by clicking Make a New Folder, which is listed under File and Folder Tasks.
Type johnmurphy as the name for the new folder and press Enter.

Start Notepad

Start Notepad by selecting Start, followed by Programs or All Programs and select Accessories, followed by Notepad. (You can also start Notepad by selecting Start, followed by Run. Type Notepad and press Enter.)

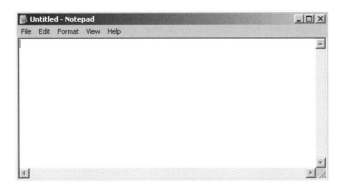

Fig. 1.4   A blank Notepad document

A new Notepad window appears. We will enter HTML tags in a Notepad document each time we create a web page. (In Web Projects 1, 2 and 3 we type all the HTML tags into a Notepad document. In Web Projects 4 and 5 we will use Dreamweaver, which will generate most of the HTML tags for us.)

For You To Do

Create the structure of your web page by typing the opening and closing HTML, head and body tags, as shown in Fig. 1.5.

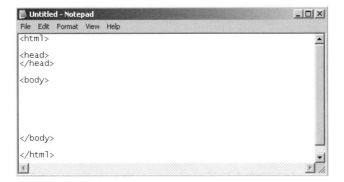

Fig. 1.5   The basic web page structure entered in Notepad

Rule: All HTML code must be written in lower case, not in capital letters.

Saving a Web Page

 To save a web page correctly you must:
- Specify the drive and the folder where the page will be stored.
- Enter the name of the web page.

All web pages stored in your PC must have an .htm file extension. When you enter the name of the web page you must add .htm after the name. For example, if you want to save a web page as **menu**, you should type menu.htm in the Save As dialog box.

 1. Save the web page by selecting File, followed by Save from the menu. The Save As dialog box is shown in Fig. 1.6.
2. Select the drive (hard drive, floppy drive, zip drive or USB drive) and then the **johnmurphy** folder.

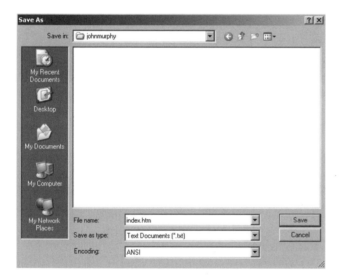

Fig. 1.6 Enter the web page name and the .htm extension in the Save As dialog box

3. Type index.htm as the name for the web page and click the Save button.
4. Close Notepad.

 Tip: If you don't enter the .htm file extension, you will not be able to view the web page in Internet Explorer.

Note:
- The first web pages that were made were stored on computers using the Unix operating system. In Unix all files have four-letter file extensions. Web pages had **.html** extensions, e.g. index.html. Because the Windows operating system uses three letters for the file extension, most web pages now use the three-letter **.htm** file extension. Note that web pages created on a Macintosh computer will have an **.html** extension. Both .html and .htm can be used as a file extension for a web page.
- The home page is the first page viewers see when they access your web site. The home page must be named either **index.htm** or **default.htm**. This causes it to load automatically as soon as your web site is accessed on the World Wide Web.

Naming a Web Page

Once your web site goes live on the World Wide Web, the web pages seen by visitors to your site are stored on your Internet service provider's computer and not on your own PC. Although everything may work well when you view your web pages on your own PC, there are rules about naming web pages that should be followed to make sure that there are no unexpected errors when you copy files from your own PC to your Internet service provider's computer.

Rules:
1. **All web page names must end with .htm or .html.**
   When you are uploading your web site to the World Wide Web, the company hosting your web site will tell you whether its server requires .htm or .html file extensions. Most servers now use .htm extensions, but there are some UNIX-based servers that use .html extensions.
2. **Do not include spaces in your web page names.**
   Instead of typing a space, use underscore or hyphen.
3. **Keep web page names relevant and short.**
   This makes it easier to create a link to a specific web page. Longer names increase the possibility of errors when creating links to web pages. Longer filenames also require more storage space and will be slower to download.
4. **If you choose to use capital letters in your web page names, be consistent.**
   This is because some Internet service providers (ISPs) computers are case sensitive. **Index.htm** and **index.htm** would be understood as completely different files. The safest method is to use lower case letters for all your web page names.
5. **Do not use special characters such as % or # in web page names. Use only letters and numbers, together with either the underscore or the hyphen.**

Viewing a Web Page in Internet Explorer

The easiest way to view a web page that you have created is by double clicking the icon for that web page in My Computer.

1. Double click the My Computer icon on the Desktop. (If you have a special Windows theme installed, My Computer will be represented by a different icon to the one shown.)
2. Select the drive where the web page is stored. If, for example, you have stored the web page on the hard drive, you should double click the icon for the hard drive.

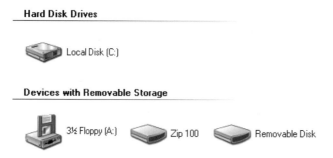

Fig. 1.7 Double click the drive where your web page is stored

3. johnmurphy Double click the **johnmurphy** folder to see the web pages stored there.
4. Each web page is represented by a blue Internet icon. Double click the Internet icon for the **index.htm** web page to view this page in Internet Explorer.

Internet Explorer starts and your web page, which is blank for the time being, is displayed.

C:\johnmurphy\index.htm – Microsoft Internet Explorer – [Working Offline]

Fig. 1.8 The title bar of Internet Explorer displays the web page name

Notice that the title bar (at the top of the Internet Explorer Window) has the name of the web page: C:\johnmurphy\index.htm, and that Internet Explorer is working offline, meaning that the web page is not 'live' on the World Wide Web. In Fig. 1.8, the web page is stored on the computer's hard disk.

Note: You can also open your web page directly in Internet Explorer like this:
1. Start Internet Explorer by clicking the blue Internet icon. When prompted, choose to work offline. (There is no need to connect to the Internet to view a web page stored on a local folder i.e. a folder stored in one of your PC' s drives.)
2. In Internet Explorer select File, followed by Open.
3. Click the Browse button, then double click My Computer.
4. Select the correct drive by double clicking the icon for the drive, then select **index.htm** from the **johnmurphy** folder.

Add Text to Your Web Page

1. With the **index.htm** web page displayed in Internet Explorer, select View, followed by Source from the menu.

    Notepad opens and displays the HTML code for the web page currently displayed in Internet Explorer.

2. Text that appears on a web page is entered in the Body section of a HTML document. Click in a blank line between the opening and closing body tags and type:

   ```
   Welcome To My Web Site
   My name is John Murphy
   ```

3. To view the changes to your web page, first save the HTML document. Select File, followed by Save.

4. Switch back to Internet Explorer by selecting Internet Explorer from the taskbar, as shown in Fig. 1.9.

Fig. 1.9   Use the taskbar to switch between Notepad and Internet Explorer

5. The changes that you made in Notepad will not be displayed in Internet Explorer until the web page is 'refreshed'.

6. Click the Refresh button to refresh the web page. Notice that all the text is on the same line (see Fig. 1.10).

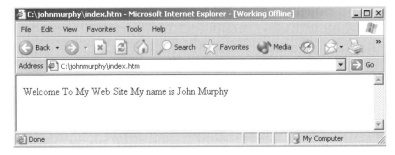

Fig. 1.10   Internet Explorer does not recognise that the Enter key was pressed in the HTML code

Tip: If you have more than one application running, you can switch between applications by holding down the ALT key and pressing the TAB key.

The Break Tag

 Pressing the Enter key in Notepad does not result in a new line being displayed in your web page. The break tag <br/> instructs Internet Explorer to go to the next line in a web page. Each <br /> tag is equivalent to pressing the Enter key once. The <br /> tag is one of the HTML tags that does not need a closing tag.

 Note: One of the rules of XHTML is that / (forward slash) must be included in tags that do not have a closing tag. For this reason, <br /> is used instead of <br> in XHTML. If you know some HTML, you will have used <br>.

Although the <br> tag works in the current versions of Internet Explorer and Netscape Navigator (Internet Explorer 6, Netscape Navigator 7.0), future versions may only recognise <br />.

 For You To Do

1. View the source of your web page and add a <br /> tag to the HTML code in the Body section so that it looks like this:

```
<body>
Welcome To My Web Site<br />
My name is John Murphy
</body>
```

 Note: When the source has been viewed once, the HTML code can be displayed by selecting Notepad in the taskbar (see Fig. 1.11.). If you view the source more than once, there will be multiple versions of the same HTML document open in Notepad, which can lead to errors.

Click here to view the HTML code.

Fig. 1.11 View the HTML code by selecting Index – Notepad in the taskbar

2. Save the changes to the HTML document by selecting File, followed by Save.

3. Switch to Internet Explorer and refresh the web page. The text is now displayed on two separate lines.

Tip: A web page can be refreshed by pressing the F5 key.

The Title Tag

 Title tags <title> are entered in the Head section of a HTML document. Normally, the results of HTML code entered in the Head section of a HTML document cannot be seen by the person viewing the page on the web. The <title> tag is the exception to this rule. Text entered between the opening and closing <title> tags appears in the title bar of Internet Explorer.

 For You To Do

1. Display the HTML code of your web page and edit the HTML code in the Head section so that it looks like this:

```
<head>
<title>
John Murphy's home page
</title>
</head>
```

2. 💾 Save the HTML document.

3. 🅔 Switch to Internet Explorer and refresh the web page. Text entered between the opening and closing <title> tags appears in the title bar of the Internet Explorer window, as in Fig. 1.12.

John Murphy's homepage - Microsoft Internet Explorer - [Working Offline]

Fig. 1.12 John Murphy's home page has replaced C:\johnmurphy\index.htm

NOTE **Note:** The web page title and the web page's file name are not the same thing. The title is a short description typed between opening and closing <title> tags in the Head section of the HTML code. It appears in the title bar when the web page is viewed in Internet Explorer. The file name is the name that you gave the web page the first time you saved it. If Internet Explorer does not find <title> </title> tags in the Head section of the HTML code, it will show the file name in the title bar.

 For You To Do

1. Edit the HTML code so that the web page appears as:

Welcome To My Web Site
My name is John Murphy

Where I Live

Slievemore View
Achill Sound
Co. Mayo

Achill is an island off the west coast of Ireland. It is the largest offshore island in Ireland but is connected to the mainland by a bridge. Achill is world famous for its beautiful scenery. If you are into the outdoors, this is the place for you! Keel Beach is a great place to go surfing, with huge waves rolling in from the Atlantic. Slievemore and Croaghan are two of the highest mountains in Mayo and are a challenging day's hillwalking. The cliffs of Achill Head are the highest cliffs in Europe. Achill has some great pubs, with traditional sessions every weekend.

Where I Study

I am in the second year of a four-year Business Studies degree in University College Galway. We study lots of different subjects, such as Accounting, Law and Psychology. The area I am most interested in is Information Technology and I hope to specialise in E-Commerce. I share a house with three other lads from Galway, who are great craic. It's hard to get any study done because they are always dragging me out to the pub!

My Hobbies

I like listening to music and going to concerts. My favourite bands are Coldplay and Badly Drawn Boy. There's a great live music scene in Galway and you can catch a live band practically every night of the week. Unfortunately, I can't afford to do that! I love to go surfing when I'm back in Achill and during the summer, I work as a lifeguard on Keel Beach. The rest of my time is taken up with studying. Study! Study! Study! I'm sure it will be worth it some day!

2. Allow the text to wrap naturally. It will not necessarily wrap as the text here wraps.
3. Use <br /> tags to insert blank lines in the web page.
4. View the changes you have made to the web page in Internet Explorer. The completed web page should look something like Fig. 1.13. (Remember: The text will not necessarily wrap as shown.)

 Tip: Spacing out your HTML code by including blank lines in Notepad makes it easier to read and understand.

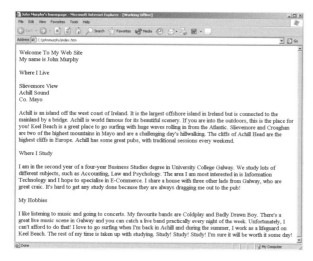

Fig. 1.13   The completed **index.htm** web page

Formatting Text in a Web Page

There are many ways that text can be formatted in a web page. We will start by learning how to make text bold, underline text and display text in italics.

Emphasising Text in Bold

Tag Name	Bold
HTML Code	<b> </b>
Effect	Text enclosed in <b> </b> tags is displayed in bold print in Internet Explorer.

Example:

HTML Code in Notepad	Result in Internet Explorer
`<b>Welcome To My Web Site</b>` `My name is John Murphy`	**Welcome To My Web Site** My name is John Murphy

Underlining Text

Tag Name	Underline
HTML Code	<u> </u>
Effect	Text enclosed in <u> <u/> tags is underlined when displayed in Internet Explorer.

Example:

HTML Code in Notepad	Result in Internet Explorer
`<u>Achill</u> is an island off the west coast of Ireland.`	<u>Achill</u> is an island off the west coast of Ireland.

Text in Italics

Tag Name	Italics
HTML Code	`<i> </i>`
Effect	Text enclosed in `<i>` `<i/>` tags is displayed in italics in Internet Explorer.

Example:

HTML Code in Notepad	Result in Internet Explorer
`<i>Slievemore</i> and <i>Croaghan</i> are two of the highest mountains in Mayo.`	*Slievemore* and *Croaghan* are two of the highest mountains in Mayo.

 For You To Do

1. 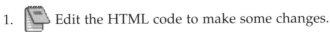 Edit the HTML code to make some changes.
2. Put the headings Welcome To My Web Site, Where I Live, Where I Study and My Hobbies in bold.
3. Put John Murphy's name in bold.
4. Underline Achill every time it appears, except in Achill Head and Achill Sound.
5. In the Where I Live paragraph, put Slievemore, Croaghan and Achill Head in italics.
6. In the Where I Study paragraph, put University College Galway in italics.
7. In the My Hobbies paragraph, put Coldplay and Badly Drawn Boy in italics.
8. Check your changes by refreshing the web page in Internet Explorer.

Tip: When you are editing the HTML for a web page, it is best to make changes to the HTML code one or two at a time. Check each change you make to the HTML code by saving the page, then refreshing it in Internet Explorer. It is much easier to find errors in your HTML code, if you edit and refresh in stages.

Add More Web Pages to the Web Site

A 'web site' gets its name from the fact that it consists of web pages that are interlinked, just like a spider's web. All web pages in the web site should be stored in the same folder. (In large corporate web sites with hundreds of web pages, the pages are usually stored in many folders.)

In this exercise, we add two web pages to John Murphy's web site. Each additional web page will be created using Notepad. It is important to save these new web pages in the **johnmurphy** folder.

Create the Mayo Page

1. 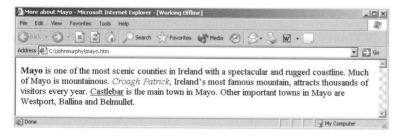 In Notepad, select File, followed by New and add opening and closing <html>, <head> and <body> tags to the new Notepad file.

2. 💾 Save this file as **mayo.htm** in the **johnmurphy** folder.

3. Add HTML code so that the web page appears as:

> **Mayo** is one of the most scenic counties in Ireland with a spectacular and rugged coastline. Much of Mayo is mountainous. *Croagh Patrick*, Ireland's most famous mountain, attracts thousands of visitors every year. <u>Castlebar</u> is the main town in Mayo. Other important towns in Mayo are Westport, Ballina and Belmullet.

Remember:
- Put text in bold, italics and underline as shown.
- Add <title></title> tags to the Head section so that the text More about Mayo appears in the title bar of the Internet Explorer window when the web page is previewed.
- 💾 🅔 Save the changes to **mayo.htm** and view the web page in Internet Explorer. The completed web page should look something like Fig. 1.14.

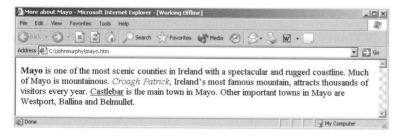

Fig. 1.14 The completed **mayo.htm** web page

 Note: Allow the text to wrap naturally. It will not necessarily wrap as shown in Fig. 1.14.

Create the Galway Page

1. In Notepad, create a new file by selecting File, followed by New.

2. 💾 Save the HTML document as **galway.htm** in the johnmurphy folder.

3. Add opening and closing <html>, <head> and <body> tags and add HTML code so that the web page appears as:

> **Galway** is one of the liveliest cities in Ireland and is famous for its arts and culture. It has many famous pubs and restaurants and was once the wine capital of Ireland. The world-renowned *Galway International Oyster Festival* takes place in Galway City every September.

Remember:
- Put text in bold and italics as shown above.
- Add <title></title> tags to the Head section so that the text More about Galway appears in the title bar of the Internet Explorer window when the web page is previewed.

- 💾 🅴 Save the changes to **galway.htm** and view the web page in Internet Explorer. The completed **galway.htm** page should look something like Fig. 1.15.

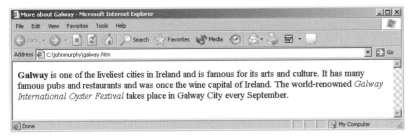

Fig. 1.15 The completed **galway.htm** web page

Hyperlinks

Hyperlinks make web sites on the World Wide Web much more interesting and fun to use by allowing you to 'jump' from one web page to another, or from one web site to another. Many web sites on the World Wide Web have hyperlinks to other related sites. You may often find yourself surfing the web for some information and ending up in a completely unrelated web site, simply by following hyperlinks that look interesting.

A hyperlink can be a word or a phrase, a button, an image or part of an image. When the mouse pointer is positioned over the hyperlink text, button or image, it changes to a pointing hand. Clicking the hyperlink brings up in a different web page on screen.

There are four main ways of displaying a hyperlink.

Text Hyperlink

A particular word or phrase displayed on a web page is used as a 'link' to another web page. When the web page viewer clicks the hyperlink text, the target web page is displayed in Internet Explorer. The usual style for hyperlink text is underlined.

Example:

 **Return to Homepage**

Clicking the underlined text with the pointing-hand mouse pointer makes Internet Explorer display a different web page, in this case the home page. Internet Explorer displays hyperlink text in blue, but this can be changed by the web page designer.

Button Hyperlink

An image of a button is used as a link to another web page. This method is normally used to create a navigation menu made up of buttons, usually displayed on the left hand side or across the top of a web page.

Example:

Clicking the button with the pointing-hand mouse pointer makes Internet Explorer display the home page.

Image Hyperlink

An image is used as a link to another web page. The image usually symbolises the other web page in some way. For example, an image of a house could be used as a hyperlink to the home page. An image of a mailbox could be used as a link to a Contact Us page.

Example:

Clicking the house image with the pointing-hand mouse pointer causes Internet Explorer to display the home page.

Hotspot Hyperlink

This is where a single image is divided into clickable areas, each area being a hyperlink to another web page. The clickable areas are called hotspots. Using hotspots, we can create multiple hyperlinks from a single image. A common example of this where a single image of a map of Ireland contains 32 hotspot hyperlinks (one for each county in Ireland).

 Note: Button and Image hyperlinks will be covered in Web Project 4.

Creating a Hyperlink

The anchor tag is used to create a hyperlink from one web page to another. The hyperlink text, button or image is enclosed in <a></a> tags. The opening anchor tag also includes the hypertext reference to the target web page.

Tag Name	Anchor
HTML Code	`<a href="name of target web page"> </a>`
Effect	The text, button or image enclosed in anchor tags becomes a hyperlink to the target web page, which will be displayed when the text, button or image is selected with the mouse.

Example:

HTML Code in Notepad	Result in Internet Explorer

`<a href="mayo.htm">`
`Find out more about Mayo`
`</a>`
	'Find out more about Mayo' is underlined and displayed in blue. The mouse pointer changes to a pointing hand when placed over this text. Clicking this text displays the **mayo.htm** web page.

 Tip: Storing all your web pages in one folder means that you do not have to refer to the folder name in the opening anchor tag. In larger web sites the web pages will be stored in a number of folders to make managing the web site easier.

 Note:
- Because Internet Explorer displays hyperlink text as underlined, use the underline tag with care to avoid any confusion between hyperlink text and text that is underlined for emphasis.
- Pressing the Enter key in Notepad does not move the cursor to a new line in Internet Explorer.

Example:

`<a href="mayo.htm">Find out more about Mayo</a>`

`has exactly the same effect as:`

`<a href="mayo.htm">`
`Find out more about Mayo`
`</a>`

 Create a Text Hyperlink

1. Open **index.htm** in Notepad and add the text `Find out more about Mayo` in between the Where I Live and Where I Study paragraphs. Use `<br />` tags to create blank lines, as shown.

Achill has some great pubs, with traditional sessions every weekend.

Find out more about Mayo

Where I study

2. Edit the HTML code so that it appears as:

```
<a href="mayo.htm">
Find out more about Mayo
</a>
```

3. ▣ 🅔 Save the changes to **index.htm** and then refresh the web page in Internet Explorer. Find out more about Mayo appears in blue underlined text. When the mouse pointer is positioned over this text, it changes to a pointing hand.
4. Test the Find out more about Mayo hyperlink in Internet Explorer. Once clicked, the **mayo.htm** web page should be displayed.

 Create a Return to Homepage Text Hyperlink

🔙 Back   At the moment, the only way of getting back to the index page from the Mayo page is by clicking the Back button in the Internet Explorer toolbar. In a well-designed web site, the web site visitor should always be able to get back to a previously viewed web page by using a hyperlink.

1. 🅔 In Internet Explorer, display the **mayo.htm** page if it is not already displayed.
2. View the Source of the web page.
3. Use <br /> tags to add a blank line at the end of the web page.
4. 📝 Add the text Return to Homepage, as shown below.

Other important towns in Mayo are Westport, Ballina and Belmullet.

Return to Homepage

5. Using anchor tags, set up this text as a hyperlink to **index.htm.**
6. 🅔 Test the Return to Homepage hyperlink in Internet Explorer.

For You To Do

1. In **index.htm,** add the text Find out more about Galway after the Where I Study paragraph and before the My Hobbies heading.

2. Edit the HTML code so that Find out more about Galway is a hyperlink to **galway.htm.**

3. In the **galway.htm** web page, type Return to Homepage and set this up as a hyperlink to **index.htm.**

4. Test all hyperlinks in Internet Explorer.

Centre Text in a Web Page

To centre text in a web page, first separate off that text by enclosing the text in paragraph tags. The text can then be centred by adding the align="center" attribute to the opening paragraph tag.

An attribute is an additional piece of HTML code that can be added to an opening tag. Adding attributes to a tag usually makes the job of the tag more specific. For a paragraph tag, adding the align attribute instructs HTML to create a paragraph and position it in a certain place on the web page.

Tag Name	Paragraph
HTML Code	`<p> </p>`
Attributes	`align="center" or align="right"`
Effect	Text enclosed in paragraph tags can be treated as one unit separate from other text on the page, for alignment and formatting purposes.

Example:

HTML Code in Notepad	Result in Internet Explorer
`<p align="center">` `<b>Welcome To My Web Site</b> ` `My name is <b>John Murphy</b>` `</p>`	Welcome To My Web Site My name is John Murphy is identified as a paragraph. The align="center" attribute causes all text between the opening and closing paragraph tags to be centred on the web page.

Tip: The `<p>` tag adds a line of space after each paragraph. If you want to start a new paragraph without inserting a blank line, use the `<br/>` tag instead.

Note: 'Center' is spelled the American way. Typing 'centre' in HTML causes an error.

 For You To Do

1. In **index.htm** use paragraph tags to centre the text `Welcome To My Web Site` and `My name is John Murphy.`
2. In **mayo.htm** and **galway.htm,** centre the text `Return to Homepage.`
3. Check your changes by viewing all web pages in Internet Explorer.

Revision Exercise

1. Create a new folder named **whitewater** on a floppy disk, zip disk, USB storage device or hard disk.

2. Create a new web page in Notepad. Save this web page as **index.htm** in the **whitewater** folder.
3. Using HTML tags, make the web page title Find out about Wicklow's mountain rivers.
4. Using HTML code, set up the **index.htm** web page so that it looks like Fig. 1.16. (Allow the text to wrap naturally. It will not necessarily wrap in the same positions as Fig. 1.16.)

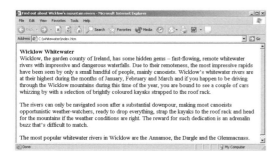

Fig. 1.16 The completed **index.htm** web page

5. Create a second web page in Notepad. Save this web page as **annamoe.htm** in the **whitewater** folder.
6. Using HTML tags, make the web page title Annamoe Whitewater.

7. Using HTML code, set up the **annamoe.htm** web page so that it looks like Fig. 1.17. Display the main heading in bold print. Allow the text to wrap naturally.

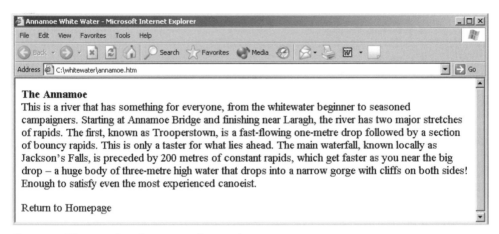

Fig. 1.17 The completed **annamoe.htm** web page

8. Create a third web page in Notepad. Save this web page as **dargle.htm** in the **whitewater** folder.
9. Using HTML tags, make the web page title Dargle Whitewater.
10. Using HTML code, set up the **dargle.htm** web page so that it looks like Fig. 1.18. Display the main heading in bold. Allow the text to wrap naturally.

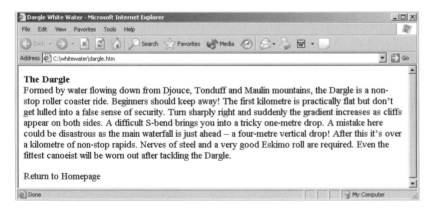

Fig. 1.18 The completed **dargle.htm** web page

11. Create a fourth web page in Notepad. Save this web page as **glen.htm** in the **whitewater** folder.
12. Using HTML tags, make the web page title Glenmacnass Whitewater.
13. Using HTML code, set up the **glen.htm** web page so that it looks like Fig. 1.19. Display the main heading in bold. Allow the text to wrap naturally.

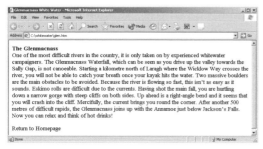

Fig. 1.19   The completed **glen.htm** web page

14. 📄 index.htm Using HTML tags, set up hyperlinks in the **index.htm** page as in Table 1.1.

Table 1.1

Text	Hyperlink to:
Annamoe	annamoe.htm
Dargle	dargle.htm
Glenmacnass	glen.htm

15. 📄 annamoe.htm In the **annamoe.htm** web page, set up the text Return to Homepage as a hyperlink to **index.htm.**

16. 📄 dargle.htm In the same way, create hyperlinks from the **dargle.htm** and **glen.htm**
    📄 glen.htm   web pages back to **index.htm.**

17. 🖥 Open **index.htm** in Internet Explorer. Test all the hyperlinks.

Progress Test 1

Finish the review of Web Project 1 by answering these questions.

1. What does the acronym HTML stand for?
   _____

2. Every HTML web page has two main sections. What are these sections called?

   a. _____
   b. _____

3. What file extension is normally given to web pages created using a PC with a Microsoft Windows operating system?
   _____

4. What name should you give to the home page of your web site?
    _____

5. Text that appears on the web page should be entered in the _____ section of the HTML code.

6. To see the HTML code of any web page, select _____, followed by _____ in Internet Explorer.

7. List three important points to remember when naming web pages.

    a. _____
    b. _____
    c. _____

8. Text enclosed in <title> </title> tags appears:

    a. On the web page.
    b. In the status bar of Internet Explorer.
    c. In the address bar of Internet Explorer.
    d. In the title bar of Internet Explorer.

9. When you make changes to your HTML code, these changes will not appear on the web page until you:

    a. _____
    and
    b. _____

10. Which HTML tag is equivalent to pressing the Return or Enter key on the keyboard?
    _____

11. Identify the error in this HTML code:

    ```
    <b>Bold Tag
    <br /><br />
    The bold tag is used to display text in heavy print.
    ```

12. Text or images which you click to take you to another web page are called:
    _____

13. Identify the errors in this HTML code:

    ```
    <a href=index.htm>Return to Homepage<a>
    ```

14. When you view a web page in Internet Explorer, what makes hyperlink text look different from other text on the web page?
    _____

15. Text can be centred on a web page by enclosing the text in _____ tags and adding the align="_____" attribute to the opening _____ tag.

Check Your Work

 To see the completed version of John Murphy's web site, the Whitewater web site and the answers to Progress Test 1, log on to **www.gillmacmillan.ie.**

New in Web Project 1

HTML Tags

Tag Name	HTML Code	Description
HTML	`<html></html>`	Every web page begins with an opening HTML tag and ends with a closing HTML tag.
Head	`<head></head>`	The Head section of a HTML document contains the page title.
Body	`<body></body>`	The Body section of a HTML document contains text that appears on the web page when it is viewed in Internet Explorer.
Break	` `	The tag instructs Internet Explorer to go to a new line in a web page. Each tag is equivalent to pressing the Enter key once.
Title	`<title></title>`	Text entered between the opening and closing <title> tags appears in the title bar of the Internet Explorer window. <title> tags are added to the Head section of a HTML document.
Bold	`<b></b>`	Text enclosed in <b> </b> tags is displayed in bold print in Internet Explorer.
Underline	`<u></u>`	Text enclosed in <u> </u> tags is underlined when displayed in Internet Explorer.
Italics	`<i></i>`	Text enclosed in <i> </i> tags is displayed in italics in Internet Explorer.
Anchor	`<a href=" "></a>`	The anchor tag is used to create a hyperlink between two web pages. The opening anchor tag contains the hypertext reference to the target web page. Text enclosed in the opening and closing anchor tags becomes a hyperlink.
Paragraph	`<p></p>`	For aligning and formatting, text enclosed in paragraph tags can be treated as one unit separate from other text on the page.

Toolbar Buttons

Refresh button When you edit the HTML code of a web page currently open in Internet Explorer, click the Refresh button to see the effect of the changes to the HTML code.

Back button Internet Explorer remembers all the web pages you have viewed in a session. Clicking the Back button shows the web page that was viewed before the web page being displayed now. Keep clicking the Back button to display all the web pages that you viewed in the session.

Mouse Pointer When the mouse pointer changes to a pointing hand, it shows that you are pointing at a hyperlink. Clicking the left mouse button will tell Internet Explorer to display a different web page.

Web Project 2

Mike's Motors Web Site

Scenario

Mike Grogan sells second-hand cars, bikes and vans. Over the last year he has noticed that a lot of his customers have asked him to email them details of cars, bikes and vans on offer. He finds it very time-consuming to send so many emails. In this project you will set up a web site to advertise the cars, bikes and vans that Mike has on offer. Once the web site has been created, Mike's customers can access the information they need from the web site and Mike will not have to send so many emails.

Learning Objectives

By completing this web project, you will learn how to:
- Develop a menu system using hyperlinks.
- Create a horizontal rule.
- Format text using heading styles.
- Create a basic table.
- Create a marquee.
- Create a Return to Top bookmark.

To complete the Mike's Motors web site, you need these software tools:

 Notepad

 Internet Explorer

Planning a Web Site

 The secret of a good web site is planning. A little time spent on planning can save lots of hassle and heartbreak later on. It always takes less time to plan than to correct an error caused by lack of planning.

A useful technique is to draw a diagram of how all the pages in your web site are linked, using a 'family tree', or hierarchical structure. Look at the structure of Mike's Motors web site in Fig. 2.1.

Four web pages will be accessible from the home page (index.htm). We will use hyperlinks to link each web page to the home page.

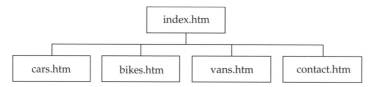

Fig. 2.1   The structure of Mike's Motors web site

Create the Home Page

Now you know how many pages are in Mike's Motors web site, you can create the individual web pages and store them in a folder. Because all the web pages, except for the Contact page, have the same structure, the easiest way to do this is first to create the home page and make a copy of it.

1. Create a new folder named **mikesmotors** on a floppy disk, zip disk, USB storage device or hard disk.

2. Start Notepad. In a blank Notepad document set up a web page by entering opening and closing <html>, <head> and <body> tags.

3. Enter <title> tags in the Head section so that the text `Welcome to Mike's Motors Web Site` appears in the title bar of Internet Explorer. Save this page as **index.htm** in the **mikesmotors** folder.

4. Rather than typing the <html>, <head>, <body> and <title> tags for all the other web pages in the web site, you can save the structure of the **index.htm** page using different file names. (This is one of the benefits of planning.)

5. With **index.htm** open in Notepad, select File, followed by Save As from the menu. Enter **cars.htm** as the file name and click Save. Edit the text in the <title> tags so that it reads `Current Selection of Cars on Offer` and then select File, followed by Save from the menu.

6. To set up the **bikes.htm** web page, first make sure that **cars.htm** is open in Notepad. Now select File, followed by Save As from the menu. Enter **bikes.htm** as the file name and click Save. Edit the text in the <title> tags so that it reads `Current Selection of Bikes on Offer` and then select File, followed by Save from the menu.

7. Set up the **vans.htm** web page and **contact.htm** web page in the same way, using this information.

Table 2.1   Page titles for the vans.htm and contact.htm web pages

Page Name	Page Title
vans.htm	Current Selection of Vans on Offer
contact.htm	Contact Details

Create the Navigation Menu System

The navigation system is used to access the Cars, Bikes and Vans pages. It appears on the home page - **index.htm -** for the Mike's Motors web site (see Fig. 2.2).

Mike's Motors

Cars | Bikes | Vans

Fig. 2.2 Hyperlinks in the home page navigation menu

Cars, Bikes and Vans are underlined to show that each of these words is a hyperlink to another web page.

For You To Do

 1. Open **index.htm** in Notepad and enter HTML code so that the web page appears as in Fig. 2.2
2. Use the paragraph tag together with the align attribute to centre all of the text.
3. Put the heading in bold.
4. Use anchor tags to create hyperlinks to **cars.htm, bikes.htm** and **vans.htm.**
5. Test the hyperlinks in Internet Explorer.

 Tip: You can use the Back button in Internet Explorer to return to the Home page after you click a hyperlink.

 Note: The vertical lines separating Cars, Bikes and Vans are called pipe symbols. To type a pipe symbol, hold down the shift key, then press the backslash key, which is to the left of the letter Z.

Creating a Horizontal Line

 A horizontal line is a line drawn horizontally across a web page. Horizontal lines can be used to break your web page into sections.

Tag Name	Horizontal Rule	
HTML Code	`<hr />`	
Attributes	`size`	Determines the thickness of the line, measured in pixels.
	`color`	Determines the colour of the line. If the colour attribute is left out, the line will be black.
	`width`	Determines how much of the web page the line spans across.
Effect	Creates a horizontal line using the colour and width specified. The thickness of the line depends on the size specified in pixels.	

Example:

HTML Code in Notepad	Result in Internet Explorer
`<hr size="3" width="80%">`	Displays a black line which is 3 pixels thick and which takes up 80 per cent of the width of the screen.

Note:

- As there is no closing <hr> tag, for XHTML the tag should be written as <hr />.
- Entering a <hr /> tag without attributes creates a line across the entire width of the web page.

What is a Pixel?

The monitor screen of your PC has an invisible grid, made up of columns and rows, something like a sheet of graph paper. Each square in the grid is called a pixel (see Fig. 2.3).

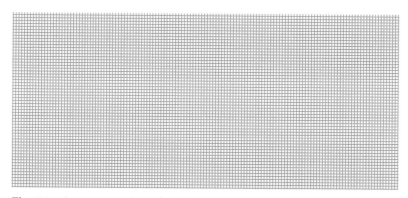

Fig. 2.3   A representation of pixels on a computer monitor

Text and images are displayed on the monitor by 'colouring in' certain pixels. The image in Fig. 2.4 has been enlarged to emphasise the pixels. Notice how the curves are jagged because they are drawn with square pixels along a diagonal line.

When text and images are viewed on a screen, curves are smooth because the pixels are much smaller and closer together than those in Fig. 2.4.

The resolution of your monitor specifies how many pixels your screen can show. Most monitors have a resolution of 1024 × 768, meaning that 1024 pixels can be shown horizontally and 768 pixels vertically (think of a spreadsheet with 1024 columns and 768 rows).

Older monitors have a resolution of 800 × 600. With this resolution, the pixels are bigger, so the image displayed on the monitor is not as sharp. Later, in Web Project 5 you will see that screen resolution is very important when you try to 'simulate' how a web site will look on different monitors.

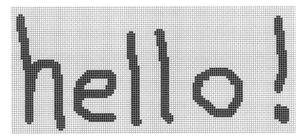

Fig. 2.4   When text or images are enlarged, the pixels become more obvious

In web design, it is important to understand what a pixel is because the width and height of items such as horizontal lines, tables and images are often given in pixels. For example, the code <hr size="3"> creates a horizontal line with a thickness of 3 pixels.

For You To Do

Edit the HTML code of the **index.htm** file to show a horizontal line with a thickness of three pixels as in Fig. 2.5.

Mike's Motors

Cars | Bikes | Vans

Fig. 2.5   A horizontal line has been added below the navigation menu

Formatting Text Using Heading Styles

There are six ready-made heading styles in HTML: Heading 1, Heading 2, Heading 3, Heading 4, Heading 5 and Heading 6. In Fig. 2.6 you can see that each heading style is a different size, Heading 1 being the biggest and Heading 6 being the smallest.

This text is formatted in Heading 1 style

This text is formatted in Heading 2 style

This text is formatted in Heading 3 style

This text is formatted in Heading 4 style

This text is formatted in Heading 5 style

This text is formatted in Heading 6 style

This is body text

Fig. 2.6   The six ready-made heading styles in HTML

Text can be displayed in a heading style by enclosing that text in heading tags. If you do not enclose text in heading tags, Internet Explorer will display that text without any style. This is referred to as body text.

Applying a Heading Style

Tag Name	Heading
HTML Code	`<h1></h1> or <h2></h2> or <h3></h3> or <h4></h4> or` `<h5></h5> or <h6></h6>`
Attributes	`align="center" or align="right"`
Effect	Formats text in the specified heading style.

Example:

HTML Code in Notepad	Result in Internet Explorer

`<h1 align="center">`
`This text is formatted in`
`Heading 1 style`
`</h1>`
	Text enclosed in heading tags is displayed in the style specified with "center" alignment.

  For You To Do

1. Open **index.htm** in Notepad and remove the paragraph tags and the bold tags from the text `Mike's Motors`.
2. Edit the HTML code so that the title Mike's Motors is displayed as centred Heading 1 style.
3. In **cars.htm,** display the heading Mike's Cars as centred Heading 1 style.
4. In **bikes.htm,** display the heading Mike's Bikes as centred Heading 1 style.
5. In **vans.htm,** display the heading Mike's Vans as centred Heading 1 style.
6. Use paragraph tags to centre the hyperlinks in **cars.htm, bikes.htm** and **vans.htm.**
7. Test each web page in Internet Explorer.

Complete the Navigation Menu System

1. Add hyperlinks to **cars.htm**, as in Fig. 2.7.
2. Add a horizontal rule tag in the position indicated.
3. Centre the hyperlinks and horizontal rule using paragraph tags.

Mike's Cars

Home | Bikes | Vans

Fig. 2.7   Navigation menu in the **cars.htm** web page

Tip: You can copy HTML code from **index.htm** and edit it to create the menu system in **cars.htm**.

3. Add hyperlinks to **bikes.htm**, as in Fig. 2.8.
4. Add a horizontal rule tag in the position indicated.
5. Centre the hyperlinks and horizontal rule using paragraph tags.

Mike's Bikes

Home | Cars | Vans

Fig. 2.8 Navigation menu in the **bikes.htm** web page

5. Add hyperlinks to **vans.htm**, as displayed in Fig. 2.9.
6. Add a horizontal rule tag in the position indicated.
7. Centre the hyperlinks and horizontal rule using paragraph tags.

Mike's Vans

Home | Cars | Bikes

Fig. 2.9 Navigation menu in the **vans.htm** web page

7. Test all hyperlinks in Internet Explorer.

Create the Contact Page

1. Open **contact.htm**.
2. Set up the **contact.htm** web page, as in Fig. 2.10, by entering HTML code in Notepad.
3. Format the heading using <h1> tags.
4. Centre all text using <p> tags.
5. Use <a> tags to set up the text Return to Home page as a hyperlink to **index.htm**.
6. Save the **contact.htm** web page.
7. Open **contact.htm** in Internet Explorer. Test the Return to Home page hyperlink.

Mike's Motors

25 Oldcourt Road
Waterford
Tel: (051) 227 3098
Fax: (051) 227 3099
Email: mikesmotors@eircom.net

Return to Homepage

Fig. 2.10 The **contact.htm** web page

 Add Text to the Home Page

1. Open **index.htm** in Notepad and insert the following text below the horizontal line.

> We have a great selection of quality used cars, bikes and vans. Click a link above to see what we have on offer or contact one of our expert staff.

2. Centre this text using paragraph tags.
3. Edit the HTML code so that the word `contact` is a hyperlink to **contact.htm.**

Creating Tables with HTML

 In a word processing document, text can easily be arranged in columns by setting up tabs. In web pages, however, tabs are not available. For this reason, tables are used to display text in columns. Later, in Web Project 3, we will see that tables can be used to position images and paragraphs of text in multiple columns. For web page layout, tables are extremely important. Almost every web site has at least one web page with a table.

To create a table in HTML, there are three HTML tags to use.

```
<table></table>
```

The beginning of the table is indicated with an opening table tag. The end of the table is indicated with a closing table tag.

```
<tr></tr>
```

Each row in the table is specified with opening and closing table row tags.

```
<td></td>
```

Each cell in a particular row is specified with opening and closing table data tags.

Creating a Table

It is always a good idea to draw the structure of your table before you try to write the HTML. Look at the table below with two rows and two columns.

To create this table, there are three steps.

1. Show the beginning and end of the table using table tags.

   ```
   <table>

   </table>
   ```

2. Add a set of opening and closing <tr> tags for each row in the table.

   ```
   <table>

     <tr>

     </tr>

     <tr>

     </tr>

   </table>
   ```

3. For each cell add a set of opening and closing <td> tags. Because there are two cells in each row, put two sets of opening and closing <td> tags in each row.

   ```
   <table>

     <tr>
       <td></td>
       <td></td>
     </tr>

     <tr>
       <td></td>
       <td></td>
     </tr>

   </table>
   ```

 Tip: Indenting <tr> and <td> tags makes it much easier to understand the HTML code. Developing this technique now will save you a lot of time later on, especially when you start to develop more complex tables.

Entering Data in a Table

To enter data in a cell, type the data between the opening and closing <td> tags.

```
<table>

  <tr>
    <td>This is cell 1</td>
    <td>This is cell 2</td>
  </tr>

  <tr>
    <td>This is cell 3</td>
    <td>This is cell 4</td>
  </tr>

</table>
```

The HTML code above produces the output in Fig. 2.11:

This is cell 1 This is cell 2

This is cell 3 This is cell 4

Fig. 2.11 The 2 × 2 table viewed in Internet Explorer

Adding a Border to a Table

The outside border of the table and the borders between cells in the table will not be seen unless the border width is specified in the opening <table> tag.

```
<table border="1">
```

The thickness of the border has been given in pixels. When the border attribute is added to the opening <table> tag, the table appears like Fig. 2.12 in Internet Explorer.

This is cell 1	This is cell 2
This is cell 3	This is cell 4

Fig. 2.12 A 2 × 2 table with a border thickness of 1 pixel

Specifying the Width of a Table

Usually the column widths adjust automatically to accommodate the longest cell entry in each column. The result is that information in the columns is very close together, with little or no blank space in individual cells. The table appears cramped.

This problem is solved by specifying the width of the table in the opening <table> tag. Once the width of the table is specified, each column is allocated an equal share of the overall table width. If there are three columns in the table, each column will be allocated a third of the overall width. This makes each column wider, as long as a large enough table width has been specified, giving the table a less cramped appearance.

The width of the table is specified in the opening <table> tag:

```
<table width="60%">
```

| This is cell 1 | This is cell 2 |
| This is cell 3 | This is cell 4 |

Fig. 2.13   Setting the table width to 60 per cent widens both columns

In this case the width of the table has been specified in relation to the width of the computer screen. An advantage of this method is that the table will always take up the same part of the screen whether the resolution is 800×600 or 1024×768.

The width of the table can also be specified in pixels:

```
<table width="500">
```

The disadvantage of this method is that there will be more space to the right of the table when the screen resolution is 1024×768.

Aligning Data in Table Cells

Data can be aligned to the left, centred or aligned to the right in each table cell. The default alignment is to the left. To align data in a cell, add the align="center" or align="right" attribute to the opening <td> tag of the cell.

Example:

```
<td align="center">This is cell 1</td>
```

Below is the adjusted HTML code for the table. Border and width attributes have been added to the opening <table> tag. The align attribute has been added to each opening <td> tag.

```
<table border="1" width="60%">

  <tr>
    <td align="center">This is cell 1</td>
    <td align="center">This is cell 2</td>
  </tr>

  <tr>
    <td align="center">This is cell 3</td>
    <td align="center">This is cell 4</td>
  </tr>

</table>
```

The HTML code above produces a table (in Fig. 2.14) in Internet Explorer.

This is cell 1	This is cell 2
This is cell 3	This is cell 4

Fig. 2.14   Align="center" has been added to each opening <td> tag

Create a Table to Display Cars For Sale

1.   Open **cars.htm** in Notepad.
2. Add HTML code to create the table displayed below. (Remember to put the table below the horizontal line.)

 Tip: Count the number of rows in the table. Set up the HTML code for the first row and copy this code to create the remaining rows.

 Note: The euro sign is not fully supported by all browsers and fonts. The best way to display a euro sign is to type € in HTML. For example, if you type €1000 in HTML, it shows up as €1000 in Internet Explorer.

Description	Price
Renault Clio 1.2 Sport 17,500 miles Airbag, alloy wheels, ABS, alarm	€10,000
Volkswagen Polo 1.4 38,000 miles Power steering, electric mirrors, adjustable steering wheel	€11,750
Volkswagen Golf 1.9d 80,000 miles Central locking, driver airbag, radio-cassette, power steering	€8,999
Opel Astra 1.4L Saloon 61,000 miles Power steering, electric mirrors, driver airbag, immobiliser	€12,750

3. Set the alignment of the table to centre by adding align="center" to the opening <table> tag. Set the width of the table to 75% and the border to 1.
4. Display text in italics as above.
5. Centre all the prices.

Create a Table to Display Bikes For Sale

1. Open **bikes.htm** in Notepad.
2. Add HTML code to create the table shown below. (Put the table below the horizontal line.)

Tip: Copy the HTML code for the table from **cars.htm** and edit the cell contents.

Description	Price
BMW F Series F650GS 12,000 miles ABS, heated grips	€12,000
Suzuki GSXR 1000 38,000 mile Red and white, immaculate condition	€9,950
Honda VFR 800i 10,000 miles New tyres, racing lines, lots of extras	€11,750
Suzuki GSXR 600 OZ 45,000 miles Very clean bike, new front tyre, new chain and sprockets	€12,750
Honda VTR 1000 SP1 8,000 miles Red, immaculate condition	€8,950

3. Set the alignment of the table to 'center', the width to 75% and the border to 1.
4. Display text in italics as above.
5. Centre all the prices.

Create a Table to Display Vans For Sale

1. Open **vans.htm** in Notepad.
2. Add HTML code to create the table shown below. (Put the table below the horizontal line.)

Tip: Rather than writing the HTML code for the entire table and then previewing the web page, it is better to preview the table in stages. Create the first three rows and preview them in Internet Explorer, then create the next three rows and so on. This approach makes it easier to find errors.

Description	Price
Renault Kangoo 1.7 Diesel 30,000 miles Blue, radio-cassette, power steering	€7,250
Ford Transit 42,000 miles White, one owner, power steering, radio-cassette, airbag	€12,750
Opel Combo 6,000 miles Green, power steering, ABS, CD player	€12,500
Ford Transit 12,000 miles Red, new model, ABS, power steering, CD player	€13,500
Citroen Berlingo 50,000 miles White, 1.9 diesel, very clean van	€5,500
Ford Transit Turbo 190 50,000 miles Diesel, turbo, very good condition	€9,250
Land Rover Discovery Tdi Base 85,000 miles Alloys, metallic paint, electric windows, remote central locking, alarm, immobiliser	€5,250
VW Transporter 42,000 miles Red, short wheelbase, plywood lined, solid tailgate rear door	€9000
VW Transporter 2.4 SWB 31,000 miles Remote central locking, electric windows, electric mirrors	€14,500

3. Set the alignment of the table to 'center', the width to 75% and the border to 1.
4. Display text in italics as above.
5. Centre all the prices.

Creating a Marquee with HTML

Marquees are often used to draw attention to something, such as a special offer. They allow you to do this by displaying text that moves horizontally across a web page.

There are three ways that marquee text can appear on a web page. In all cases, the text first appears on the left or right of the web page and then:

1. Scrolls across the page, disappears off the edge of the screen and then reappears on the other side of the screen, or;
2. Scrolls across the page, bounces off the edge of the screen and then scrolls in the opposite direction, or;
3. Scrolls across the page and stops when it reaches the edge of the screen.

The way that you display a marquee depends on the effect you want to achieve.

Tag Name	Marquee		
HTML Code	`<marquee></marquee>`		
Attributes	behavior	Specifies how the marquee text moves across the web page	
		`behavior="scroll"`	Text disappears off one side of the screen and then reappears at the other side.
		`behavior="alternate"`	Text bounces off the edges of the screen.
		`behavior="slide"`	Text slides in and stops once it hits the edge of the screen.
	loop	Specifies the number of times the marquee is to move across the screen. loop="infinite" causes the marquee to move as long as the web page is open in Internet Explorer.	
	width	Determines how much of the page the marquee moves across. This can be specified in pixels or as a percentage.	
	direction	Text normally scrolls from right to left. To make text scroll from left to right add direction="left" to the opening <marquee> tag.	

Note: 'behavior' is spelled the American way. Typing 'behaviour' in HTML causes an error.

Marquee Example 1:

```
<marquee behavior="scroll" loop="2">
Welcome To My Web Page
</marquee>
```

Welcome To My Web Page appears on the right of the screen, scrolls across to the left and disappears. It then reappears on the right, scrolls across again and disappears altogether.

Marquee Example 2:

```
<marquee behavior="slide" width="80%">
Welcome To My Web Page
</marquee>
```

Welcome To My Web Page appears at a point, which is 80 per cent across the width of the screen, scrolls across to the left and stops once it hits the left edge of the screen.

Marquee Example 3:

```
<marquee behavior="alternate" loop="infinite">
Welcome To My Web Page
</marquee>
```

Welcome To My Web Page appears on the right of the screen, scrolls across to the left, bounces off the edge of the screen and then scrolls to the right until it bounces off the right edge of the screen. This marquee will continue bouncing off the edges of the screen as long as the web page is open in Internet Explorer.

 Note: With a marquee that has the 'behavior' to scroll, the text will eventually disappear from the screen unless an infinite loop is specified.

 Tip: Use marquees sparingly. Too many moving items on a web page can distract the web page visitor. If you are using a marquee, remember that it can attract attention by sliding in and stopping or by looping two or three times. Marquees that loop infinitely can become annoying.

 **Add a Marquee to the Home Page**

1. Open **index.htm** in Notepad and create a marquee using the text below.

On special offer this week: **Renault Clio 1.2 Sport**

2. Position the marquee below the text Click a link above to see what we have on offer or contact one of our expert staff.
3. Set up the marquee so that it appears on the right hand side of the screen and scrolls infinitely.
4. Display Renault Clio 1.2 Sport in bold.
5. Test the marquee in Internet Explorer.

Add Marquees to the Cars, Bikes and Vans Pages

Create marquees, using the text below in **cars.htm, bikes.htm** and **vans.htm.**

Table 2.2 **Marquees to be added to the** *cars.htm, bikes.htm* **and** *vans.htm* **web pages**

Marquee Text	Web Page
We currently have **4** cars on offer	cars.htm
We currently have **5** bikes on offer	bikes.htm
We currently have **9** vans on offer	vans.htm

In each case, position the marquee between the horizontal line and the table. Each marquee should slide in from the right and scroll infinitely. Ensure that there is a blank line between the marquee and the table.

Named Anchors

You have already seen that a hyperlink allows you to 'jump' from one web page to any other web page in a web site. Named anchors allow you to 'jump' from one part of a web page to another part of the **same web page.**

A named anchor identifies a specific place on a web page. Once the anchor has been created, using a hyperlink you can instantly move to that anchor from any other part of the web page. This is especially useful where a web page is too big to fit on one screen. The Return to Top hyperlink appears at the bottom of many web pages, so you can move straight from the bottom of a web page to the top of a web page without having to use the vertical scroll bar.

If a web page that goes over several screens does not have anchors, the web page viewer will have to use the vertical scroll bar while reading the contents of the web page. This can be slow and frustrating and can leave people feeling 'lost in space' somewhere in a web page without any visible directions. This can turn visitors away from your web site. Named anchors are sometimes referred to as bookmarks.

Creating a Hyperlink to a Named Anchor

1. Identify a specific position on the web page using a named anchor. A named anchor is created using the anchor tag together with the name attribute. To create an anchor at the top of a web page, put the cursor just below the opening <body> tag and enter this HTML code:

```
<body>
<a name="topofpage"> </a>
```

Note: It is better not to include spaces in anchor names. You should also use names that have some meaning to make it easier to remember your anchors.

2. Put text on the page that will be a hyperlink to the anchor. In the example below, the text Return to Top is displayed at the bottom of the web page. To make this a hyperlink to the named anchor, it is enclosed in anchor tags. The opening anchor tag includes a hypertext reference to the named anchor.

```
<a href="#topofpage">Return to Top</a>
```

 Note: When hyperlinking to a named anchor, the # symbol comes before the anchor name.

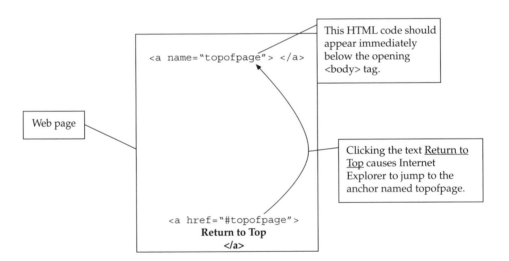

Add a Return to Top Hyperlink to the Vans Page

1. Open **vans.htm** in Notepad and create a named anchor in the line after the opening <body> tag using this HTML code:

```
<a name="topofpage"> </a>
```

2. Enter HTML code so that the text Return to Top is displayed at the bottom of the web page after the table listing vans and prices. Make sure that Return to Top is displayed in the centre of the screen. (Remember: use <p> tags to centre text.)

3. Create a hyperlink to the anchor named `topofpage` by enclosing the text `Return to Top` in anchor tags.

4. Test the Return to Top hyperlink in Internet Explorer.

Revision Exercise

1.
   My Computer

   Create a new folder named **rugby** on a floppy disk, zip disk, USB storage device or hard disk.

2. Create a new web page in Notepad. Save this web page as **index.htm** in the **rugby** folder.

3. Using HTML tags, make the web page title Ireland's Rugby World Cup – Pool A Matches.

4. Using HTML code, set up the **index.htm** web page so that it looks like Fig. 2.15.

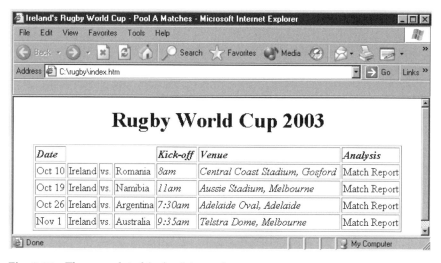

Fig. 2.15 The completed **index.htm** web page

5. Create a second web page in Notepad. Save this web page as **romania.htm** in the **rugby** folder.

6. Using HTML tags, make the web page title Ireland vs. Romania.

7. Using HTML code, set up the **romania.htm** web page so that it appears like Fig. 2.16. (Allow the text to wrap naturally. It will not necessarily wrap like Fig. 2.16.)

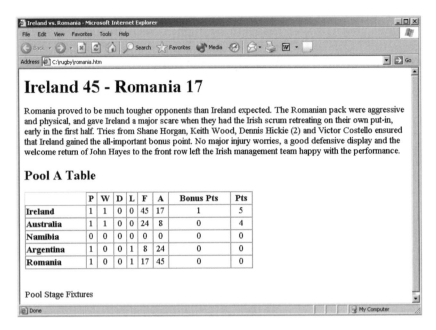

Fig. 2.16   The completed **romania.htm** web page

8.   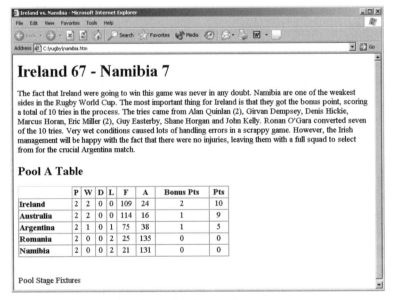 Create a third web page in Notepad. Save this web page as **namibia.htm** in the **rugby** folder.
9.   Using HTML tags, make the web page title Ireland vs. Namibia.
10. Using HTML code, set up the **namibia.htm** web page so that it looks like Fig. 2.17. Allow the text to wrap naturally.

Fig. 2.17   The completed **namibia.htm** web page

11. Create a fourth web page in Notepad. Save this web page as **argentina.htm** in the **rugby** folder.

12. Using HTML tags, make the web page title Ireland vs. Argentina.

13. Using HTML code, set up the **argentina.htm** web page so that it looks like Fig. 2.18. Allow the text to wrap naturally.

Fig. 2.18   The completed **argentina.htm** web page

14. Create a fifth web page in Notepad. Save this web page as **australia.htm** in the **rugby** folder.

15. Using HTML tags, make the web page title Ireland vs. Australia.

16. Using HTML code, set up the **australia.htm** web page so that it looks like Fig. 2.19. Allow the text to wrap naturally.

17. index.htm In the **index.htm** page, set up the text Match Report as a hyperlink for each match, see Table 2.3.

Table 2.3   Hyperlinks from the home page to the match report web pages

Table Row	Text	Hyperlink to:
2	Match Report	romania.htm
3	Match Report	namibia.htm
4	Match Report	argentina.htm
5	Match Report	australia.htm

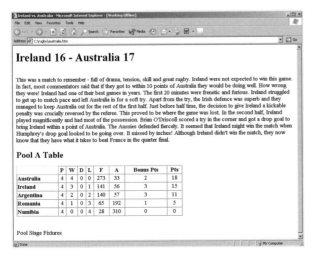

Fig. 2.19 The completed **australia.htm** web page

18. In the **romania.htm** web page, set up the text Pool Stage Fixtures as a hyperlink to **index.htm**.

19. In the same way, create hyperlinks from the **argentina.htm**, **australia.htm** and **namibia.htm** web pages back **to index.htm**.

20. Open **index.htm** in Internet Explorer and test all hyperlinks.

Progress Test 2

Finish the review of Web Project 2 by answering these questions.

1. Text that scrolls across a web page is called a _____.

2. Screen resolution depends on the number of _____ that can be displayed horizontally and vertically.

3. Creating a table in HTML requires three different tags. List the tags:

   a. _____

   b. _____

   c. _____

4. When a tag does not have a closing tag, XHTML requires that the _____ symbol is added to the tag.

5. Identify the errors in this HTML code.

```
<table>
  <tr>
    <td>Summer
    <td>Winter
  </tr>

  <tr>
    <td>28 C</td>
    <td>-5 C</td>
</table>
```

6. Study this HTML code:

```
<table border="1">
  <tr>
    <td>Day</td>
    <td>Fruit</td>
    <td>Drink</td>
    <td>Hardware</td>
  </tr>
  <tr>
    <td>Monday</td>
    <td>100</td>
    <td>20</td>
    <td>15</td>
  </tr>
  <tr>
    <td>Tuesday</td>
    <td>95</td>
    <td>15</td>
    <td>10</td>
  </tr>
</table>
```

This HTML code creates the following table (Table 2.4):

Table 2.4

Day	Fruit	Drink	Hardware
Monday	100	20	15
Tuesday	95	15	10

What changes would you need to make to the HTML code to add another column to the table, as in Table 2.5?

Table 2.5

Day	Fruit	Drink	Hardware	Dairy
Monday	100	20	15	150
Tuesday	95	15	10	125

7. A named _____ identifies a specific position on a web page. The web page viewer can move straight to this position by clicking a _____.

8. The six pre-defined styles available in HTML are referred to as _____ styles.

9. This HTML code displays Welcome To My Web Page twice.

```
<h6>Welcome To My Web Page</h6>
<h1>Welcome To My Web Page<h1>
```

Which line of text will appear bigger on the web page?

10. A named anchor has been created at the top of the web page using the HTML code: `<a name="top"> </a>`. The text `Return to Top` appears at the bottom of the web page. Write the HTML code to convert the text `Return to Top` into a hyperlink to the anchor named **top.**

Check your work

 To see the completed version of the Mike's Motors web site, the Rugby web site and the answers to Progress Test 2, log on to **www.gillmacmillan.ie.**

New in Web Project 2

HTML Tags

Tag Name	HTML Code	Description
Horizontal rule	`<hr />`	Creates a horizontal line in a web page.
Heading	`<h1></h1>`	Text enclosed in <h1></h1> tags will be displayed in Heading 1 style in Internet Explorer. <h2>, <h3>, <h4>, <h5> and <h6> tags can also be used.
Table	`<table></table>`	Indicates the beginning and the end of a table.
Table row	`<tr></tr>`	Each row in a table is specified with <tr></tr> tags.
Table data	`<td></td>`	Each cell in a table is specified with <td></td> tags.
Marquee	`<marquee></marquee>`	Text enclosed in <marquee></marquee> tags moves across the screen.
Named anchor	`<a name=" ">`	Marks a position on a web page that is accessed by a hyperlink.

Web Project 3

Southern Estate Agents Web Site

Scenario

Southern Estate Agents is located in South Dublin and specialises in the residential market. In a typical day, they receive up to a hundred queries by telephone from potential buyers. Answering these queries is very time-consuming, leaving a growing amount of paperwork to be done.

In this project, you will create a web site that shows photographs and details of houses for sale. Once the web site has been completed, potential house buyers will be able to get all the information they need by accessing this web site.

Project Objectives

By completing this web project, you will learn how to:
- Plan the structure of individual web pages.
- Merge table cells.
- Display text using a variety of font styles and colours.
- Change the background colour of table cells.
- Add comments to your HTML code.
- Display images on a web page.
- Display text in a bulleted list.
- Create a mailto hyperlink.

To complete the Southern Estate Agents web site, you need:

 Notepad

 Internet Explorer

 *Step by Step Web Design* CD

Site Structure

Look at the site structure for Southern Estate Agents web site in Fig. 3.1. The Southern Estate Agents web site has three levels of navigation. The home page has hyperlinks to four web pages. One of these web pages (property.htm) also has hyperlinks to some individual property details pages.

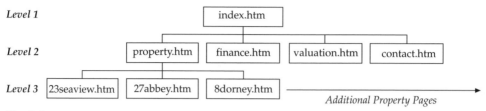

Fig. 3.1

Create a Folder to Store Your Web Pages

- Create a new folder named **estate** (on a floppy disk, zip disk, USB storage device or hard disk).

Displaying Images in a Web Page

One of the features that make web pages really interesting is the way you can present a range of media to the web page viewer. You can get your message across to your audience, using a mixture of text, images and sound that can exist side by side on a web page.

In this section, you learn how to display a digital photograph on a web page. All the photos for the Southern Estate Agents web site are on the *Step by Step Web Design* CD. In later projects you will get the chance to create your own digital photos.

Storing An Image

Before you can display an image on a web page, it must be stored on computer disk. To avoid confusion, it is best to store your images in a separate folder named **images.** The **images** folder should be a sub-folder of the folder that stores your web pages.

For You To Do

1. In the **estate** folder, create a sub-folder named **images.**

2. Open the **Project 3** folder on the *Step by Step Web Design* CD. It has two sub-folders: **Graphics** and **Web Pages**. Copy all the files from the **Graphics** folder to your **images** folder.

Referring to an Image with HTML

 In HTML, the image tag allows you to display images and graphics on a web page.

Tag Name	Image	
HTML Code	`<img src="image name" />`	
Effect	Displays an image on a web page.	
Attributes	`alt`	If an image is slow to load in Internet Explorer, alternative text can be displayed while the image is loading. Alt can also be used to display a message when the mouse pointer is over the image. The alt attribute can also assist visually impaired users who are accessing web pages using a text-to-voice converter.
	`height`	The height of an image can be specified in pixels or as a percentage.
	`width`	The width of an image can be specified in pixels or as a percentage.
	`vspace`	Space can be added above and below the image by specifying vspace in pixels.
	`hspace`	Space can be added to the left and to the right of the image by specifying hspace in pixels.

Example:

HTML Code in Notepad	Result in Internet Explorer
`<img src="images/estate.jpg" alt="Southern Estate Agents Sales Office" />`	Displays **estate.jpg** in a web page. If the photo is slow to load, the text Southern Estate Agents Sales Office is displayed while it is loading. This text will also be displayed when the mouse pointer is over the image.

 Note: As there is no closing <img> tag, in XHTML the tag is written as <img src="image name" />.

 Tip: Rather than using the height and width attributes to change the size of an image, it is better to edit the image in graphics software. The time it takes Internet Explorer to display an image is directly related to the size of the image in bytes. Bytes are used to measure the amount of space needed to store the image on disk. Larger images take longer to download. Reducing the size of an image using the height and width attributes makes the size of an image smaller on the page but does not affect the size of the image in bytes.

What happens is that your image looks smaller on the web page but still takes the same time to download. You will learn how to edit images in Section 2 of *Step by Step Web Design*.

Specifying the Path to an Image

All the images for the Southern Estates Agents web site are now stored in the **images** folder on your own disk, as in Fig. 3.2.

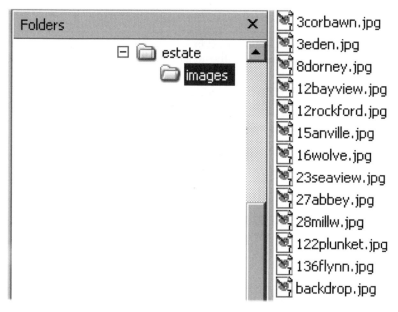

Fig. 3.2 All images used in the web site are stored in the **images** sub-folder

The **estate** folder will store the web pages. In Fig. 3.3, there is one web page **index.htm** in the **estate** folder. The **estate** folder also stores the **images** sub-folder.

Fig. 3.3 All web pages will be stored in the **estate** folder

To display an image in the **index.htm** web page, use the <img /> tag. The <img/> tag must first refer to the **images** sub-folder and then to the name of the image file you want to display.

Example:

```
<img src="images/backdrop.jpg" />
```

This HTML code entered **in index.htm** displays an image named **backdrop.jpg** stored in a sub-folder named **images.**

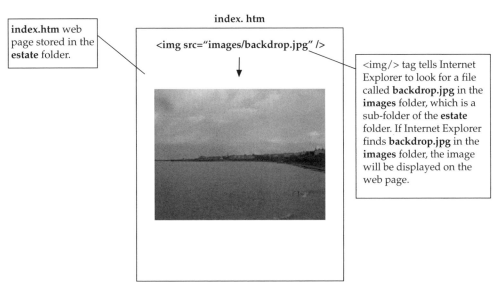

Fig. 3.4 How Internet Explorer displays an image on a web page

Note:
- Because the **index.htm** file is stored in the **estate** folder, there is no need to refer to the **estate** folder in the <img /> tag. You only need to refer to the **images** folder.
- For a detailed explanation of the JPEG and GIF image types, see Web Project 4.

Tip: Never include upper case letters or spaces in folder and file names. This can cause problems when you make your web site live on the World Wide Web.

Planning Individual Web Pages

In the Southern Estate Agents web site, you will create a more advanced page layout using tables. No matter how complex your page layout is, always plan the structure of each web page before trying to create the web page with HTML.

Planning web page structure has three major advantages:
- HTML code is much easier to write when you know exactly what the structure of the web page is.

- When you create HTML code based on a planned web page, you will make fewer errors. It is also easier to edit HTML code when it is based on a plan.
- The HTML code will be more efficient and easier to understand. When HTML code is written without any planning, there is often duplication and unnecessary code.

The structure of a web page can be planned by doing a rough sketch of the page, showing the position of headings, hyperlinks, text and pictures. For a web page based on a table, the rows and columns in the table should be clearly shown. You can also plan web page structure using a word processing package.

The layout of the Southern Estate Agents home page is shown below. The layout was created using Microsoft Word.

Layout of the Home Page (index.htm)

Table 1 (width=100%)

← width=40px →	Southern Estate Agents			
	← Merge cell across 4 columns →			
	Property Details	Financial Services	Property Valuation	Contact Details
	Horizontal Line ← Merge cell across 4 columns →			

1 blank line

Table 2 (width=100%)

← width=40px →	Marquee Text

1 blank line

Table 3 (width=100%)

← width=40px →	Photo	← width=40px →	**Estate Agents** Text **Financial Services** Text **Valuation** Text

2 blank lines

Table 4 (width=100%)

← width=40px →	Text describing services

As you can see, the whole web page will be based on tables. This allows us to structure a page and line up text and images. Notice that the first column in every table is 40 pixels wide and does not have any text or images. This moves all the text 40 pixels in from the left edge of the screen, giving the web page a less cluttered appearance.

Merging Cells in a Table

Before creating the HTML for the home page, you need to learn how to merge cells in a table.

Merging Cells Horizontally

My Web Site		
News	Comments	Analysis

In the table above, three cells in the top row have been merged together to form one big cell. This technique is often used to centre a title in a web page.

To merge cells horizontally, add the colspan attribute to the opening <td> tag. In Row 1 of the table, the first cell spans three columns so we need to add colspan="3" to the opening <td> tag of that cell. The HTML code would be:

```
<table>
  <tr>
    <td colspan "3">My Web Site</td>
  </tr>

  <tr>
    <td>News</td>
    <td>Comments</td>
    <td>Analysis</td>
  </tr>
</table>
```

Note that Row 1 of the table has only one set of <td> tags. This is because the cell in Row 1 goes across three columns.

Create the Home Page

1. Start Notepad. In a blank Notepad document set up a web page by entering opening and closing <html>, <head> and <body> tags.

2. 💾 Enter <title> tags in the Head section so that the text `Welcome to Southern Estate Agents` appears in the title bar of Internet Explorer. Save this page as **index.htm** in the **estate** folder.

3. Create a table in the <body> section, as below. Set the width of the table to 100%.

← width=40px →	Southern Estate Agents			
	←——— *Merge cell across 4 columns* ———→			
	Property Details	Financial Services	Property Valuation	Contact Details
	Horizontal Line			
	←— *Merge cell across 4 columns* —→			

*First table in **index.htm** page*

Remember:
- `<td width="40"></td>` sets the width of a cell to 40 pixels. No data is entered in this cell.
- `<td colspan="4">` merges a cell across four columns.
- Row 1 and Row 3 of the table have only two sets of `<td></td>` tags. Row 2 of the table has five sets of `<td></td>` tags.
- Use `<hr />` to create a horizontal line.
- Add a `<br />` tag after the closing `</table>` tag to create a blank line below the table.
- Check the table by opening **index.htm** in Internet Explorer.

Create a Marquee in the Home Page

1. Open **index.htm** in Notepad, if it is not already open. Create a second table after the `<br />` tag. The layout of the table is shown below. Set the width of the table to 100%.

← width=40px →	Welcome To Our Web Site

*Second table in **index.htm** page*

Remember:
- The text Welcome To Our Website should appear on the right of the screen, and stop when it reaches the border of the 40-pixel wide blank cell.
- The table has only two cells. There is no need to use colspan in the cell containing the marquee. This cell will automatically adjust to the width of the screen minus 40 pixels because the width of the table is 100 per cent.
- Add a `<br />` tag after the closing `</table>` tag to create a blank line below the table.
- Check the table by opening **index.htm** in Internet Explorer.

Display a Photograph and Text Side by Side

 Open **index.htm** in Notepad, if it is not already open. Create a third table below the table with the marquee. The layout of the table is shown below. Set the width of the table to 100%.

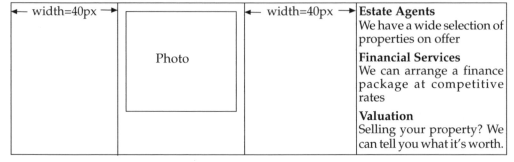

← width=40px →	Photo	← width=40px →	**Estate Agents** We have a wide selection of properties on offer **Financial Services** We can arrange a finance package at competitive rates **Valuation** Selling your property? We can tell you what it's worth.

*Third table in **index.htm** page*

Remember:

- Display the photo **backdrop.jpg** in the second cell of the table. Add the alt attribute so that the text `Dun Laoghaire Harbour` is displayed when the mouse pointer is over the image.
- Display the text in the fourth cell of the table. Use two <br /> tags to create a blank line between paragraphs.
- Add a <br /> tag after the closing </table> tag to create a blank line below the table.
- Check the table by opening **index.htm** in Internet Explorer.

 **Note:** Do not use <br /> tags in the middle of a sentence or paragraph. Allow text to wrap naturally. Depending on your monitor size and its resolution, your text may or may not wrap in the same way as the text shown above. If your text wraps differently, it is OK. Only add <br/> tags after the headings and at the end of each paragraph.

Add Descriptive Text to the Home Page

 1. 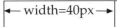 Open **index.htm** in Notepad, if it is not already open. Create a fourth table under the table with the photograph. The layout of the table is shown below. Set the width of the table to 100%.

← width=40px →	Southern Estate Agents is the leading estate agent in South Dublin and has been established since 1973. We specialise in the residential market and will also arrange a finance package to suit your needs. We offer a top quality service and have a very high level of customer satisfaction.

Fourth table in index.htm page

2. Use a <br /> tag at the end of each sentence.

3. Check your work by opening **index.htm** in Internet Explorer.

 Note: Paragraphs of text can also be indented using <blockquote> </blockquote>. Put in a <blockquote> tag before the beginning of the paragraph and a </blockquote> tag after the paragraph.

Example:

```
<blockquote>
When this web page is previewed in Internet Explorer, the entire left
edge of this paragraph will be indented from the left edge of the
screen.
</blockquote>
```

The only disadvantage of using <blockquote> is that you cannot specify by how much you want to indent the text.

Working with Web Colours

 Each colour on a web page is defined by how much red, green and blue are mixed together to make that colour. It is something like taking a tin of red paint, a tin of green paint and a tin of blue paint and mixing the three colours in a fourth tin to make a new colour. The colour that you get depends on how much red, how much green and how much blue is in the mix.

The computer can understand 256 different shades of red, green and blue. The number 0 is no colour, 1 is the lightest shade of red, green or blue and 255 is the deepest shade of red, green or blue. Mixing these in different proportions offers the potential to create millions of colours.

At one end of the colour spectrum is black, where all the colours are turned off. At the other end of the spectrum is white. This is where red, green and blue are all at their deepest shade. When they are mixed together, the resulting colour is white. In between these two extremes are all the possible shades in the colour spectrum.

Table 3.1   Web colours are made by mixing red, green and blue in different proportions

Black (all colours turned off)				White (equal amounts of red, green, blue)		
R	**G**	**B**		**R**	**G**	**B**
0	0	0		255	255	255

RGB Colour System

Instead of using three numbers, each between 0 and 255, to specify the amount red, green and blue in a colour, HTML uses a six-character RGB code. RGB codes, also known as hex codes, are used in HTML to specify the colour of elements in a web page, such as text, tables and backgrounds. In an RGB code, the first two characters represent how much is red, the second two characters represent how much is green and the final two characters represent how much is blue. RGB code shows colours as:

```
#rrggbb
```

where:
rr = the amount of red in the mix
gg = the amount of green in the mix
bb = the amount of blue in the mix.

Each set of characters representing red, green and blue uses the hexadecimal system of counting. Hexadecimal is a number system with 16 different numbers. A combination of numbers and characters is used to represent these 16 numbers.

(Remember we normally use the decimal number system, which has 10 different numbers.) Table 3.2 shows the 16 numbers in the hexadecimal system. The decimal equivalent of each hexadecimal number is shown in the shaded cell below.

Table 3.2   Hexadecimal numbers and their decimal equivalents

Hexadecimal Numbers	0	1	2	3	4	5	6	7	8	9	A	B	C	D	E	F
Decimal Numbers	0	1	2	3	4	5	6	7	8	9	10	11	12	13	14	15

The number F in the hexadecimal system corresponds to the number 15 in the decimal system. Let's look at a couple of examples.

Specifying Font Colours

Colour Example 1:

```
<font color="#FFFFFF">
```

The RGB code #FFFFFF creates a colour which depends on the amounts of red, green and blue that are mixed together. FF is the amount of red in the mix. This is converted to a decimal number as:

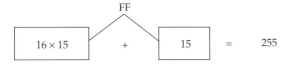

Fig. 3.5

As the amounts of green and blue are also FF, the entire RGB code can be written in decimal as 255, 255, 255 – the maximum amounts of red, green and blue, which creates white. So <font color="#FFFFFF"> sets the colour of the text to white.

Colour Example 2:

```
<font color="#E62B88">
```

This sets the colour of the text to dark red. E6 is the amount of red in the mix. The decimal equivalent of E6 is $(16 \times 14) + 6 = 230$. 2B is the amount of green in the mix. The decimal equivalent of 2B is $(16 \times 2) + 11 = 43$. 88 is the amount of blue in the mix. The decimal equivalent of 88 is $(16 \times 8) + 8 = 136$.

The RGB code can be written in decimal as 230, 43, 136, which is a dark red. This is because there is much more red in the mix than green and blue. So <font color="#E62B88"> sets the colour of the text to dark red.

Specifying Background Colours

As well as specifying font colour, RGB codes can also be used to specify the background colours of tables, individual table cells or entire web pages. Background colour is specified by adding `bgcolor="#rrggbb"`, where #rrggbb is any RGB code, to the opening <table> tag, opening <tr> tag or opening <td> tag when formatting tables. When setting the background colour for an entire web page, add `bgcolor="#rrggbb"` to the opening <body> tag.

Colour Example 3:

```
<table bgcolor="#FF6600">
  <tr>
    <td>Name</td>
    <td>Class</td>
  </tr>

  <tr>
    <td>Alan</td>
    <td>Web Design</td>
  </tr>
</table>
```

sets the background colour of the entire table to orange.

Colour Example 4:

```
<table>
  <tr bgcolor="#FF6600">
    <td>Name</td>
    <td>Class</td>
  </tr>

  <tr>
    <td>Alan</td>
    <td>Web Design</td>
  </tr>
</table>
```

sets the background colour of Row 1 of the table to orange.

Colour Example 5:

```
<table>
  <tr>
    <td>Name</td>
    <td>Class</td>
  </tr>

  <tr>
    <td>Alan</td>
    <td bgcolor="#FF6600">Web Design</td>
  </tr>
</table>
```

sets the background colour of the second cell in Row 2 of the table to orange.

Colour Example 6:

```
<body bgcolor="#FF6600">
```

sets the background colour of the entire web page to orange.

Web Safe Colours

If you like working with colour, and you are excited by the idea of playing with millions of colours, prepare to be disappointed. The number of colours that a monitor can display depends on the power of the PC's graphics card. You may have a relatively new PC with a powerful graphics card and design your web page with lots of great colours. When you preview the web page, all the colours are displayed perfectly on your monitor. The problem occurs when your web page goes live on the World Wide Web.

There are millions of PCs ranging from new ones to ones over 20 years old. In general, older PC's will have less powerful graphics cards, so they will not be able to display as many colours as newer PCs. When people view your web page, their PC's graphics card may not be able to produce the colour that you specified in your HTML code.

To overcome this problem, Internet Explorer either chooses the closest match to the colour specified in the HTML code or makes a new colour by mixing available colours together. This is called **dithering**. The result of dithering is that different people viewing your web page may see different colours to the ones you specified in your HTML code.

Older computers have 8-bit graphics cards. These graphics cards are only able to display 256 different colours. Netscape Navigator uses 216 of these for web pages. These 216 colours are called **web safe colours**. They will appear the same on every monitor regardless of the age of the graphics card.

There is good news for colour enthusiasts. With time more people buy new PCs and the ratio of PCs with low quality graphics cards goes down, dithering will become less and less of a problem. For this reason, many commercial web sites are now using colours outside the 216 web-safe colour range.

 For a complete list of web safe colours, access the support material on **www.gillmacmillan.ie.**

Pre-defined Colours

Sixteen colours can be called by name in HTML code. (They can also be described with RGB codes.)

Table 3.3   **The pre-defined colours in HTML**

Black (#000000)	Silver (#C0C0C0)	Gray (#808080)	White (#FFFFFF)
Maroon (#800000)	Red (#FF0000)	Purple (#800080)	Fuchsia (#FF00FF)
Green (#008000)	Lime (#00FF00)	Olive (#808000)	Yellow (#FFFF00)
Navy (#000080)	Blue (#0000FF)	Teal (#008080)	Aqua (#00FFFF)

Formatting a Web Page

One of the main differences between HTML and XHTML is the way that web pages are formatted. In HTML, most formatting is done locally, that is in the web page itself using HTML formatting tags. In XHTML, all formatting is carried out using Cascading Style Sheets (CSS). With CSS, individual styles can be created and named by the web page designer. The number of characteristics, including font size, font color, font style, background colour, etc., for each style is up to the web page designer.

Once a style has been created, it can be applied to individual words, sentences, paragraphs, sections or entire web pages. The advantage of styles is that editing is much easier and quicker. By changing the style definition, all elements linked to that style change automatically.

In HTML, most text formatting is applied using the <font> tag. Although the <font> tag is being phased out, it is important to know about it for two reasons. Firstly, it is still used in lots of web pages. Secondly it will be some years before it is phased out altogether. The new way to format web pages is CSS (Cascading Style Sheets). This will be covered in detail in Web Project 4.

A Crash Course in Printing Theory

 Text can be displayed in many different styles on a computer screen. These styles are called fonts. In general, fonts can be divided into two main categories: serif fonts and sans-serif fonts.

Serif Fonts

In a serif font a decorative curve is added to the end of each stroke in a letter. These decorative curves are called serifs.

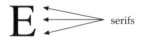

Fig. 3.6   Times New Roman is one of the most popular serif fonts

Sans-Serif Fonts

In a sans-serif font, there are no decorative curves at the end of each stroke.

 no serifs

Fig. 3.7   Arial is one of the most popular sans-serif fonts

There are some well-established rules for making text easier to read on a printed page. These are:

- Sans-serif fonts have a stronger emphasis and should be used for headlines and headings.
- Serif fonts are easier to read and should be used for the body text in a piece of writing.
- Differences in letter shapes help us to read individual words in a sentence. THIS SENTENCE IS VERY DIFFICULT TO READ BECAUSE ALL THE LETTERS ARE THE SAME HEIGHT.

These rules work very well for printed text but there are problems when they are applied to text for a computer screen. The majority of printed matter has a resolution of 600 dots per inch, so the letters are dense and clear to read. On a computer screen, letters appear at a resolution of less than 100 dots per inch. This lower resolution makes very small serif characters difficult to read. Small text on screen is best in a sans-serif font.

Choosing Fonts for Your Web Site

Producing text on a computer screen is not the same as producing text on a printed page. There are two major technical issues to consider when choosing fonts for text in your web site.

Curves are not 'smooth'

When text is displayed on a computer screen, curves in individual letters look jagged, or pixellated. This is because individual letters are made up of a number of pixels, each of which is square in shape.

In the large letter C in Fig. 3.8 you can see that the curves are not perfectly formed. This makes text on a computer screen difficult to read at small font sizes. The Verdana and Georgia fonts were specially designed for use in web pages. With these fonts, curves are more rounded and less pixellated.

Platform Inconsistency

A platform is the combination of hardware and software that makes up your PC. There are many different PCs of varying ages, with different operating systems

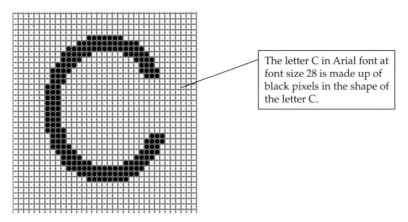

The letter C in Arial font at font size 28 is made up of black pixels in the shape of the letter C.

Fig. 3.8 Because pixels are square in shape, curves are jagged

(Windows, Mac OS, Linux) and different fonts installed. Choosing a font available to all PC users is a challenge!

When someone views your web page, they will only be able to see the fonts specified in your HTML code if those fonts are installed on **their PC**. If you specify Book Antiqua as the font, web viewers will see the text formatted in Book Antiqua as long as that font is loaded on their PC. If it does not have Book Antiqua, the text will be displayed in the default font, usually Times New Roman or Times.

There are so many different PCs and operating systems, the list of fonts that will be interpreted correctly by all PCs is very limited (see Table 3.4).

Table 3.4   Web safe fonts that that will be interpreted correctly by all PCs

Serif	Sans Serif
Georgia	Verdana
Times New Roman	Arial

This list of fonts is often called browser safe fonts, or web safe fonts. To be sure that the web page viewer will see text exactly as you format it, you should only use Georgia, Times New Roman, Verdana and Arial.

Formatting Text With The Font Tag

 The font tag <font> is used to specify the style, size and colour of text. The font style is specified by choosing a font such as Times New Roman, Arial or Verdana. The <font> tag also allows us to display text in seven different sizes in a range of colours.

Tag Name	Font	
HTML Code	`<font> </font>`	
Effect	Formats text on a web page in a variety of styles, colours and sizes.	
Attributes	`face`	Specifies the font style the text will be displayed in. More than one font can be specified. Internet Explorer will check if the first font is available on the web page of the viewer's PC. If it is not available, the second font in the list will be displayed. Always include a font that will definitely be displayed at the end of the list.
	`size`	A size from 1 to 7 can be specified, where 1 is the smallest and 7 is the biggest.
	`color`	The colour of the text can be specified with one of the 16 pre-defined colours or by using hexidecimal codes.

Example:

HTML Code in Notepad	Result in Internet Explorer
`<font face="Geneva, Arial" size="7" color="#4A2885">` `Have fun with fonts` `</font>`	When Internet Explorer sees the font tag, it checks to see if the Geneva font is loaded on the web page of the visitor's PC. If it finds Geneva, the text `Have fun with fonts` will be displayed in the Geneva font. If Geneva is not loaded on the PC, the text will be displayed in the Arial font. The text will be displayed in the largest font size and the colour of the text is dark blue.

The <font> tag can be used to format individual words, sentences or entire paragraphs.

Example:

```
<font face="Arial" size="4" color="#990000">Estate Agents</font>
<br />
<font face="Verdana">We have a wide selection of properties on
offer</font>
```

In the HTML code above, the text `Estate Agents` is enclosed in opening and closing font tags. The opening <font> tag specifies Arial as the font style, 4 as the font size and #990000 as the font colour. These attributes will be applied only to the text `Estate Agents`. The text `We have a wide selection of properties on offer` will be displayed in the Verdana font.

Format the Main Heading in the Home Page

You are going to learn about changing the background colour of the cell with the text Southern Estate Agents. The size and colour of this text will also be changed.

1. Open **index.htm** in Notepad.
2. Apply a background colour of #990000 to the cell containing the main heading Southern Estate Agents.
3. Using the <font> tag, apply a font face of Arial, a font size of 6 and a font colour of #FFFFFF to the main heading Southern Estate Agents.

> **Tip:** Put the opening <font> tag before the word 'Southern' and the closing </font> tag after the word 'Agents'.

4. Check your formatting by opening **index.htm** in Internet Explorer.

 Format the Sub-Headings in the Home Page

    1. Open **index.htm** in Notepad, if it is not already open.
2. Using the <font> tag, apply a font face of Arial, a font size 4 and a font colour of #990000 to the marquee text Welcome to our Website and to the sub-headings Estate Agents, Financial Services and Valuation.

> **Note:** The marquee text is in the second table. The sub-headings are in the third table.

> **Tip:** Holding down the CTRL key and typing C is a shortcut to Copy in the Edit menu. CTRL and V is a shortcut to Paste.

3. Put the sub-headings Estate Agents, Financial Services and Valuation in bold.
4. Check your formatting by opening **index.htm** in Internet Explorer.

 Format Remaining Text in the Home Page

    1. Open **index.htm** in Notepad, if it is not already open.
2. Using the <font> tag, apply a font face of Verdana to all the remaining text in the home page, including:

- Property Details, Financial Services, Property Valuation and Contact Details, which appear just under the main heading in the first table.

Tip: Because this text is displayed in four separate table cells, each item of text must be enclosed in <font> tags.

- Text under the sub-headings Estate Agent, Financial Services and Valuation in the third table.
- Text describing Southern Estate Agents, which appears below the photo in the fourth table.

3. Check your formatting by opening **index.htm** in Internet Explorer.

Finishing Touches

We will display the first letter of each word in the main heading Southern Estate Agents in a different colour. The RGB code for this colour is #CCCC00.

Example:

```
<font face="Arial" color="#CCCC00" size="6">S</font>
<font face="Arial" color="#FFFFFF" size="6">outhern </font>
```

The HTML code above displays the letter 'S' of Southern in a light green. The remaining letters are displayed in white. All letters are displayed in Arial font with a font size of 6.

 Tip: For the space between the 'n' of Southern and the closing </font> tag it is necessary to make sure there is space between the words 'Southern' and 'Estate'.

 For You To Do

Edit the HTML code in **index.htm** to display the first letter of each word in the main heading Southern Estate Agents in the colour #CCCC00.

Add Comments to Your HTML Code

Open **index.htm** in Notepad. Have a look at the HTML code. There is a lot of it! The more HTML code you add to a web page, the harder it becomes to understand that code. It is good programming practice to add comments to your code to help you and others understand it. Each time you enter a comment in your code, you must enclose the comment in special symbols so that Internet Explorer does not interpret the comment as HTML code. All comments begin with <!-- and end with -->.

Example:

```
<!-- This is a comment. Internet Explorer will not interpret it as
HTML code -->
```

 For You To Do

Add a comment in the line above the opening <table> tag for each table in **index.htm.** The comments should start like this:

```
<!-- Beginning of Table 1 -->
```
then
```
<!-- Beginning of Table 2 -->
```

and so on. The completed **index.htm** web page should look something like Fig. 3.9.

Southern Estate Agents

Property Details	Financial Services	Property Valuation	Contact Details

Welcome To Our Website

Estate Agents
We have a wide selection of properties on offer

Financial Services
We can arrange a finance package at competitive rates

Valuation
Selling your property? We can tell you what it's worth

Southern Estate Agents is the leading estate agent in South Dublin and has been established since 1973. We specialise in the residential market and will also arrange a finance package to suit your needs. We offer a top quality service and have a very high level of customer satisfaction.

Fig. 3.9 The completed Southern Estate Agents home page

Plan the Layout of the Property Details Page

The layout of the Property Details page is on the next page.

Table 1 (width=100%)

← width=40px →	Southern Estate Agents			
	← *Merge cell across 4 columns* →			
	Home	Financial Services	Property Valuation	Contact Details
	Horizontal Line ← *Merge cell across 4 columns* →			

1 blank line

Table 2 (width=100%)

← width=40px →	Marquee Text

1 blank line

Table 3 (width=100%)

← width=40px →	Properties Available in Dun Laoghaire		
	← *Merge cell across 3 columns* →		
	Location	Property Type	Price
	Text	Text	Text
	Text	Text	Text
	Properties Available in Shankill		
	← *Merge cell across 3 columns* →		
	Location	Property Type	Price
	Text	Text	Text
	Text	Text	Text
	Properties Available in Bray		
	← *Merge cell across 3 columns* →		
	Location	Property Type	Price
	Text	Text	Text
	Text	Text	Text

1 blank line

Table 4 (width=100%)

← width=40px →	Horizontal Line
	Top of Page

Note how Table 1 and Table 2 in the Property Details page are almost exactly the same as Table 1 and Table 2 in the home page. (One small difference is that in Table 1 Property Details has been replaced with Home.) Planning your web pages saves time in the long run. Instead of having to enter all the HTML code to create the Property Details page, you can copy existing HTML code from **index.htm** to create the first two tables and then enter additional HTML code to create the other tables.

Create the Property Details Page

To create the first two tables in the **property.htm** page, first copy HTML code from **index.htm**.

1. Start Notepad. In a blank Notepad document set up a web page by entering opening and closing <html>, <head> and <body> tags.
2. Enter <title> tags in the Head section so that the title Properties for Sale appears in the title bar of Internet Explorer. Save this page as **property.htm** in the **estate** folder.
3. Open **index.htm** in Notepad.
4. Highlight HTML code from <!--Beginning of Table 1--> down as far as but not including <!--Beginning of Table 3-->. To copy this code, select Edit followed by Copy from the menu.
5. Open **property.htm** in Notepad.
6. Put the cursor between the opening and closing <body> tags. Select Edit followed by Paste from the menu.
7. Find the line of code in Table 1 that reads:

   ```
   <td><font face="Verdana">Property Details</font></td>
   ```

   Edit this code so that it reads:

   ```
   <td><font face="Verdana">Home</font></td>
   ```

Tip: Select Edit, followed by Find from the menu.

8. Find the marquee text `Welcome to our Website` in Table 2. Change this text so that it reads `To arrange a viewing, ring 01-295 0155`.

9. Check your work by opening **property.htm** in Internet Explorer.

Create a Table to Display Property Details

Look back at Table 3 in the layout of the Properties Details page. Notice how there are two different row layouts in the table. Rows with the location name have one blank cell and a large cell that is merged across three columns. All other rows in the table have four cells. This means that we only need to create HTML code for two table rows. This code can then be copied to create all the other table rows. Another advantage of planning! A section of the table structure is shown below to help you create the HTML code.

← width=40px →	Properties Available in		
	Location	Property Type	Price
	Text	Text	Text
	Text	Text	Text

Merge cell across 3 columns

1. Open **property.htm** in Notepad, if it is not already open.
2. Put the cursor below the closing </table> of the second table.
3. Start the third table as follows. Remember to begin with a comment.

```
<!-- Beginning of Table 3 -->
<table width="100%" border="0" cellspacing="0">
  <tr>
    <td width="40"></td>
    <td colspan="3">Properties Available in </td>
  </tr>

  <tr>
    <td width="40"></td>
    <td></td>
    <td></td>
    <td></td>
  </tr>
</table>
```

Note: cellspacing="0" stops Internet Explorer from showing gaps between table cells.

4. To create the other rows in the table copy the HTML code for each row above as many times as necessary. Using this method, create the table shown below.

← width=40px →	Properties Available in Dun Laoghaire		
	Location	Property Type	Price
	23 Seaview Park	Detached House	€325,000
	27 Abbey Lane	Terraced House	€280,000
	8 Dorney Road	Semi-Detached House	€345,000
	15 Anville Wood	Semi-Detached House	€380,000
	Properties Available in Shankill		
	Location	Property Type	Price
	122 Plunkett Road	Semi-Detached House	€320,000
	3 Corbawn Terrace	Semi-Detached House	€315,000

	16 Wolverton Grove	Semi-Detached House	€343,000
	12 Bayview Mews	Semi-Detached House	€295,000
	Properties Available in Bray		
	Location	Property Type	Price
	136 O'Flynn Park	Semi-Detached House	€345,000
	28 Millwood Downs	Semi-Detached House	€415,000
	12 Rockford Manor	Semi-Detached House	€347,500
	3 Eden Lane	Semi-Detached House	€295,000

Remember:
- The first cell in every row is a blank cell with a width of 40 pixels.
- Use € to display the euro sign.
- Include three blank table rows before Shankill and Bray. Internet Explorer will not display a table row if there are cells in that row that have no data. To force Internet Explorer to display the blank rows, insert a non-breaking space in one cell in each blank row. The code for a non-breaking space is
  The HTML code for a blank row is:

```
<tr>
  <td width="40"></td>
  <td> </td>
  <td></td>
  <td></td>
</tr>
```

 Note: A non-breaking space is a space that does not force the cursor onto a new line. Each non-breaking space is equivalent to pressing the spacebar once.

- Put the headings Properties Available in Dun Laoghaire, Properties Available in Shankill and Properties Available in Bray in bold. Apply the following formatting to these headings:

```
face="Arial"
size="4"
color="#CCCC00"
```

and apply a background colour of #666666 to each of the cells with these headings.
- Display the headings Location, Property Type and Price in bold. Apply the following formatting to these headings:

```
face="Arial"
color="#FFFFFF"
```

Apply a background colour of #333333 to each of the cells with these headings.
- Put the property addresses, property types and prices of all properties in the Verdana font.
- Apply a background colour of #CCCCCC to table cells displaying the location, the property type and the price in every second row as displayed above.

Create a Table to Display a Horizontal Line and Bookmark Hyperlink

1.  Open **property.htm** in Notepad, if it is not already open.
2. Put the cursor under the closing </table> of the third table.
3. Create a fourth table to display a horizontal line and a hyperlink to a named anchor, as shown below. Remember to put in a comment before the table.

← width=40px →	Horizontal Line
	Top of Page

Remember:
- Insert the comment <!-- Beginning of Table 4 --> before the opening <table> tag.
- Set the width of the table to 100% and the border width to 0.
- Use the <hr/> tag to create a horizontal line.
- Put the text Top of Page in the Verdana font.
- To create the hyperlink to a named anchor, first create a named anchor just after the opening <body> tag. The code will be something like <a name="top"> </a>. Next, enclose the text Top of Page in anchor tags. The opening anchor tag should refer to the named anchor:

```
<a href="#top">Top of Page</a>
```

- Check your work by opening **property.htm** in Internet Explorer. The completed web page should look something like Fig. 3.10.

Note: Use <br /> tags to ensure spacing between each of the four tables.

Southern Estate Agents			
Home	Financial Services	Property Valuation	Contact Details

To arrange a viewing, ring 01-295 0155

Properties Available in Dun Laoghaire

Location	Property Type	Price
23 Seaview Park	Detached House	€325,000
27 Abbey Lane	Terraced House	€280,000
8 Dorney Road	Semi-Detached House	€345,000
15 Anville Wood	Semi-Detached House	€380,000

Properties Available in Shankill

Location	Property Type	Price
122 Plunkett Road	Semi-Detached House	€320,000
3 Corbawn Terrace	Semi-Detached House	€315,000
16 Wolverton Grove	Semi-Detached House	€343,000
12 Bayview Mews	Semi-Detached House	€295,000

Properties Available in Bray

Location	Property Type	Price
136 O'Flynn Park	Semi-Detached House	€345,000
28 Millwood Downs	Semi-Detached House	€415,000
12 Rockford Manor	Semi-Detached House	€347,500
3 Eden Lane	Semi-Detached House	€295,000

Top of Page

Fig. 3.10   The completed Property Details web page

Create a Bulleted List

If you are familiar with word processing packages, you have probably used bullets. They are used to emphasise a list of points. A bullet is a small symbol, usually a solid circle or square, that appears at the beginning of a short line of text. In HTML, bullets are created using the Unordered List tags and List Item tags.

Tag Names	Unordered List, List Item

HTML Code	<pre><ul>
	<li>List Item 1</li>
	<li>List Item 2</li>
	<li>List Item 3</li>
	etc.
	</ul></pre>

Effect	Bullets are displayed before each item enclosed in <li> tags. The default bullet style is disc.
Attributes	type="disc" (●), type="circle" (○), or type="square" (■)

Example:

HTML Code in Notepad	Result in Internet Explorer
<ul type="square"> <li>Oil fired central heating</li> <li>Parking</li> <li>Alarm</li> </ul>	■ Oil fired central heating ■ Parking ■ Alarm

Note:
- The whole list must be enclosed in <ul></ul> tags.
- If you do not specify the bullet type, it will be shown as a disc.

Plan the Layout of the Individual Property Pages

Look at the layout for each individual property page below.

Table 1 (width=100%)

◄— width=40px —►	Southern Estate Agents
	Home Property Details Next
	Horizontal Line

1 blank line

Table 2 (width=100%)

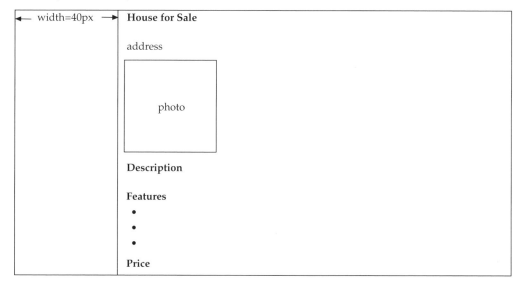

Create the Property Page

 First, we set up the table containing the company name, hyperlinks and horizontal line. The structure of this table is:

← width=40px →	Southern Estate Agents
	Home Property Details Next
	Horizontal Line

1. Start Notepad. In a blank Notepad document set up a web page by entering opening and closing <html>, <head> and <body> tags.
2. Enter <title> tags in the Head section so that the text 23 Seaview Park appears in the title bar of Internet Explorer. Save this page as **23seaview.htm** in the **estate** folder.
3. Open **index.htm** in Notepad.
4. Highlight HTML code from <!--Beginning of Table 1--> down as far as, but not including <!--Beginning of Table 2-->. Copy this code by selecting Edit, followed by Copy from the menu.
5. Open **23seaview.htm** in Notepad.
6. Put the cursor between the opening and closing <body> tags. Select Edit, followed by Paste from the menu.
7. Delete colspan="4" from the first and third rows of the table.
8. Edit the HTML code in the second row of the table so that it reads:

```
<tr>

  <td width="40"></td>
  <td>
    <font face="Verdana">
    Home     Property Details     Next
    </font>
  </td>

</tr>
```

Tip: No matter how many times you press the spacebar in Notepad, Internet Explorer will show only one space between words. To create more than one space, use   as many times as required.

Remember:
- Set up the text Home as a hyperlink to **index.htm**. Set up the text Property Details as a hyperlink to **property.htm**. (The text Next will be set up as a hyperlink to **27abbey.htm** later on in this project.)

← width=40px →	<!--main heading and address-->

<!--main heading and address-->
3-Bedroom Detached House for Sale
23 Seaview Park, Dun Laoghaire

<!--picture of house-->

<!--description of house-->
Description
3-bedroom detached house within strolling distance of Dun Laoghaire town centre

<!--main features of house-->
Features
• Oil-fired central heating
• Parking
• Alarm

<!--selling price-->
Price: €325,000

- Set up Table 2, as shown.
- This table has only one row. Use <br /> tags each time you want to move onto the next line.
- Put comments in your HTML code. This will make it easier to copy and edit the HTML code later on.
- Format the text `3-Bedroom Detached House for Sale` in Heading 1 style. Display the photo **23seaview.jpg** in the position indicated. (Use the <img /> tag.) Using the alt attribute, set up the alternative text as `23 Seaview Park`.
- Put the headings 23 Seaview Park, Dun Laoghaire, Description and Features in bold. Apply the following formatting to these headings:

```
face="Arial"
color="#990000"
```

- Put the heading Price €325,000 in bold. Format this text as follows:

```
face="Arial"
size="6"
color="#990000"
```

- Put the rest of the text in the web page in the Verdana font.
- Check your work by opening **23seaview.htm** in Internet Explorer.

Note: Use <br /> tags to create space between Tables 1 and 2.

Create Additional Property Pages

Because all individual property pages have the same structure and formatting, you can create the remaining property pages by making copies of the **23seapark.htm** web page and changing the text for the main heading, the address, description, features and price. You also need to change the file reference in the <img /> tag each time you copy **23seapark.htm.**

Copy a Web Page

Create the **27abbey.htm** web page by making a copy of the **23seaview.htm** web page and editing the copy.

1.   Open **23seaview.htm** in Notepad.

2.   Select File, followed by Save As from the menu. Enter **27abbey.htm** as the file name and then click Save.

3.   **27abbey.htm** is now open in Notepad. Using the information displayed in Table 3.5, change the page title, edit the text that appears on the web page and change the reference to the photo in the <img /> tag.

Table 3.5   Information to be displayed in the *27abbey.htm* web page

27abbey.htm					
Page Title: 27 Abbey Lane					
Main Heading	Address	Photo	Description	Features	Price
2-Bedroom Terraced House for Sale	27 Abbey Lane, Dun Laoghaire	27abbey.jpg alt="27 Abbey Lane"	Spacious 2-bedroom terraced house with parking	Oil-fired central heating PVC double glazing Parking	€280,000

4.   Check your work by opening **27abbey.htm** in Internet Explorer.

5.   Create two additional property web pages using the information displayed in Tables 3.6 and 3.7.

Table 3.6 Information to be displayed in the *8dorney.htm* web page

8dorney.htm					
Page Title: 8 Dorney Road					
Main Heading	Address	Photo	Description	Features	Price
3-Bedroom Semi-Detached House for Sale	8 Dorney Road, Dun Laoghaire	8dorney.jpg alt="8 Dorney Road"	Fully modernised family home in the heart of Dun Laoghaire	Gas-fired central heating Garage Large garden	€345,000

Table 3.7 Information to be displayed in the *15anville.htm* web page

15anville.htm					
Page Title: 15 Anville Wood					
Main Heading	Address	Photo	Description	Features	Price
4-Bedroom Semi-Detached House for Sale	15 Anville Wood, Dun Laoghaire	15anville.jpg alt="15 Anville Wood"	Exceptionally spacious house in a quiet cul-de-sac	Oil-fired central heating Security sensor lights Parking Alarm	€380,000

6. Copy the other individual property pages from the *Step by Step Web Design* CD.

 Project 3
 Graphics
 Web Pages

- Open the **Project 3** folder in the CD.
- Open the **Web Pages** folder.
- Copy all the files from the **Web Pages** folder to your **estate** folder.

Set Up Hyperlinks to Individual Property Pages

 1. Open **property.htm** in Notepad. The addresses of properties in Dun Laoghaire are in Fig. 3.11.

Properties Available in Dun Laoghaire		
Location	Property Type	Price
23 Seaview Park	Detached House	€325,000
27 Abbey Lane	Terraced House	€280,000
8 Dorney Road	Semi-Detached House	€345,000
15 Anville Wood	Semi-Detached House	€380,000

Fig. 3.11 Dun Laoghaire properties in the **Property Details** web page

2. Set up the text 23 Seaview Park as a hyperlink to **23seaview.htm.**
3. Set up the text 27 Abbey Lane as a hyperlink to **27abbey.htm.**
4. Set up all other locations as hyperlinks to the appropriate web pages, using the file names in Table 3.8.

Table 3.8   Other hyperlinks from the *Property Details* web page

Text	Hyperlink to:
8 Dorney Road	8dorney.htm
15 Anville Wood	15anville.htm
122 Plunkett Road	122plunkett.htm
3 Corbawn Terrace	3corbawn.htm
16 Wolverton Grove	16wolve.htm
12 Bayview Mews	12bayview.htm
136 O'Flynn Park	136oflynn.htm
28 Millwood Downs	28millwood.htm
12 Rockford Manor	12rockford.htm
3 Eden Lane	3eden.htm

5. Open **23seaview.htm** in Notepad. The following line of text appears just below the main heading:

   Home Property Details Next

   Set up the text Next as a hyperlink to **27abbey.htm.**
6. Set up Next hyperlinks in **27abbey.htm, 8dorney.htm** and **15anville.htm.**

Table 3.9   Next hyperlinks in the individual property web pages

Web Page	Text	Hyperlink to:
27abbey.htm	Next	8dorney.htm
8dorney.htm	Next	15anville.htm
15anville.htm	Next	122plunkett.htm

7. Test all your hyperlinks in Internet Explorer.

Plan the Layout of the Financial Services Page

This is the layout of the Financial Services page.

Table 1 (width=100%)

← width=40px →	Southern Estate Agents			
	←————— Merge cell across 4 columns —————→			
	Home	Property Details	Property Valuation	Contact Details
	←————— Horizontal Line —————→ *Merge cell across 4 columns*			

1 blank line

Table 2 (width=75%)

← width=40px →	Financial Services
	Text

1 blank line

Table 3 (width=60%)

← width=40px →	Typical Mortgage Repayments			
	←————— Merge cell across 4 columns —————→			
	Loan Amount	20 Years	25 Years	30 Years

Create the Financial Services Page

 1. Start Notepad. In a blank Notepad document set up a new web page by entering opening and closing <html>, <head> and <body> tags.

2. Enter <title> tags in the Head section so that the text We offer the complete finance package to secure your home appears in the title bar of Internet Explorer. Save this page as **finance.htm** in the **estate** folder.

3. Create Table 1 by copying the HTML code you need from **index.htm** and then pasting this code into the <body> section.

4. Open **finance.htm** in Internet Explorer. The second row of the table is:

Property Details	Financial Services	Property Valuation	Contact Details

Edit the HTML code so that this table row appears as:

Home	Property Details	Property Valuation	Contact Details

5. Set up Table 2, as below. (Use <br /> tags to create a blank line between Tables 1 and 2.)

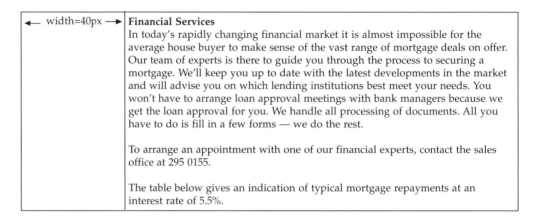

| ← width=40px → | **Financial Services**
In today's rapidly changing financial market it is almost impossible for the average house buyer to make sense of the vast range of mortgage deals on offer. Our team of experts is there to guide you through the process to securing a mortgage. We'll keep you up to date with the latest developments in the market and will advise you on which lending institutions best meet your needs. You won't have to arrange loan approval meetings with bank managers because we get the loan approval for you. We handle all processing of documents. All you have to do is fill in a few forms — we do the rest.

To arrange an appointment with one of our financial experts, contact the sales office at 295 0155.

The table below gives an indication of typical mortgage repayments at an interest rate of 5.5%. |

Note: Allow the text to wrap naturally. Use <br /> tags only after the heading and at the end of paragraphs. The text will not necessarily wrap exactly as shown. The point at which the text wraps depends on your monitor size and resolution.

Remember:
- Insert the comment <!-- Beginning of Table 2 --> before the opening <table> tag.
- Set the width of the table to 75% and the border width to 0.
- Put the heading Financial Services in bold. Apply the following formatting to the heading:

```
face="Arial"
color="#990000"
```

- Put the text starting from In today's rapidly changing financial market...5.5% in the Verdana font.

Tip: Use Copy and Paste to create Rows 3 to 7.

- Set up Table 3, as below:

← width=40px →	**Typical Mortgage Repayments** ← *Merge cell across 4 columns* →			
	Loan Amount	**20 Years**	**25 Years**	**30 Years**
	€100,000	€687.89	€614.09	€567.79
	€125,000	€859.86	€767.61	€709.74
	€150,000	€1,031.83	€921.13	€851.68
	€175,000	€1,203.80	€1,074.65	€993.63
	€200,000	€1,375.77	€1,228.17	€1,135.58

Remember:

- Insert the comment <!-- Beginning of Table 3 --> before the opening <table> tag. Set the width of the table to 60%, the border width to 0 and the cell spacing to 0.
- Include a blank cell with a width of 40 pixels at the beginning of each row.
- Put the heading Typical Mortgage Repayments in bold. Centre this heading in the merged cell. Apply the following formatting to this heading:

```
face="Arial"
size="4"
color="#CCCC00"
```

Apply a background colour of #666666 to the cell with this heading.
- Put the headings Loan Amount, 20 Years, 25 Years and 30 Years in bold. Apply the following formatting to these headings:

```
face="Arial"
color="#FFFFFF"
```

Apply a background colour of #333333 to each of the cells with these headings.
- Set the alignment of all table cells to 'center'.
- Put all payment amounts in the Verdana font.
- Apply a background colour of #CCCCCC to table cells showing Loan and Repayment amounts in every second row, as in Fig. 3.12.
- The completed Financial Services page should look something like Fig. 3.12.

Southern Estate Agents

Home   Property Details   Property Valuation   Contact Details

Financial Services
In today's rapidly changing financial market it is almost impossible for the average house buyer to make sense of the vast range of mortgage deals on offer. Our team of experts is there to guide you through the process of securing a mortgage. We'll keep you up to date with the latest developments in the market and will advise you on which lending institutions best meet your needs. You won't have to arrange loan approval meetings with bank managers because we get the loan approval for you. We handle all processing of documents. All you have to do is fill in a few forms - we do all the rest.

To arrange an appointment with one of financial experts, contact the sales office at 295 0155.

The table below gives an indication of typical mortgage repayments at an interest rate of 5.5%.

Typical Mortgage Repayments			
Loan Amount	20 Years	25 Years	30 Years
€100,000	€687.89	€614.09	€567.79
€125,000	€859.86	€767.61	€709.74
€150,000	€1,031.83	€921.13	€851.68
€175,000	€1,203.80	€1,074.65	€993.63
€200,000	€1,375.77	€1,228.17	€1135.58

Fig. 3.12   The completed Financial Services web page

Plan the Layout of the Property Valuation Page

The following is the layout of the Property Valuation page.

Table 1 (width=100%)

← width=40px →	Southern Estate Agents			
	← ————— *Merge cell across 4 columns* ————— →			
	Home	Property Details	Financial Services	Contact Details
	Horizontal Line			
	← ————— *Merge cell across 4 columns* ————— →			

Table 2 (width=75%)

← width=40px →	Property Valuation
	Text

Create the Property Valuation Page

1. 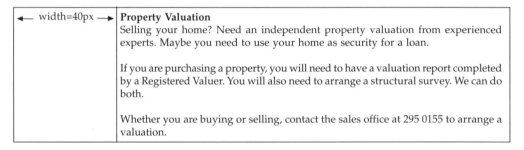 Create a new file in Notepad, as before.
2. Enter <title> tags in the Head section so that the text `We'll tell you what your property is worth` appears in the title bar of Internet Explorer. Save this page as **valuation.htm** in the **estate** folder.
3. Create Table 1 by copying the HTML code you need from **index.htm** and pasting this code into the <body> section.
4. Edit the HTML code in the second row of the table so that it appears as:

    Home   Property Details   Financial Services   Contact Details

5. Set up Table 2, as below:

← width=40px →	Property Valuation
	Selling your home? Need an independent property valuation from experienced experts. Maybe you need to use your home as security for a loan.
	If you are purchasing a property, you will need to have a valuation report completed by a Registered Valuer. You will also need to arrange a structural survey. We can do both.
	Whether you are buying or selling, contact the sales office at 295 0155 to arrange a valuation.

Remember:
- Insert the comment <!-- Beginning of Table 2 --> before the opening <table> tag.
- Set the width of the Table to 75% and the border width to 0.
- Put the heading Property Valuation in bold. Apply the following formatting to this heading:

```
face="Arial"
color="#990000"
```

- Put the text `Selling your...arrange a valuation.` in the Verdana font.
- The completed Property Valuation page should look something like Fig. 3.13.

Southern Estate Agents

Home   Property Details   Financial Services   Contact Details

Property Valuation
Selling your home? Need an independent property valuation from experienced experts?
Maybe you need to use your home as security for a loan.

If you are purchasing a property, you will need to have a valuation report completed by a
Registered Valuer. You will also need to arrange a structural survey. We can do both.

Whether you are buying or selling, contact the sales office at 295 0155 to arrange a
valuation.

Fig. 3.13   The completed Property Valuation web page

Mailto Hyperlinks

In Web Project 1, you learned how to create a hyperlink to another web page using
the anchor tag. Hyperlink text is enclosed in anchor tags and the opening anchor
tag refers to the target web page. For example:

```
<a href="23seaview.htm">23 Seaview Park</a>
```

sets up the text 23 Seaview Park as a hyperlink to the web page named
23seaview.htm. When the web page viewer clicks on this text, the web page named
23seaview.htm will open in Internet Explorer.

The anchor tag can also be used to set up a hyperlink to an email address. When
the web page viewer clicks the hyperlink text, the default email software (normally
Outlook Express) opens up with the email address already entered in the To: box.

Tag Name	Anchor
HTML Code	<a href="mailto:email address"> </a>
Effect	When the web page viewer clicks the hyperlink text, the default email software opens up with the email address referred to in the opening anchor tag already entered in the To: box.

Example:

HTML Code in Notepad	Result in Internet Explorer

`<a href="mailto:`
`someone@somewhere.ie">`
`Contact Us`
`<a>`
	Contact Us is underlined and displayed in blue. The mouse pointer changes to a pointing hand when over this text. Clicking this text opens Outlook Express with someone@somewhere.ie already entered in the To: box. The web page viewer can then type their email message.

Plan the Layout of the Contact Details Page

The following is the layout of the Contact Details page.

Table 1 (width=100%)

◄— width=40px —►	Southern Estate Agents			
	◄——————— *Merge cell across 4 columns* ———————►			
	Home	Property Details	Financial Services	Property Valuation
	◄————— Horizontal Line *Merge cell across 4 columns* —————►			

Table 2 (width=75%)

◄— width=40px —►	**Contact Details**
	Text

Create the Contact Details Page

1. Create a new file in Notepad, as before.
2. Enter <title> tags in the Head section so that the text Contact Us appears in the title bar of Internet Explorer. Save this page as **contact.htm** in the **estate** folder.
3. Create Table 1 by copying the HTML code you need from **index.htm** and pasting this code into the <body> section.
4. Edit the HTML code in the second row of the table so that it appears as:

   Home   Property Details   Financial Services   Property Valuation

5. Set up Table 2, as below:

◄— width=40px —►	Contact Details For all your property, mortgage and financial needs, contact our sales office. 1 Main Street, Ballybrack, Co. Dublin Tel: 01-295 0155 Fax: 01-295 0156 Email: info@southernestates.net

Remember:
- Insert the comment <!-- Beginning of Table 2 --> before the opening <table> tag.
- Put the heading Contact Details in bold. Apply the following formatting to the heading:

```
face="Arial"
color="#990000"
```

- Put the text For all your . . . info@southernestates.net. in the Verdana font.

- Set up the text `info@southernestates.net` as a mailto hyperlink to the email address info@southernestates.net
- Save the web page, then open it in Internet Explorer. The completed Contact Details page should look something like Fig. 3.14.

Fig. 3.14 The completed Contact Details web page

- Test your mailto hyperlink by clicking the hyperlink text. The default email software should open with info@southernestates.net entered in the To: box, as in Fig. 3.15.

Fig. 3.15 The result of clicking the mailto hyperlink

Set Up Hyperlinks

 1.  Open **index.htm** in Internet Explorer. The navigation menu is in Fig. 3.16.

Southern Estate Agents			
Property Details	Financial Services	Property Valuation	Contact Details

Fig. 3.16 Navigation menu in the home page

2. Set up the heading Property Details as a hyperlink to **property.htm.**
3. Set up the heading Financial Services as a hyperlink to **finance.htm.**
4. Set up the heading Property Valuation as a hyperlink to **valuation.htm.**
5. Set up the heading Contact Details as a hyperlink to **contact.htm.**

6. Test all your hyperlinks in Internet Explorer.

7. Open **property.htm** in Notepad. The menu bar is in Fig. 3.17.

Southern Estate Agents			
Home	Financial Services	Property Valuation	Contact Details

Fig. 3.17 Navigation menu in the Property Details web page

8. Set up these hyperlinks:

Table 3.10 Hyperlinks in the Property Details web page

Text	Hyperlink to:
Home	index.htm
Financial Services	finance.htm
Property Valuation	valuation.htm
Contact Details	contact.htm

9. Test all your hyperlinks in Internet Explorer.
10. In the same way, set up hyperlinks using the text in the navigation menus of **finance.htm, valuation.htm** and **contact.htm.** Test all your hyperlinks when you are finished.

Check Your Work

 To see the completed version of Southern Estate Agents web site, log on to **www.gillmacmillan.ie.**

Section 1 Revision Exercises

Revision Exercise 1

In this exercise you add formatting, horizontal lines and images to the web site that you created in Web Project 1.

On The John Murphy Home Page

1. Start Notepad and open the home page you created in Web Project 1, **index.htm** in the **johnmurphy** folder.
2. Take the underlining off the word 'Achill' every time it appears in the text, as it may be confused with hyperlinks.
3. Align all text to the left.
4. Put the headings Welcome To My Web Site and My name is John Murphy in bold. Apply the following formatting to these headings:

   ```
   face="Arial"
   size="4"
   ```

5. Put the headings Where I live, Where I study and My Hobbies in bold. Apply the following formatting to these headings:

   ```
   face="Arial"
   size="4"
   ```

6. Put all the rest of the text into the Verdana font.
7. Put in a horizontal line just under the text My name is John Murphy. The colour of this horizontal line is #0084A5. Set the size of this horizontal line to 4.
8. Put horizontal lines under the text Find out more about Mayo and Find out more out about Galway. Set the size of both horizontal lines to 4 and the colour to #0084A5.
9. Create an **images** sub-folder in the **johnmurphy** folder

10.  Open the **Section 1 Revision Exercises** folder on the *Step by Step Web Design* CD. Find the files **cliffs.jpg, mountain.jpg** and **surf.jpg** in the **Revision Exercise 1** sub-folder. Copy these files to the **images** sub-folder you created in 9 above.

11. Using tables, indent all text 30 pixels from the left edge of the screen. Put the images **cliffs.jpg, mountain.jpg** and **surf.jpg** in the position as shown on the following page.

Table 1 (width= "100%" border="0")

| ← width=30px → | Welcome To My Web Site |
| | My name is John Murphy |

Table 2 (width= "100%" border="0")

| ← width=30px → | Where I live | |
| | Text | cliffs.jpg |

Table 3 (width= "100%" border="0")

| ← width=30px → | Where I study | |
| | Text | mountain.jpg |

Table 4 (width= "100%" border="0")

| ← width=30px → | My Hobbies | |
| | Text | surf.jpg |

12. Add the alt attribute to each <img /> tag as follows:

Image	**alt**
cliffs.jpg	The cliffs of Achill Head
mountain.jpg	Slievemore mountain
surf.jpg	Surfer catches a wave in Keel Bay

13. Insert a Return to Top hyperlink at the bottom of the web page.
14. Add comments to your HTML code so that you and others will be able to understand it easily in the future. A section of the completed web page is shown in Fig. 3.18.

Welcome To My Web Site
My name is John Murphy

Where I Live

Slievemore View
Achill Sound
Co. Mayo

Achill is an island off the west coast of Ireland. It is the largest offshore island in Ireland but is connected to the mainland by a bridge. Achill is world famous for its beautiful scenery. If you are into the outdoors, this is the place for you! Keel Beach is a great place to go surfing with huge waves rolling in from the Atlantic. *Slievemore* and *Croaghan* are two of the highest mountains in Mayo and are a challenging day's hillwalking. The cliffs of *Achill Head* are the highest cliffs in Europe. Achill has some great pubs, with traditional sessions every weekend.

Find out more about Mayo

Fig. 3.18 The updated home page

On The mayo.htm Web Page

1. Open **mayo.htm** in Notepad.
2. Take the underlining off the word 'Castlebar' in the text, as it may be confused with a hyperlink.
3. Put all the rest of the text into the Verdana font.
4. Align the hyperlink text to the left.
5. Open the **Section 1 Revision Exercises** folder on the *Step by Step Web Design* CD. Find the file **house.jpg** in the **Revision Exercise 1** sub-folder. Copy this file to the **images** sub-folder on your disk.
6. Using a table, indent the text 30 pixels from the left edge of the screen. Put the image **house.jpg** in the position shown below.

Table (width= "100%" border="0")

← width=30px →	Mayo is one of the most scenic . . .	house.jpg
	Return to Home page	

7. Add the alt attribute to the <img /> tag so that the text `Farmhouse near Castlebar` is displayed while the image is loading or when the mouse pointer is positioned over the image.
8. Add comments to your HTML code so that you and others will be able to understand it easily in the future. The completed web page should look something like Fig. 3.19.

Mayo is one of the most scenic counties in Ireland with a spectacular and rugged coastline. Much of Mayo is mountainous. *Croagh Patrick*, Ireland's most famous mountain, attracts thousands of visitors every year. Castlebar is the main town in Mayo. Other important towns in Mayo are Westport, Ballina and Belmullet.

Return to Homepage

Fig. 3.19   The updated Mayo web page

On The galway.htm Web Page

1. Open **galway.htm** in Notepad.
2. Put all the text into the Verdana font.
3. Align the hyperlink text to the left.
4. Open the **Section 1 Revision Exercises** folder on the *Step by Step Web Design* CD. Find the file **sunset.jpg** in the **Revision Exercise 1** sub-folder. Copy this file to the **images** sub-folder on your own disk.
5. Using a table, indent the text 30 pixels from the left edge of the screen. Put the image **sunset.jpg** in the position shown below.

Table (width= "100%" border="0")

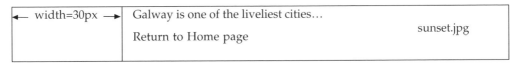

← width=30px →	Galway is one of the liveliest cities...	sunset.jpg
	Return to Home page	

6. Add the alt attribute to the <img /> tag so that the text `Sunset over Galway Bay` is displayed while the image is loading or when the mouse pointer is positioned over the image.
7. Add comments to your HTML code so that you and others will be able to understand it easily in the future. The completed web page should look something like Fig. 3.20.

Galway is one of the liveliest cities in Ireland and is famous for its arts and culture. It has many famous pubs and restaurants and was once the wine capital of Ireland. The world-renowned *Galway International Oyster Festival* takes place in Galway City every September.

Return to Homepage

Fig. 3.20   The updated Galway web page

Revision Exercise 2

In this exercise, you add formatting and images to the web site that you created in Web Project 2.

1. Create an **images** sub-folder in the **mikesmotors** folder.

2. 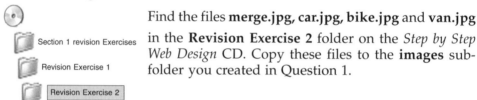 Find the files **merge.jpg, car.jpg, bike.jpg** and **van.jpg** in the **Revision Exercise 2** folder on the *Step by Step Web Design* CD. Copy these files to the **images** sub-folder you created in Question 1.

3. Start Notepad and open the home page created in Web Project 2, **index.htm** in the **mikesmotors** folder.
4. Put all the text into the Arial font.
5. Put the heading Mike's Motors in bold. Apply the following formatting to this heading:

    ```
    size="7"
    color="#005796"
    ```

6. Apply the following formatting to the horizontal line and to the marquee text:

    ```
    color="#005796"
    ```

7. Put the image **merge.jpg** under marquee text. Align the image to "center".
8. Add comments to your HTML code so that you and others will be able to understand it easily in the future. The completed web page should look something like Fig. 3.21.

On The cars.htm Web Page

1. Put all the text into the Arial font.

Mike's Motors

Cars | Bikes | Vans

We have the a great selection of quality used cars, bikes and vans.
Click a link below to see what we have on offer or contact one of our expert staff

On Special Offer this week: **Renault Clio 1.2 Sport**

Fig. 3.21 The updated Mike's Motors home page

2. Put the heading Mike's Cars in bold. Apply the following formatting to this heading:

```
size="7"
color="#7D7D7D"
```

3. Put the image **car.jpg** in between *Mike's* and *Cars*, as in Fig. 3.22.
4. Apply the following formatting to the horizontal line and to the marquee text:

```
color="#7D7D7D"
```

Home | Bikes | Vans

We currently have **4** cars on offer

Description	Price
Renault Clio 1.2 Sport 17,500 miles Airbag, alloy wheels, ABS, alarm	€10,000
Volkswagen Polo 1.4 138,000 miles Power steering, adjustable steering wheel, electric mirrors	€11,750
Volkswagen Golf 1.9d 80,000 miles Central locking, driver air bag, radio-cassette, power steering	€8,999
Opel Astra 1.4L Saloon 61,000 miles Power steering, electric mirrors, driver air bag, immobiliser	€12,750

Fig. 3.22 The updated Mike's Cars web page

5. Add comments to your HTML code so that you and others will be able to understand it easily in the future. The completed web page should look something like Fig. 3.22.

On The bikes.htm Web Page

1. Put all the text into the Arial font.
2. Put the heading Mike's Bikes in bold. Apply this formatting to this heading:

   ```
   size="7"
   color="#9C2C86"
   ```

3. Put the image **bike.jpg** in between Mike's and Bikes, as in Fig. 3.23.
4. Apply the following formatting to the horizontal line and to the marquee text:

   ```
   color="#9C2C86"
   ```

5. Add comments to your HTML code so that you and others will be able to understand it easily in the future. The completed web page should look something like Fig. 3.23:

Mike's Bikes

Home | Cars | Vans

We currently have **5** bikes on offer

Description	Price
BMW F Series F650GS 12,000 miles ABS, heated grips	€12,000
Suzuki GSXR 1000 38,000 miles Red and White, immaculate condition	€9,950
Honda VFR 800i 10,000 miles New tyres, racing lines, lots of extras	€11,750
Suzuki GSXR 600 OZ 45,000 miles Very clean bike, new front tyre, new chain	€12,750
Honda VTR 1000 SP1 8,000 miles Red, immaculate condition	€8,950

Fig. 3.23   The updated Mike's Bikes web page

On The vans.htm Web Page

1. Put all the text into the Arial font.
2. Put the heading Mike's Vans in bold. Apply this formatting to this heading:

   ```
   size="7"
   color="#7BC618"
   ```

3. Put the image **van.jpg** in between Mike's and Vans, as in Fig. 3.24.
4. Apply the following formatting to the horizontal line and to the marquee text:

   ```
   color="#7BC618"
   ```

5. Add comments to your HTML code so that you and others will be able to understand it easily in the future. The completed web page should look something like Fig. 3.24.

Mike's Vans

Home | Cars | Bikes

We currently have 9 vans on offer

Description	Price
Renault Kangoo 1.7 Diesel 30,000 miles Blue, radio-cassette, power steering	€7,250
Ford Transit 42,000 miles White, one owner, power steering, radio-cassette, airbag	€12,750
Opel Combo 6,000 miles Green, power steering, ABS, CD player	€12,500
Ford Transit 12,000 miles Red, new model, ABS, power steering, CD player	€13,500
Citroen Berlingo 50,000 miles White, 1.9 diesel, very clean van	€5,500

Fig. 3.24   The updated Mike's Vans web page

On The Contact.htm Web Page

1. Put all the text into the Arial font.
2. Put the heading Mike's Motors in bold. Apply the following formatting to this heading:

```
size="7"
color="#005796"
```

3. Put the image **merge.jpg** under the address. The completed web page should look something like Fig. 3.25.

Mike's Motors

25 Oldcourt Road
Waterford
Tel: (051) 227 3098
Fax: (051) 227 3099
Email: mikesmotors@eircom.net

Return to Homepage

Fig. 3.25   The updated Contact web page

Progress Test 3

Finish the review of Web Project 3 by answering these questions.

1. The home page in a web site should be saved as _____.

2. The euro sign can be displayed on a web page by entering _____ in the HTML code.

3. Text that scrolls across a web page is called a _____.

4. Creating a hyperlink to a _____ allows the web page viewer to 'jump' to another part of a web page.

5. Find the errors in these file names:
   a. my web page.htm _____
   b. page#4.htm _____

6. The HTML code for any web page currently displayed in Internet Explorer can be viewed by selecting View, followed by _____ from the menu.

7. Find the errors in this HTML code:

```
<table>
  <tr>
    <td>Day</td>
    <td>Temp</td>
  </tr>
    <td>Monday</td>
    <td>15.6</td>
</table>
```

8. <title> tags should be entered in the _____ section of the HTML code.

9. HTML code that displays text and images on a web page should be entered in the _____ section.

10. Web colours are created by mixing _____, _____ and _____ in different proportions.

11. A _____ allows the web page viewer to 'jump' from one web page to another by clicking the left mouse button.

12. Write the HTML code to create this bulleted list:
    - 30,000 miles
    - Metallic paint
    - One owner
    _____
    _____
    _____

13. List three items essential for viewing a web page on the World Wide Web.

    a. _____

b. _____

c. _____

14. The image **house.jpg** is stored in the **images** folder. This **images** folder is a sub-folder of the **estate** folder where all the web pages are stored. The HTML code below is from the **index.htm** page, stored in the **estate** folder.

```
<img src="house.jpg" />
```

Why is the image not displayed correctly on the web page?

_____

_____

15. Write the HTML code to create this table:

Temperature Averages	
January	**July**
5	21

_____

_____

_____

_____

16. Complete this HTML code so that the background colour of Cell 1 is red (#FF0000) and the background colour of Cell 2 is yellow (#FFFF00).

```
<table>
  <tr>
    <td              >Cell 1</td>

    <td              >Cell 2</td>
  </tr>
</table>
```

17. To merge cells horizontally in a table, add the _____ attribute to the opening <td> tag. To merge cells vertically, add the _____ attribute.

18. What is wrong with this comment?

```
<-- Beginning of Table 1 -->
```

_____

19. The number of colours that can be displayed on a PC's monitor depends on which item of hardware?

_____

20. When Internet Explorer cannot display a colour correctly, it either selects a close match to the colour or makes a new colour by mixing available colours together. This process is called _____.

Check Your Work

 To view the answers to the progress test together with the updated versions of the John Murphy and Mike's Motors web sites log onto **www.gillmacmillan.ie.**

New in Web Project 3

HTML Tags

Tag Name	HTML Code	Description
Image	<img src="image name" />	Displays a digital photo or a graphic in a web page.
Font	<font face=" " size=" " color= " "> </font>	Text enclosed in <font> </font> tags will be displayed in the style, size and colour specified in the opening <font> tag.
Comment	<!-- Text between these symbols is not interpreted as HTML code -->	Allows you to insert descriptive comments in your HTML code.
Unordered List	<ul> </ul>	Shows the beginning and end of a bulleted list.
List Item	<li> </li>	Each item in a bulleted list must be enclosed in <li> </li> tags.
Anchor	<a href="mailto:email address> </a>	The anchor tag is used to create a mailto hyperlink to an email address. The opening anchor tag refers to the email address. Text enclosed in the opening and closing anchor tags becomes a hyperlink to the email address.

SECTION 2

More Advanced
Web Design Projects

Main Objectives: Create web pages using Dreamweaver and HTML
Apply formatting using Inline CSS styles
Use Paint Shop Pro as an image editor
Create web graphics using Paint Shop Pro

Web Project 4: Online Computer Tutorial Web Site

General Project Objectives
- Develop a web site colour scheme
- Learn about web image formats (GIF and JPEG)
- Format a web page using Inline CSS styles
- Use a digital camera

Dreamweaver Objectives
- Define a site
- Enter text on a web page
- Create tables and insert images
- Use Dreamweaver as a HTML editor
- Use the Properties Toolbar to specify colour and alignment

Paint Shop Pro Objectives
- Resize an image
- Optimise an image
- Create navigation buttons
- Create a drop cap

Revision Exercises
- CSS Styles Revision Exercise 1
- CSS Styles Revision Exercise 2
- Progress Test 4

New in Web Project 4: Dreamweaver and Paint Shop Pro toolbar buttons

Web Project 5: Online Database Web Site

General Project Objectives
- Scan an image for the web
- Test download times
- Test a web page at different screen resolutions
- Test web pages in Internet Explorer and Netscape Navigator

Dreamweaver Objectives
- Control hyperlink text with styles
- Create a rollover image
- Create anchors
- Create a site map
- Add meta tags to web pages

Paint Shop Pro Objectives
- Edit images
- Create a web page background image
- Create graphics and bullet symbols

Revision Exercises
- HTML Tags web site
- Progress Test 5

New in Web Project 5: Dreamweaver toolbar buttons

Web Assignment 1

Insert multimedia files in a web page

Web Assignment 2

Create an image map

Web Project 4

Online Computer Tutorial Web Site

Scenario

Learn IT is a training company specialising in computer skills. The growth in popularity of the Internet and advances in communications technology has opened up new distance learning markets for Learn IT. They are offering an introductory computer course in their training centre but now wish to deliver the same training material through their web site.

In this project you develop an online computer tutorial web site with a series of lessons and tests. You create all the digital images and graphics to be used in the site. Once the web site is ready, students on the computer-skills course will have the option of accessing training material on line.

Project Objectives

By completing this web project, you will learn how to:
- Develop a web site colour scheme.
- Learn about web image formats (GIF and JPEG).
- Format a web page using Inline CSS styles.
- Use a digital camera.

In **Dreamweaver**, you will learn how to:
- Define a web site.
- Enter text on a web page.
- Create tables and insert images.
- Use Dreamweaver as a HTML editor.
- Use the Properties Toolbar to specify colour and alignment.

In **Paint Shop Pro**, you will learn how to:
- Resize an image.
- Optimise an image.
- Create navigation buttons.
- Create a drop cap.

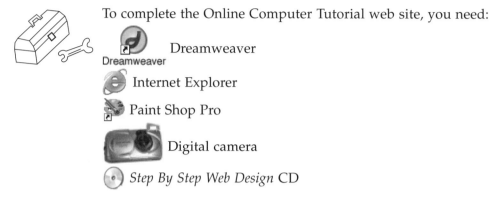

To complete the Online Computer Tutorial web site, you need:

Dreamweaver

Internet Explorer

Paint Shop Pro

Digital camera

Step By Step Web Design CD

Site Structure

In this web project, you create the home page and all of the lesson pages. The test and solution web pages for the web site are on the *Step by Step Web Design* CD. Later in this assignment, you add navigation buttons to the test and solution web pages.

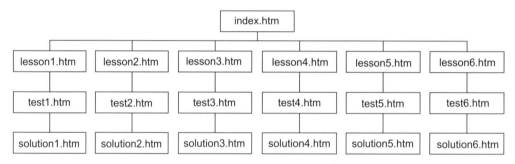

Fig. 4.1   This is the site structure for Online Computer Tutorial web site

Colour Palette

The colours you use in your web site will have a lot of effect on its impact and readability. Always use a mix of colours that are known to work together. This is not as easy as it sounds, as not everyone has a background in art or design.

So how do non-experts find colour combinations that work? The best method is to look at existing web sites and to make a note of the colour schemes that you like and that work well. Have a look around you. If you see a colour scheme on a book cover or in room decoration, make a note of it.

General Colour Scheme Guidelines

- Web pages with dark text on light backgrounds are easier to read.
- Less is more – try not to use more than four colours.

- Use colours consistently across the web pages of a web site. For example, if the body text is blue on the home page, it should be blue on the other web pages.
- Although most PCs now have graphics cards with 16.7 million colours, choosing web safe colours means consistency across all hardware platforms.

The Online Computer Tutorial web site will have a white background with blue body text on all lesson web pages. All headings and navigation buttons are orange. For variety, some of the table cells in the home page are light grey. The text in the table cells is dark grey. The colour scheme is summarised in Table 4.1.

Table 4.1 Online Computer Tutorial web site colour scheme

Item	Colour	Hex Code
Headings, buttons	Orange	#FF6600
Body text	Blue	#330099
Sections of Table in Home Page	Light Grey	#CCCCCC
Text displayed in light grey cells	Dark Grey	#666666

Web Image File Types – GIF and JPEG

 Each time you create an image to be displayed on a web page, you should save the image either as a GIF or a JPEG. These are the two major image file formats supported by web pages: GIF (Graphics Interchange Format) and JPEG (Joint Photographic Experts Group).

• **JPEG File Format:** Each pixel is represented by 24 bits. This means that each pixel in a JPEG image can be one of 16.7 million colours.
• **GIF File Format:** Each pixel is represented by 8 bits. This means that each pixel in a GIF image can be one of 256 colours.

Choosing GIF or JPEG

The image file format you choose depends on a number of factors. Use Table 4.2 to decide which file format is most suitable.

When a digital photograph is saved as a JPEG format, there is a small loss of quality because JPEG file compression removes some data from the image to make the file size smaller. There is no loss of quality with the GIF format, but it is not suitable for photographs because it can only display 256 colours.

The way that Internet Explorer downloads the image is also important. **GIF** images are **interlaced**. This means that the whole image appears first in low resolution and becomes gradually sharper as Internet Explorer downloads more of the image. **JPEG** images are **non-interlaced**, meaning that the image downloads section by section.

Table 4.2 Guidelines for choosing an image format

Use JPEG for:	Use GIF for:
Images with lots of colours and shades with subtle transitions between shades and colours.	Images with large areas of solid colour with no transitions between colours.
Examples: • digital photographs • scanned photographs	*Examples:* • menu buttons, company logos and banner headings • scanned images with large areas of solid colour

Fig. 4.2 shows how a non-interlaced image downloads in stages when a web page with the image is opened in Internet Explorer.

Fig. 4.2 A non-interlaced JPEG image downloading on a web page in Internet Explorer

JPEG images can be made 'progressive' using the JPEG optimiser in Paint Shop Pro. This means that they will appear as interlaced images when they are being downloaded. This is useful for large JPEG images because it allows the web page viewer to get an idea of what the image is like while waiting for it to download.

Note: As the Windows operating system only supports three-letter file extensions, **.jpg** is used as the file extension for JPEG files

Create a Folder to Store Your Web Pages

1. **My Computer** Create a new folder named **tutorial** on a floppy disk, zip disk, USB storage device or hard disk.

2. tutorial Create an **images** sub-folder inside the **tutorial** folder.

images

Take Pictures with a Digital Camera

 1. Using a digital camera, take photographs of:

- a PC
- a mouse
- a keyboard
- a monitor
- a CPU
- a printer.

Sample pictures and their file names are in Table 4.3.

Table 4.3   Digital photographs with their file names

pc.jpg

mouse.jpg

keyboard.jpg

monitor.jpg

cpu.jpg

printer.jpg

2.  Save each digital photograph to the **images** sub-folder, using the file names in Table 4.3.

 Note: If you do not have access to a digital camera, you can copy these images from the *Step by Step Web Design* CD. Open the **Project 4** folder in the CD. It has a sub-folder named **digital photos**. Copy the **pc.jpg, mouse.jpg, keyboard.jpg, monitor.jpg, cpu.jpg** and **printer.jpg** images from the **digital photos** folder to your **images** folder.

 Photography Tips
- Place the mouse, keyboard and printer on a white background, such a blank sheet of A3 paper. The white background will blend in with the background colour of the web page.

- Put the object to be photographed on the floor with the side you want to photograph showing. Take the photograph while looking straight down at it.
- Be aware of lighting and how it reflects off each item that you photograph.

Paint Shop Pro

 As a web page designer, you will need to create graphics, logos or digital photographs for your web site. For copyright reasons, you cannot copy graphics or digital photographs from other web sites (unless they are from a free web graphics site) – you must create them yourself.

Paint Shop Pro is a powerful graphics package with many features, including animation. Using Paint Shop Pro, you can create and edit images for the Web. Because this is not a book about web graphics, we will only look at some of Paint Shop Pro's tools. This should give you a general understanding of image creation and editing. Once you understand the basic principles of image creation and editing, it is relatively easy to learn how to use other graphics packages.

View a Digital Photograph in Paint Shop Pro

 View details of the digital photograph **pc.jpg** in Paint Shop Pro to decide how the image can be optimised for web page viewing.

1.   Open **pc.jpg** in Paint Shop Pro.
2. Select Image, followed by Image Information from the menu to display the details of **pc.jpg.** The Current Image Information dialog box in Fig. 4.3 gives some important information about the digital photograph:
   - It is 1280 pixels wide and 960 pixels high.
   - The resolution of the image is 72 pixels per inch.
   - Each pixel is represented by 24 bits in memory, giving a total 16.7 million possible colours (2^{24} = 16.7 million).
   - The image needs 3600 Kb of memory in order to display it on your PC screen.
   - The image requires 213 kilobytes of storage space on disk.

This information can be found by viewing the **tutorial** folder in My Computer, see Fig. 4.4.

For web design, there are a number of important points.

- The physical size of the image (1280 × 960 pixels) is far too big and would not fit on a monitor with a resolution of 800 × 600 pixels.
- The size of the image in bytes is also too big, and this would increase the download time of the web page.
- The resolution of the image is 72 pixels per inch, which is the standard for web design.

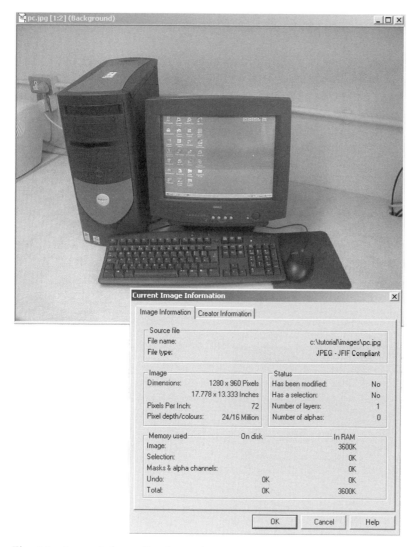

Fig. 4.3   Image information for **pc.jpg**

	Name ▲	Size	Type	Dimensions
My Computer	pc.jpg	213 KB	Paint Shop Pro 7 Image	1280 x 960

Fig. 4.4   Details for **pc.jpg**, which can be found in My Computer

> **NOTE**
>
> **Note:** The dimensions of the digital photos from your camera depend on how it is set up. Most cameras offer a range of resolutions from 640 × 480 pixels to 2560 × 1920 pixels. If possible, set the resolution of your digital camera to 1280 × 960 before doing this project.

If this is not possible, you can still do the project but your digital photos may not have the same dimensions as in the *Step by Step Web Design* solutions web site.

Resize a Digital Photograph in Paint Shop Pro

 Here you resize the **pc.jpg** image using Paint Shop Pro. The resized image will take up less space on the web page and need less storage space on disk.

1. Open **pc.jpg** in Paint Shop Pro, if it is not already open.
2. Select Image, followed by Resize from the menu. The Resize dialog box is displayed.
3. In the Resize dialog box, select Pixel Size and enter 128 as the width. The height displayed depends on the original proportions of your digital photograph. If the height is not exactly as in Fig. 4.5, it does not really matter.

Note: Make sure that the Maintain aspect ratio box is ticked in the Resize dialog box. The image will be resized proportionately.

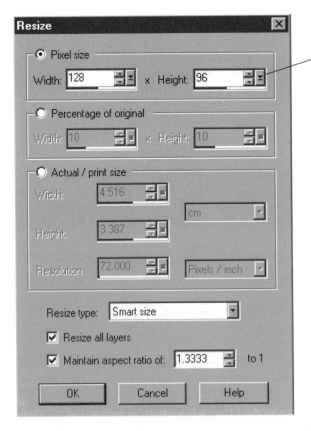

At 128 × 96 pixels, the resized image is 10 per cent of the original size (assuming that the resolution of your camera is set to 1280 × 960 pixels).

Fig. 4.5 The Resize dialog box allows you to change the physical size of an image

4. Click OK to resize the image.
5. Select File, followed by Save As from the menu. Enter **smallpc.jpg** as the name of the resized image. Saving the image under a different name means that the original image is still intact and can be used for further editing.

Note:
*   Smart size is a method of image resizing where Paint Shop Pro chooses the best algorithm based on the current image characteristics.
*   The Resize All Layers box relates to images with more than one layer. As our image has only one layer, this feature has no effect.

Optimise a Digital Photograph in Paint Shop Pro

To reduce the file size of a digital photograph, use the JPEG Optimiser. The JPEG optimiser is part of the web toolbar, which is shown in Fig. 4.6.

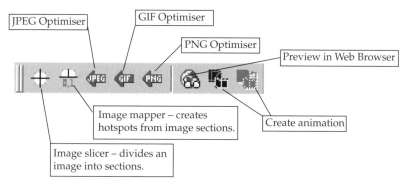

Fig. 4.6   Paint Shop Pro's web toolbar

Note:
*   **PNG** (Portable Network Graphics) is another type of graphic file for the Web. Like JPEG, it uses 24-bit colour, but unlike JPEG it does not compress images so there is no loss of quality. Because of this, PNG file sizes are much larger than JPEG file sizes and the download times are much longer, and the PNG file format is not widely used in web design.
*   A **hotspot** is where a section of an image is used as a hyperlink to another web page. Using hotspots, a single image can contain many hyperlinks to different web pages. This is often called an image map. Hotspots will be introduced in the Image Map assignment.

1. Open **smallpc.jpg** if it is not already open.
2. Select View, followed by Toolbars from the menu. Display the Web Toolbar by ticking the appropriate check box and close the Toolbars dialog box.

Fig. 4.7 The Web Toolbar

3. In the Web Toolbar, click the Export JPEG button. The JPEG Optimiser is displayed.
4. Set the compression value to 2. This makes the size of the file smaller but with some loss of image quality. If you compress a file more (higher compression value), the file size and image quality are reduced. As a web page designer you need to reach a compromise between image quality and file size. Larger files size mean slower download times.
5. Click the Format tab and select Progressive as the file type. This means that the image will look quite blurred on the web page at first but become progressively sharper as more of the image is downloaded.
6. Click the Download Times tab. The download times for viewing this image in a browser are shown across different modem speeds.
7. Click OK and enter **smallpc.jpg** as the name of the optimised image. Click the Save button to save the optimised image. Click Yes when Paint Shop Pro asks if you want to overwrite the original image.
8. View the details for **smallpc.jpg** in My Computer. They should be more or less the same as the details in Fig. 4.8. Notice how the file size has been reduced from 213Kb to 9Kb. This will reduce download time when the image is displayed on a web page. The dimensions of the image have also been reduced from 1280 × 960 to 128 × 96.

Name ▲	Size	Type	Dimensions
smallpc.jpg	9 KB	Paint Shop Pro 7 Image	128 x 96

Fig. 4.8 Details of **smallpc.jpg** after resizing and optimising

JPEG images usually have a larger file size than GIF images. This is because the JPEG format has more colours, so there is more data to store. As a web page designer you must balance the need for image quality with the need for small image file sizes. Good image quality makes your web pages more attractive and professional. Higher image quality needs a larger file size and a longer download time. Long download times are bad because they frustrate the web page visitor and can cause people to leave your web site. As a general rule, try to keep the file size of all your images below 15Kb. File sizes of 10Kb or less are best.

Rule:
Limit the file sizes of all images to 15Kb or less.

For You To Do

1. Resize each of the following images so the height is 96 pixels. (Make sure that the Maintain aspect ratio box is ticked so that each image is resized proportionately.) In each case accept the width in pixels that is automatically entered by Paint Shop Pro.
   - mouse.jpg
   - keyboard.jpg
   - monitor.jpg
   - cpu.jpg
   - printer.jpg.

2. Save each resized image in the **images** sub-folder, using the file names in Table 4.4. **For each image, File and Save As, so you do not overwrite the original image.**

Table 4.4   **File names for resized images**

Original Image	Resized Image
mouse.jpg	smallmouse.jpg
keyboard.jpg	smallkeyboard.jpg
monitor.jpg	smallmonitor.jpg
cpu.jpg	smallcpu.jpg
printer.jpg	smallprinter.jpg

3. Using the JPEG Optimiser, set the compression value to 2 and the file type to Progressive for each image. Save each optimised image using the original file names; when you optimise **smallmouse.jpg,** save the optimised image as **smallmouse.jpg,** and so on. (Click Yes when Paint Shop Pro asks if you want to overwrite the original image.)

Note: We will use the original images again later on in this project so do not delete them from the **images** folder!

Dreamweaver

Dreamweaver is a powerful web-development package used by web design professionals. It can be used as a HTML generator, writing HTML as you place text or graphics on a web page. Dreamweaver can also be used as a HTML editor, where HTML code can be edited or typed directly. It has a range of toolbar buttons and menu options, which reduce the amount of direct HTML coding to be done, as well as powerful web-site management tools that keep track of hyperlinks and web page names.

If you are into web design, you should know Dreamweaver. The only disadvantage is that, as a web site designer, you will experience a very small loss of control due to the fact that Dreamweaver adds in some additional HTML code.

Dreamweaver Toolbars

The most important toolbars to know about in Dreamweaver are the Insert Toolbar, the Document Toolbar and the Properties Toolbar.

 Note: If you are using an earlier version of Dreamweaver, your toolbars will look slightly different to those in Figs. 4.9 and 4.10.

The Insert Toolbar

The Insert toolbar is divided into a number of tabs, each of which you click to display a range of toolbar buttons. For example, when the Tables tab is selected, Dreamweaver displays buttons that allow you to insert a table together with buttons that insert various table tags. Fig. 4.9 shows the Insert Toolbar with the Common tab selected.

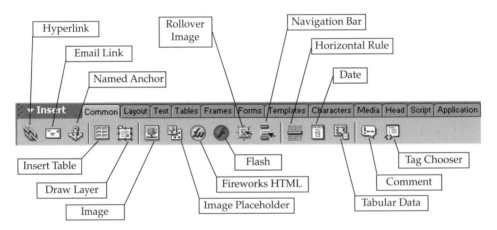

Fig. 4.9 The Insert toolbar with the Common tab selected

The Document Toolbar

The Document toolbar allows you to view your web page in different ways, carry out file management, preview your web page in a browser, get help from a reference manual and select items that you want to display in the Dreamweaver window.

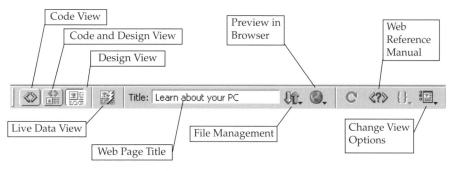

Fig. 4.10   The Document toolbar

The Properties Toolbar

The Properties toolbar enables you to alter the properties of the item you have selected in the web page. The Properties toolbar adjusts as you select different items. In Fig. 4.11, the Properties toolbar is displaying the properties of selected text.

Fig. 4.11   The Properties toolbar displaying the properties of selected text

In Fig. 4.12, the Properties toolbar is displaying the properties of a table. Additional properties, specific to tables, are displayed in the lower half of the toolbar.

Fig. 4.12   The Properties toolbar displaying the properties of a selected table

Fig. 4.13 is an example of the Properties toolbar displaying the properties of an image. Notice how all sections of the toolbar relate to the selected image.

Fig. 4.13   The Properties toolbar displaying the properties of a selected image

Viewing A Dreamweaver Web Page

Dreamweaver allows you to create and view your web pages using three different methods. These are Code View, Design View and Code and Design View.

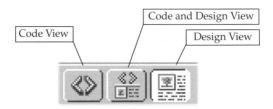

Fig. 4.14   Code View, Design View and Code and Design View buttons

Design View

Working in Design View in Dreamweaver is very similar to using a word processing package. Web page text can be typed in directly, as in Fig. 4.15.

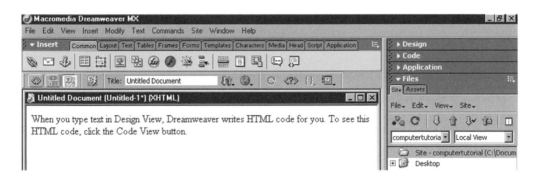

Fig. 4.15   Creating a web page in Design View

Toolbar buttons and menu options can be used to format text, insert tables and images. As you work in Design View, Dreamweaver writes all the HTML code for you.

Code View

When Code View is selected, any HTML, XHTML or other code used to create the current web page is displayed.

One very useful feature of Code View is that the line numbers are shown on the left. Fig. 4.16 shows our web page in Code View. Notice how Dreamweaver has inserted code relating to XHTML in the Head section. This is because the Make document XHTML compliant check box was ticked when creating the web page.

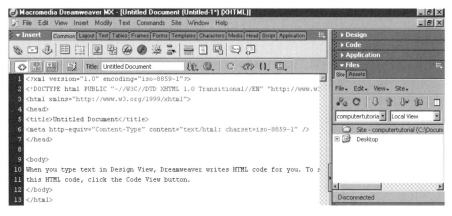

Fig. 4.16 Creating a web page in Code View

Code and Design View

This is a useful way of looking at your web page if you want to see a web page and the HTML code that created the web page at the same time. Fig. 4.17 is an example of a web page viewed in Code and Design view. HTML code appears in the upper section of the Dreamweaver window as text is typed in the lower section.

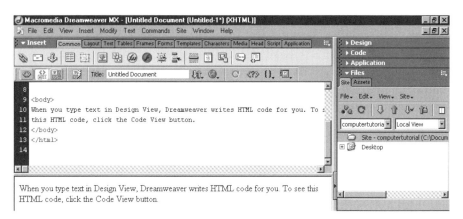

Fig. 4.17 Creating a web page in Code and Design View

Define a Site in Dreamweaver

1. In Dreamweaver, select Site followed by New Site from the menu.

   Dreamweaver

2. In the Site Definition dialog box (see Fig. 4.18), make sure that the Basic tab is selected. Now type **computertutorial** as the name for the site. Click Next (Fig. 4.18).

3. Select No, I do not want to use a server technology and click Next.

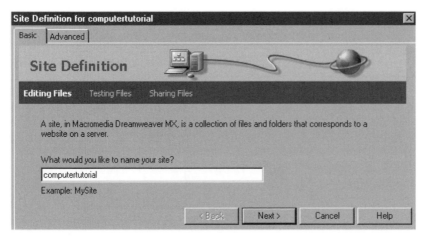

Fig. 4.18 Step 1 of Dreamweaver's Site Definition Wizard

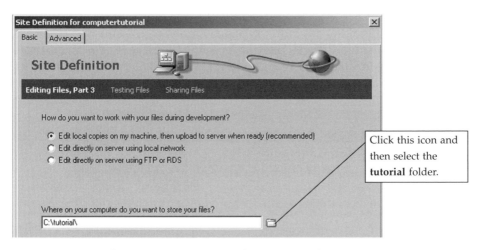

Fig. 4.19 Step 3 of Dreamweaver's Site Definition wizard

4. Select Edit local copies on my machine as in Fig. 4.19. Now click the folder icon and navigate to your **tutorial** folder that you created at the beginning of this web project. This tells Dreamweaver that all your web pages will be saved in the **tutorial** folder. Click Next.

5. Step 4 of the Site Definition wizard asks you to specify how to connect to the remote server. As you will not be making this web site 'live' on the Internet, select None from the list.

6. Click Next to see the summary information for your site, then click Done.

Create the Home Page

  1. In Dreamweaver, select File, followed by New from the menu. The New Document dialog box is displayed in Fig. 4.20.

Dreamweaver

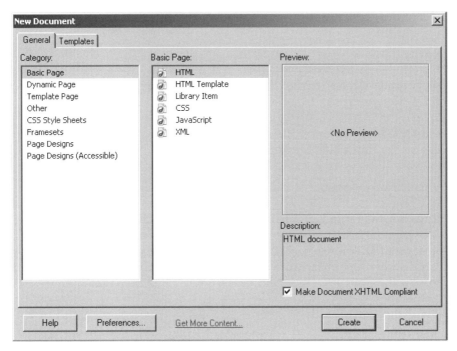

Fig. 4.20 The New Document dialog box

2. Set up your web page by clicking Create. (Make sure that the Make Document XHTML Compliant check box is selected.)
3. A new blank web page is displayed in Dreamweaver.

Add Text to the Home Page Using Design View

1.   Dreamweaver   Make sure that your Dreamweaver web page is open and that you are in Design View. Enter the text `Online Computer . . . enjoy the tutorial` as shown below.

Design View

> Online Computer Tutorial
> Need computer terms explained in plain English? Look no further! We explain everything from the absolute beginning so it does not matter if you've never used a computer before. Maybe you've just bought a computer or you need to use a computer in your new job. Whatever your reason for learning, we'll get you started! The main areas of your computer are displayed below. We have designed comprehensive lessons to introduce you to each area. We hope you enjoy the tutorial. For further information contact us by email.

Note: Allow the text to wrap naturally. It may not necessarily wrap as displayed.

2. Select File, followed by Save from the menu. Enter **index.htm** as the file name and click the Save button.

 Note: When you enter the text `Online Computer Tutorial` and press the Enter key, Dreamweaver inserts the code:

```
<p>Online Computer Tutorial</p>
```

Pressing the Enter key causes Dreamweaver to enclose the text `Online Computer Tutorial` in opening and closing paragraph tags. HTML inserts a blank line after the closing paragraph tag. To move the cursor onto a new line in Dreamweaver, without inserting a blank line, hold down the Shift key and then press Enter. Dreamweaver then inserts the HTML code:

```
Online Computer Tutorial<br />
```

Add a Title to Your Web Page

 Adding a title is easy in Dreamweaver. You do not have to type the <title> </title> tags in the Head section. Simply enter the text in the Title section of Dreamweaver's Document toolbar and it will automatically appear in the title bar of Internet Explorer.

1. Open the **index.htm** web page in Dreamweaver, if it is not already
   Dreamweaver open. Make sure that you are viewing the web page in Design View.
2. Using the Document toolbar, enter the text `Welcome to the Online Computer Tutorial` as the title, as in Fig. 4.21.

Fig. 4.21 Using the Document toolbar to insert a page title

3. Check your spelling by selecting Text, followed by Check Spelling from the menu.
4. Save the changes by selecting File, followed by Save from the menu.

Test Your Web Page in Internet Explorer

1. Click the Preview/Debug in Browser button on the Document toolbar as in Fig. 4.22.

Fig. 4.22 Test your web page with the Preview/Debug in Browser button

2. Select Preview in iexplore as in Fig. 4.22. Your web page opens in Internet Explorer.

Cascading Style Sheets (CSS)

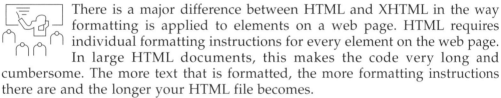 There is a major difference between HTML and XHTML in the way formatting is applied to elements on a web page. HTML requires individual formatting instructions for every element on the web page. In large HTML documents, this makes the code very long and cumbersome. The more text that is formatted, the more formatting instructions there are and the longer your HTML file becomes.

XHTML incorporates CSS (Cascading Style Sheets), which handle formatting in a completely different way. In CSS, the formatting instructions are separated from the elements that are being formatted. Formatting instructions are specified once in the Head section and are then applied many times to elements on the web page. This is achieved by identifying and naming specific elements or sections of the web page using special tags and then linking these named elements or sections to formatting instructions contained in the Head section.

By separating formatting instructions from the elements to be formatted, CSS makes the code easier to construct and understand. CSS styles are quite similar to HTML in the way they are written. Once you know how to write HTML, it is relatively easy to learn about CSS styles.

Advantages of CSS Styles

* Each set of formatting instructions is specified only once. This greatly reduces the amount of code and makes the code easier to understand and edit.
* Using CSS styles forces you into planning the way your web page will be formatted before you actually create it. For example, you will have to decide the style, size and colour of headings, sub-headings and body text. In the long run, this makes your web pages easier to create and, more importantly, easier to edit.

Formatting with CSS Styles

This is done in two separate steps:

Create A CSS Style

A CSS style is a set of formatting instructions. For example, it could be a CSS style that specifies the font style as Verdana, the font weight as Bold and the font colour as #FF0000.

Apply Formatting Using the CSS Style Created in Step 1

Once a CSS style has been created, it can be applied as many times as you want within a web page.

Dreamweaver's properties toolbar has two modes: HTML mode and CSS mode. When the properties toolbar is in HTML mode, a capital letter A button is shown between the Format and Font boxes, as in Fig. 4.23. Dreamweaver writes HTML

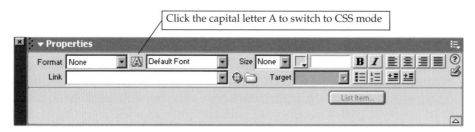

Fig. 4.23   The Properties toolbar in HTML mode

formatting code when the properties toolbar is in HTML mode. For example, if you highlight some text and click the Bold button, the text would be enclosed in <b> </b> tags. To switch the Properties toolbar to CSS mode, click the capital letter A button. The Properties toolbar now appears as in Fig. 4.24.

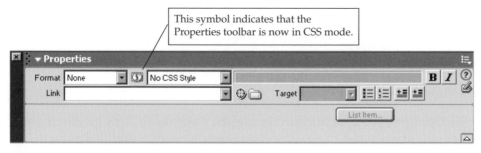

Fig. 4.24   The Properties toolbar in CSS mode

When the Properties toolbar is in CSS mode, it controls the format of the web page by writing CSS code in the Head section instead of HTML code in the Body section.

Worked Example Step 1: Create a CSS Style

 Now create a CSS style to format the main heading of the home page. Each CSS style can have as many formatting instructions as you decide is appropriate. In this case, you will add three formatting instructions to the CSS style to specify the font style, size and colour.

1.
   Dreamweaver
   Open the **index.htm** web page in Design View, if it is not already open, and make sure that the Properties toolbar is in CSS mode.

2. Select New CSS Style from the Properties toolbar, as shown in Fig. 4.25.

Fig. 4.25   Creating a new CSS style

3. The New CSS Style dialog box is now displayed (see Fig. 4.26.)

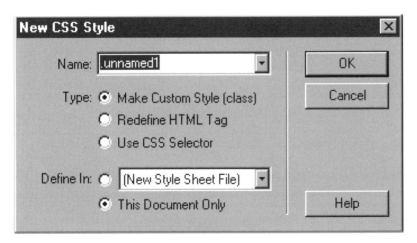

Fig. 4.26   The New CSS Style dialog box

4. Each CSS style should be given a name. The name of the CSS style should have a full stop in front of it. Enter **.main** as the name of the new CSS style, as in Fig. 4.27.

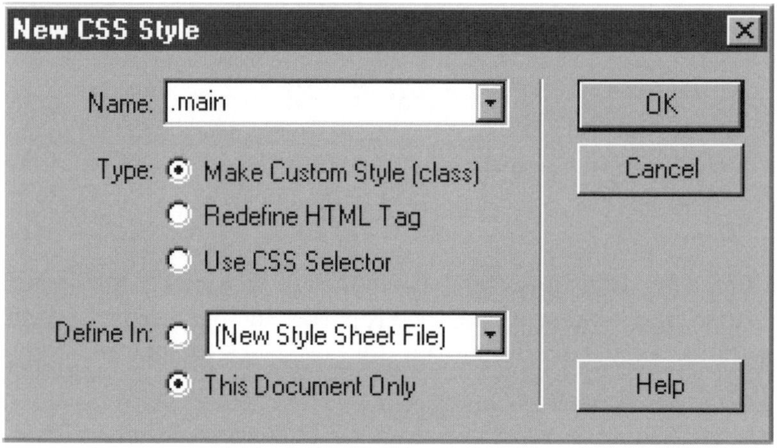

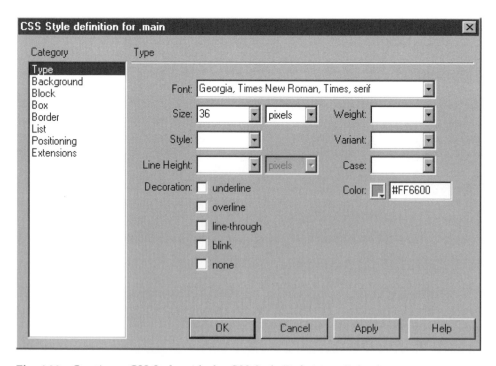

Fig. 4.27   Assigning a name to a CSS style

Make sure that the Make Custom Style (class) option is selected and that the style is defined in This Document Only. The means that the CSS code will be added to the Head section of the web page. Click OK to go on to the next step, where you add formatting instructions to the CSS style.

5. The CSS Style Definition dialog box (Fig. 4.28) allows us to add formatting instructions to a CSS style.

Fig. 4.28   Creating a CSS Style with the CSS Style Definition dialog box

6. Select Georgia, Times New Roman, Times, serif as the font, 36 as the size and #FF6600 as the colour, as in Fig. 4.28. Click OK to set up the CSS style.

7. Click the Code View button to display the HTML and CSS code. The code is in the Head section and should appear as:

```
<style type="text/css">
<!--
.main {
  font-family: Georgia, "Times New roman", times, serif;
  font-size: 36px;
  color: #FF6600;

}
-->
</style>
```
property-value pairs

Fig. 4.29 CSS code for the **.main** style

The CSS code is written between opening and closing <style> tags. Each CSS style consists of a number of properties and values. Property and value pairs are separated using semi-colons.

Each property included in the CSS style has a name and is followed by the value assigned to that property. For example in Fig. 4.29, the font-size property is followed by a value of 36px. A colon is used to separate the property and the value. In the **.main** style there are three property-value pairs because we specified the font, size and colour in the CSS Style Definition dialog box.

CSS code can also be entered directly in the Head section in code view. As you become more familiar with CSS styles, you will be able to able to edit and eventually create your own CSS styles by doing your own coding.

Worked Example Step 2: Format Text Using a CSS Style

We now apply the formatting instructions in the **.main** CSS style to the main heading in the **index.htm** web page.

1.
   Dreamweaver
   Open the **index.htm** web page in Design View, if it is not already open, and make sure that the Properties toolbar is in CSS mode.

2. Highlight the text Online Computer Tutorial and select **main** from the Properties toolbar, as in Fig. 4.30. Dreamweaver applies the three formatting instructions in the **.main** style to the text Online Computer Tutorial. The result should look something like Fig. 4.31.

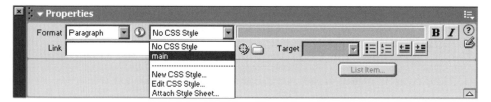

Fig. 4.30 Using the Properties toolbar to apply the **.main** style

Online Computer Tutorial

Need computer terms explained in plain English? Look no further! We explain everything from the absolute beginning so it doesn't matter if you've never used a computer before. Maybe you've just bought a computer or you need to use a computer in your new job. Whatever your reason for learning, we'll get you started! The main areas of your computer are displayed below. We have designed comprehensive lessons to introduce you to each area. We hope you enjoy the tutorial. For further information, contact us by email.

Fig. 4.31 The **.main** style has been applied to Online Computer Tutorial

3. Click the Code View button and look at the HTML code in the Body section:

```
<p class="main">Online Computer Tutorial</p>
```

Dreamweaver has linked the text Online Computer Tutorial to the **.main** style by adding class="main" to the opening paragraph tag

CSS Properties and Values

In this project, you will use the CSS properties and values listed in Table 4.5. Additional CSS properties and values will be introduced in Web Project 5.

Table 4.5 CSS properties and values

Property	Associated Values	Example
font-family	any valid font name	font-family: Arial, Helvetica, sans-serif;
font-size	any size in pixels	font-size: 12px;
font-weight	normal, bold, bolder, lighter	font-weight: bold;
color	any hexadecimal colour code	color: #330099

Note:
- In CSS styles hexidecimal codes are not enclosed in inverted commas.
- A font-size of 12px in a CSS style roughly corresponds to <font size="2">. A font-size of 16px in a style rule roughly corresponds to <font size="3">. A font-size of 32px in a style rule roughly corresponds to <font size="6">.

- The style and size of text can be set for the whole web page by creating CSS styles for the <body> tag:

```
body{
font-family: "Verdana";
font-size: 12px;
}
```

This CSS style sets a default text format of Verdana, 12px for the whole web page. However, these formats will not be applied to text in table cells.
- Each time you select a font in the Style Definition dialog box, Dreamweaver specifies more than one font in the CSS code. For example, when you choose the Georgia font, Dreamweaver writes the CSS code:

```
font-family: Georgia, "Times New Roman", Times, serif;
```

Internet Explorer will display the text in Georgia as long as the Georgia font is loaded on the web page viewer's PC. If Georgia is not on the PC, Internet Explorer will try to display the text in Times New Roman. If neither Georgia nor Times New Roman are available, Internet Explorer will attempt to display the text in the Times font. In the case of a very old PC, with neither Georgia, Times New Roman nor Times, the text will be displayed in a basic serif font.

Create a CSS Style to Format Text in the Home Page

 1. Open the **index.htm** web page in Design View, if it
Dreamweaver   is not already open, and make sure that the Properties
toolbar is in CSS mode.
2. Using the Properties toolbar, create a CSS style named **.text** that includes these properties:
font: Verdana, Arial, Helvetica, sans serif
size: 12px
color: #330099
3. Apply the **.text** style to the paragraph beginning `Need computer terms explained...`
4. 🖫 🌀. Save the changes and preview the web page in Internet Explorer using the Preview/Debug in Browser button. The text should appear as in Fig. 4.32.

Online Computer Tutorial

Need computer terms explained in plain English? Look no further! We explain everything from the absolute beginning so it doesn't matter if you've never used a computer before. Maybe you've just bought a computer or you need to use a computer in your new job. Whatever your reason for learning, we'll get you started! The main areas of your computer are displayed below. We have designed comprehensive lessons to introduce you to each area. We hope you enjoy the tutorial. For further information, contact us by email.

Fig. 4.32 The **.text** style has been applied to the paragraph of text

Plan the Layout of the Home Page

The layout of the home page is displayed below. We have already entered the main title and a paragraph of text. We will create a table below the paragraph, as shown below, to position text and images on the home page.

Online Computer Tutorial ⟩━ main title

Need computer terms............contact us by email. ⟩━ paragraph of text

Table 1 (width=100%)

Lesson 1 Your PC	smallpc.jpg	Lesson 2 Using The Mouse	smallmouse.jpg	Lesson 3 Using The Keyboard	smallkeyboard.jpg
Text text text text Text text text text Text text text text		Text text text text text Text text text text text Text text text text text		Text text text text text Text text text text text Text text text text text	
Start Lesson 1		Start Lesson 2		Start Lesson 3	
Blank Table row					
Lesson 4 The Monitor	smallmonitor.jpg	Lesson 5 The CPU	smallcpu.jpg	Lesson 6 Using Your Printer	smallprinter.jpg
Text text text text text Text text text text text Text text text text text		Text text text text text Text text text text text Text text text text text		Text text text text text Text text text text text Text text text text text	
Start Lesson 4		Start Lesson 5		Start Lesson 6	

Create a Table in Dreamweaver

1. Make sure that the cursor is in a blank line below the text We hope you enjoy the tutorial.

2. ▦ Click the Insert Table button on the Insert toolbar. Specify the following properties in the Insert Table dialog box as in Fig. 4.33.

3. Click OK to insert the table. Dreamweaver inserts HTML code to create a table with seven rows and six columns (see Fig. 4.33).

Insert Table ☒

Rows: 7   Cell Padding: 0   OK

Columns: 6   Cell Spacing: 3   Cancel

Width: 99 Percent ▼   Help

Border: 0

Fig. 4.33 The Insert Table dialog box

Note: Cell spacing sets the gap between table cells. A cell spacing of 3 means there will be a 3-pixel gap between each cell in the table. **Cell padding** is the amount of empty space between the cell contents and the borders of the cell.

Increasing the cell spacing pushes the cells away from each other. Increasing the cell padding pushes the cell borders outwards from the cell contents.

4.   To make sure that text and images in the table are spaced out evenly on the page, we will set the column widths, using the opening <td> tags in the top row of the table. Our table has six columns. Six does not divide exactly into 100, so we set the column widths to 17%, 16%, 17%, 16%, 17%, 16%. These numbers add up to 99 per cent, which is the width of the table. Click the Code View button and edit the HTML code for the first row of the table as shown in Fig. 4.34.

```
<table width="99%" border="0" cellspacing="3" cellpadding="0">
  <tr>
    <td width="17%"> </td>
    <td width="16%"> </td>
    <td width="17%"> </td>
    <td width="16%"> </td>
    <td width="17%"> </td>
    <td width="16%"> </td>
  </tr>
```

Fig. 4.34 Setting column widths in the table

Note:
- Without this HTML code, column widths will adjust automatically as you enter text in a Dreamweaver table.
- Each time you create a table, Dreamweaver inserts non-breaking spaces in table cells. This is because HTML will not display empty table cells on a web page.

Design View button

5.   Click the Design View button, then position the cursor in the second cell of the first table row.

Image button

6.   Click the Image button in the Insert toolbar. The Select Image Source dialog box appears, as shown in Fig. 4.35.

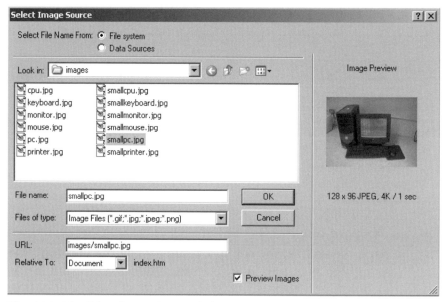

Fig. 4.35   The Select Image Source dialog box

7.   Open the **images** folder. Select **smallpc.jpg.** A preview of the image appears in the Select Image Source dialog box as in Fig. 4.35. The dimensions of the image are also given. The image is 128 pixels wide and 96 pixels high. The file size in kilobytes and the download time are also listed. The file size of this image is 4 kilobytes and the download time is 1 second.
8.   Click OK to insert this image in the table.
9.   In the same way, insert images in Row 1 and Row 5 of the table in the positions indicated in Table 4.6. (Press the Tab key to move the cursor from cell to cell.)

Table 4.6   Positions of images on the home page

	smallpc.jpg		smallmouse.jpg		smallkeyboard.jpg
	smallmonitor.jpg		smallcpu.jpg		smallprinter.jpg

Display Alternative Text

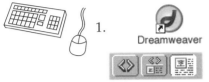 1. 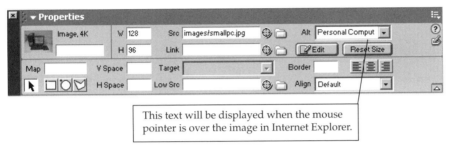 View the **index.htm** web page in Design View.

2. Select the **smallpc.jpg** image.

Fig. 4.36 showing Properties of smallpc.jpg:

> This text will be displayed when the mouse pointer is over the image in Internet Explorer.

Fig. 4.36   Properties of **smallpc.jpg** displayed in the Properties toolbar

3. Using the Properties toolbar, enter `Personal Computer` as the alternative text, as shown in Fig. 4.36.
4. Set up alternative text for the other images in **index.htm**, using the information in Table 4.7.

Table 4.7   Images and alternative text

Image Name	Alternative Text
mouse.jpg	The Mouse
keyboard.jpg	The Keyboard
monitor.jpg	The Monitor
cpu.jpg	The CPU
printer.jpg	The Printer

5. Save the web page and preview the web page in Internet Explorer using the Preview/Debug in Browser button. Check the alternative text by positioning the mouse pointer over each image.
6. Insert text as shown in Fig. 4.37. Use the left and right arrow keys on the keyboard to move the cursor from table cell to table cell. To force the cursor to a new line, hold down the Shift key on the keyboard and press Enter.

Tip: Pressing Enter in Dreamweaver moves the cursor to a new line but also inserts a blank line. To move to a new line without inserting a blank line, hold down the Shift key and press Enter.

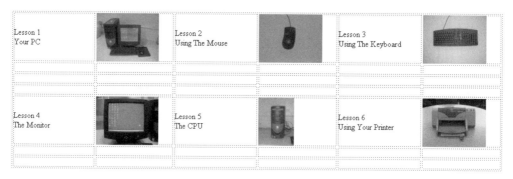

Fig. 4.37   Text and images inserted in a Dreamweaver table

Create a CSS Style to Format Headings

 1. Open the **index.htm** web page in Design View, if it is not already open, and make sure that the Properties toolbar is in CSS mode.

2. Using the Properties toolbar, create a CSS style named **.headings** that includes the following properties:
   font: Arial, Helvetica, sans-serif;
   size: 16px;
   weight: bold;
   color: #330099;

3. Apply the **.headings** style to the text in Fig. 4.37: Lesson 1 Your PC, Lesson 2 Using The Mouse, etc.

4. Save the web page and preview the web page in Internet Explorer using the Preview/Debug in Browser button.

Create a CSS Style to Format Table Text

1. Using the Properties toolbar, create a CSS style named **.tabletext** that includes the following properties:

font: Verdana, Arial, Helvetica, sans-serif;
size: 12px;
color: #666666;

Merge Table Cells

1. Open the **index.htm** web page in Dreamweaver, if it is not already open.

2. Click the Show Design View button to display the web page in Design View.

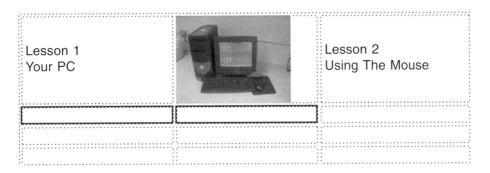

Fig. 4.38 Merging two cells in a table

3. Highlight table cells as shown in Fig. 4.38.

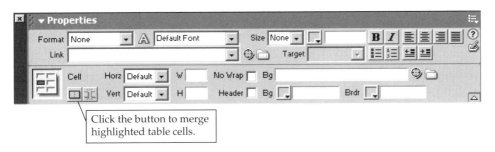

Fig. 4.39 The Properties toolbar

4. Merge the selected cells using the Merge Cells button in the Properties toolbar, as shown in Fig. 4.39.
5. Merge cells and enter text as shown in the shaded cells of Table 4.8.

Table 4.8 Main table in the home page with text entered

Lesson 1 Your PC	pc.jpg	Lesson 2 Using The Mouse	mouse.jpg	Lesson 3 Using The Keyboard	keyboard.jpg
A quick history of the PC as well as a list of things you can do with your computer.		Never used a mouse before? Look no further than this tutorial.		The main device for entering data into your PC. Click here to learn the keys!	
Start Lesson 1		Start Lesson 2		Start Lesson 3	
Lesson 4 The Monitor	monitor.jpg	Lesson 5 The CPU	cpu.jpg	Lesson 6 Using Your Printer	printer.jpg
Click here to learn how to change screensavers and backgrounds.		The CPU is the brain of your computer. Click here to learn more.		From simple documents to birthday cards. Click here to learn how.	
Start Lesson 4		Start Lesson 5		Start Lesson 6	

Apply a Background Colour to Table Cells

 Table 4.9 displays the background colours used in the table. #CCCCCC is a light grey. #FF6600 is orange. Where no background colour is specified for a table cell, the cell will be white.

Table 4.9 Background colours of table cells in the home page

Lesson 1 Your PC	pc.jpg	Lesson 2 Using The Mouse	mouse.jpg	Lesson 3 Using The Keyboard	keyboard.jpg
bgcolor="#CCCCCC"		bgcolor="#CCCCCC"		bgcolor="#CCCCCC"	
bgcolor="#FF6600"		bgcolor="#FF6600"		bgcolor="#FF6600"	
Lesson 4 The Monitor	monitor.jpg	Lesson 5 The CPU	cpu.jpg	Lesson 6 Using Your Printer	printer.jpg
bgcolor="#CCCCCC"		bgcolor="#CCCCCC"		bgcolor="#CCCCCC"	
bgcolor="#FF6600"		bgcolor="#FF6600"		bgcolor="#FF6600"	

1. Open the **index.htm** web page in Dreamweaver, if it is not already open.

Dreamweaver

2.  Click the Show Design View button to display the web page in Design View.

3. Highlight all cells in the second row of the table.

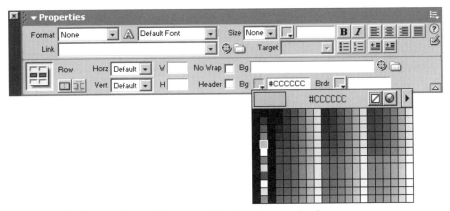

Fig. 4.40 Using the Properties toolbar to apply a background colour

4. Select #CCCCCC from the list of web safe colours in Fig. 4.40.
5. Apply background colours to the other table cells in the same way. (See Table 4.9 on page 136.)
6.  Save the changes and preview the web page in Internet Explorer.

Format Table Text

1. Open the **index.htm** web page in Design View, if it is not already open, and make sure that the Properties toolbar is in CSS mode.

Dreamweaver

2. Using the Properties toolbar, apply the **.tabletext** style to the text in each shaded cell of Table 4.9. (Except for the table containing the text Start Lesson 1, Start Lesson 2 up to Start Lesson 6.)

Align Data in Table Cells

1. Open the **index.htm** web page in Dreamweaver, if it is not already open.

Dreamweaver

2.  Click the Show Design View button to display the web page in Design View.

3. Select the text Lesson 1 Your PC.

4. Set the horizontal alignment of this table cell to Center and the vertical alignment to Middle, as in Fig. 4.41.

Fig. 4.41 Using the Properties toolbar to set horizontal and vertical alignment of table cells

5. Apply a horizontal alignment of Center and a vertical alignment of Middle to each cell that has a lesson title.

6. Save the changes and preview the web page in Internet Explorer.

Create a Mailto Hyperlink

1.  With the **index.htm** web page open in Design View, highlight the text contact us in the opening paragraph.

2. Click the Email Link button and enter info@onlinetutorial.ie in the Email Link dialog box, as in Fig. 4.42.

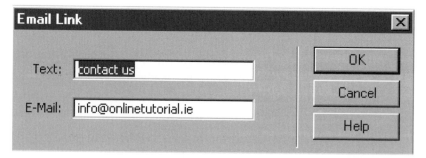

Fig. 4.42 Creating a mailto hyperlink with the Email Link dialog box

The completed home page should look something like Fig. 4.43.

Online Computer Tutorial

Need computer terms explained in plain English? Look no further! We explain everything from the absolute beginning so it doesn't matter if you've never used a computer before. Maybe you've just bought a computer or you need to use a computer in your new job. Whatever your reason for learning, we'll get you started! The main areas of your computer are displayed below. We have designed comprehensive lessons to introduce you to each area. We hope you enjoy the tutorial. For further information contact us by email.

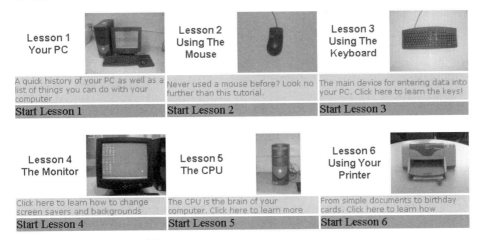

Lesson 1
Your PC

A quick history of your PC as well as a list of things you can do with your computer

Start Lesson 1

Lesson 2
Using The Mouse

Never used a mouse before? Look no further than this tutorial.

Start Lesson 2

Lesson 3
Using The Keyboard

The main device for entering data into your PC. Click here to learn the keys!

Start Lesson 3

Lesson 4
The Monitor

Click here to learn how to change screen savers and backgrounds

Start Lesson 4

Lesson 5
The CPU

The CPU is the brain of your computer. Click here to learn more

Start Lesson 5

Lesson 6
Using Your Printer

From simple documents to birthday cards. Click here to learn how

Start Lesson 6

Fig. 4.43   The completed home page

Add Comments to Your HTML Code

 In the Southern Estate Agents web site, you directly coded comments into our HTML code. In Dreamweaver, a comment can be added to the HTML code by clicking the Comment button, which is in the Insert Toolbar.

1.   Open the **index.htm** web page in Dreamweaver, if it is not already
Dreamweaver open.

2.    Click the Show Design View button to display the web page in design view.

3.   Position the cursor in the blank line immediately above the table and then click the Comment button. The Comment dialog box is displayed (see Fig. 4.44).

4.   Enter the comment shown in Fig. 4.44 and click OK to add the comment to your HTML code.

5.   Display the HTML code by clicking the Code View button. The comment begins with <!-- and ends with --> and is positioned just above the opening <table> tag.

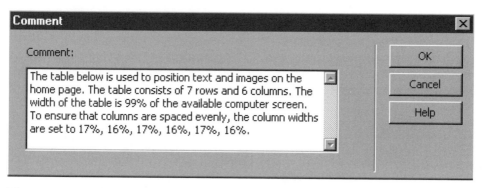

Fig. 4.44 Using the Comment dialog box to add a comment to your HTML code

Create the Lesson Web Pages

In this section you create the first lesson page. Because all lesson pages have the same format and more or less the same structure, you can create other lesson pages by copying and editing. When you have finished this section, you will have created a web page that looks something like Fig. 4.45.

Lesson 1: Your PC

The first PC was made by IBM in 1981. Back then PCs weren't very powerful and had limited graphics. Over time PCs gradually became more user-friendly and more powerful. Today millions of people use PCs at work. A huge range of sophisticated software packages can be installed on your PC. Specialised software allows you to use your PC to carry out many different tasks in the workplace. The growth in leisure-related software means that your home PC can be used to watch DVDs, play computer games and listen to music CDs, as well as creating your own CDs and DVDs!

Software that comes with your PC allows you to carry out a variety of tasks with your PC. There are two main types of software: Systems Software and Applications Software.

Systems Software

Also referred to as the operating system, this software allows the PC to organize and manage important tasks, such as saving and printing files. The most popular operating system is Microsoft Windows. Other operating systems such as Linux and Mac OS are also available. Operating systems have developed in response to advances in technology. Modern operating systems allow you to link your PC to a network of other PCs in the building. Windows 2000 and Windows XP have sophisticated security and password systems which allow you to protect your PC from unauthorised use.

Applications Software

As the name suggests, applications software relates to a specific application or task. The most popular applications are word processing, spreadsheets, databases, desktop publishing and web design. You can type a letter using a word processor, create a budget with a spreadsheet, store names and addresses of business contacts using a database, design a birthday card using desktop publishing software or create a web site using web design software. The most popular software package is Microsoft Office, which contains Word (word processing), Excel (spreadsheets), Access (databases), Publisher (desktop publishing) and Frontpage (web design).

Fig. 4.45 The completed web page will look like this

To create the **lesson1.htm** web page there are five stages.

1. Resize Images

Use the digital photographs **pc.jpg, mouse.jpg, keyboard.jpg, monitor.jpg, cpu.jpg** and **printer.jpg** that you took earlier in this project. Each digital image must be resized to 192 × 144 pixels. At 192 × 144 pixels, the images on the lesson pages are slightly larger than those on the home page, where they have been resized to 128 × 96 pixels.

 Note: A smaller version of an image used as a hyperlink to a larger version of the same image is often called a thumbnail image.

2. Create navigation buttons

Each lesson page will have some navigation buttons to allow the web page viewer to move quickly to other sections of the web site. Each button must be created in Paint Shop Pro and saved as a separate GIF file.

3. Create drop caps

A drop cap is where the first letter of a paragraph is in a font size much bigger than the other text in the paragraph. The drop cap is usually two or three lines high, with the paragraph text wrapping around it. Drop caps add style and emphasis to the start of a paragraph. In Fig. 4.45 the letter T is a drop cap.

4. Set up CSS Styles

There are three text formats in the **lesson1.htm** web page in Fig. 4.45:

- the main heading
- the body text
- the paragraph headings.

We will specify each text format using CSS styles in the Head section.

5. Enter text and position images on web pages

Having completed Steps 1 to 4, all that is left to do is positioning the text and images on the web page and setting up spacing. We will use tables to display paragraphs in columns and to position the navigation buttons.

Resize Images

 1. Using Paint Shop Pro, resize each of these images so they are 144 pixels high.
   - pc.jpg
   - mouse.jpg
   - keyboard.jpg
   - monitor.jpg
   - cpu.jpg
   - printer.jpg.

Make sure that the Maintain Aspect Ration box is ticked so each image is resized in proportion. For each image, accept the width in pixels that is automatically entered by Paint Shop Pro.

2. Using the JPEG Optimiser, set the compression value to 2 and the file type to Progressive for each image.

3. Save each optimised image using the file names in Table 4.10.

Table 4.10   **File names for optimised images**

Original Image	Optimised Image
pc.jpg	bigpc.jpg
mouse.jpg	bigmouse.jpg
keyboard.jpg	bigkeyboard.jpg
monitor.jpg	bigmonitor.jpg
cpu.jpg	bigcpu.jpg
printer.jpg	bigprinter.jpg

Create Navigation Buttons

 1. In Paint Shop Pro, create a new image with a width of 100 pixels and a height of 60 pixels. The resolution is 72 pixels per inch, the background colour is transparent and the image type is 16.7 million colours.

2. In the Tool palette, click the Preset Shapes button.

 Tip: If the Tool palette is not displayed, select View followed by Toolbars from the menu and tick the Tool Palette check box.

3. In the Tool Options dialog box, select the ellipse from the list of preset shapes. Make sure that the Retain Style and Create as vector boxes are not selected, as in Fig. 4.46.

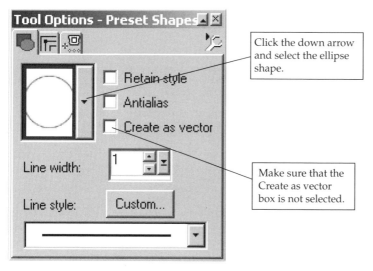

Click the down arrow and select the ellipse shape.

Make sure that the Create as vector box is not selected.

Fig. 4.46 Preset Shapes with the ellipse selected

Note:
- Ticking the Retain Style box means that the image you create will have all the styles (colour, gradient or pattern) included in the preset shape. If you take the tick off the Retain Style box, any styles that are set in the colour palette will be applied to the image.
- Paint Shop Pro can create graphics using one of two possible formats:
1. **Vector** file formats where the image is constructed from a set of mathematical instructions.
2. **Raster** file formats where the image is made up of pixels.

Tip:
- If the Tool Options dialog box is not displayed, select View followed by Toolbars from the menu and tick the Tool Options Palette check box.
- Ticking the Antialias check box before you draw the button makes the edges of the navigation button look less pixellated.

4. Set the background colour to orange by double clicking the Fill Colour box (see Fig. 4.47) and entering #FF6600 in the HTML code box. Set the border colour to orange by double clicking the Stroke Colour and entering #FF6600 as the HTML code.

Fill Colour box

Stroke colour

Styles

Fig. 4.47 The Fill Colour and Stroke Colour boxes are in the Colour palette

Tip: If the Colour palette is not displayed, select View followed by Toolbars from the menu and tick the Colour Palette check box.

5. Click and drag to draw an oval in your new image.
6. **A** Click the Text button and then click anywhere inside in the orange oval.
7. Select Verdana from the Name box, as in Fig. 4.48. Select 10 as the font size.

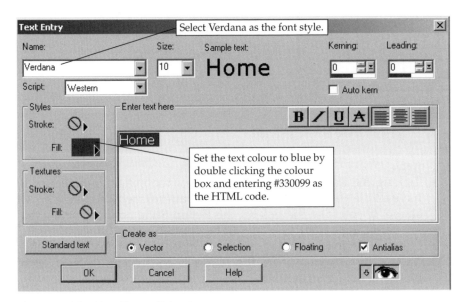

Fig. 4.48 The Text Entry dialog box

8. Double click the Fill box and enter #330099 as the HTML code, as shown in Fig. 4.49. Click OK to set the text colour.
9. Now type the text that will appear on the button, in this case Home.
10. Click OK to insert the text in the image. The completed navigation button should look something like Fig. 4.50.

 Note: If you created the button as a vector, you will not be able to position the text over the button.

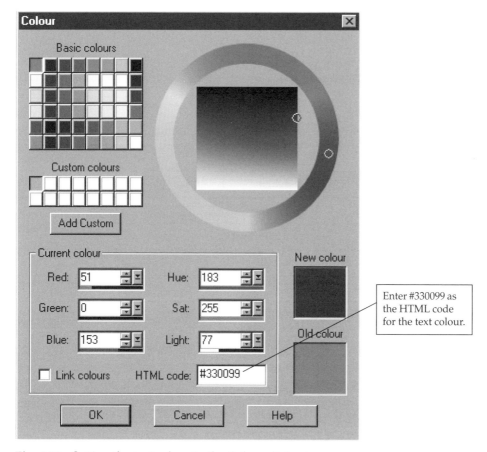

Fig. 4.49 Setting the text colour in the Colour dialog box

Fig. 4.50 The completed navigation button

Fig. 4.51 The text must be centred on the navigation button

You will probably have to move the text until it is centred on the orange ellipse shape, as in Fig. 4.51. If this is the case, put the mouse pointer in the centre of the text. When the mouse pointer changes to four black arrows, pointing up, down, left and right ✥, click and drag to move the text.

11. tutorial Click File and the Save As button. Select Compuserve Graphics images Interchange (*.gif) from the Save As Type box and enter **home** as the file name. Save the file in the **images** folder. **Do not close the file!**

12. Point the cursor at the text Home, which is still selected. Click once when the mouse pointer shows a capital [A] in square brackets.

13. Type `Previous`. If necessary, centre the text on the button. Select File followed by Save As and enter **previous** as the file name. Make sure that the file is saved in the **images** folder.
14. Create the remaining buttons using the information in Table 4.11. Each time you edit a button, save the new button in the **images** folder, using File and Save As.

Table 4.11   Individual button names with the text for each button

Button Text	Button Name
Next	next.gif
Test	test.gif
Solutions	solutions.gif
Back	back.gif
Lesson 2	lesson2.gif
Lesson 3	lesson3.gif
Lesson 4	lesson4.gif
Lesson 5	lesson5.gif
Lesson 6	lesson6.gif

 Tip: Holding down the CTRL key and typing the letter Z undoes your last action.

Create Drop Caps

 1. Create a new image in Paint Shop Pro, with these settings:
Width: 30 pixels
Height: 40 pixels
Resolution: 72 Pixels per inch
Background Colour: Transparent
Image Type: 16.7 million colours (24 bit)

2. Zoom the image by selecting View, followed by Zoom in by 5 from the menu.

 Tip: If you have a wheel mouse, you can zoom in and out by rolling the wheel with your finger.

3. **A** Click the Text button and then click anywhere in the blank image. The Text Entry dialog box is displayed.

4. Select Verdana as the font name, 28 as the font size and bold as the font weight. Set the text colour by double clicking the Fill box and entering #330099 as the HTML code.

5. Type an upper case T in the Text Entry dialog box, as shown in Fig. 4.52, and click OK.

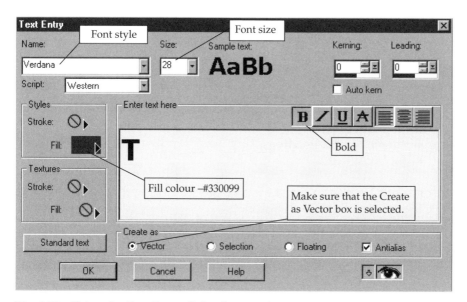

Fig. 4.52   Using the Text Entry dialog box to place text on an image

6. If necessary, move the image until you can see all of it on the screen.

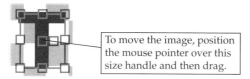

7. Select Selections, followed by Select All from the menu.

8. ▣ Click the Copy button on the Standard toolbar.

9. Select Edit, followed by Paste from the menu. Now select As New Image.

10. ▣ Click the Save button and save the image as **dropcap1.gif** in the **images** folder.

 Tip: This image is saved as a GIF because GIFs are best for images with large areas of solid colour.

For You To Do

Create an image of the letter W using the information in Create Drop Caps. Save this image as **dropcap2.gif.**

Tip: The image will need to be wider to accommodate the letter W.

Set Up CSS Styles

There are three text formats in the **lesson1.htm** web page:
- the main heading
- the paragraph headings
- the body text.

These text formats can be seen in Fig. 4.45, on page 140. We will specify each text format using CSS styles in the Head section.

1.   In Dreamweaver, make sure that the **computertutorial** site is active,
Dreamweaver   as in Fig. 4.53.

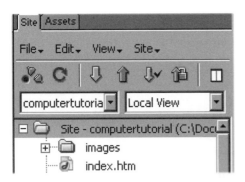

Fig. 4.53 The Site Panel with the **computertutorial** site active

2. Select File, followed by New from the menu and click Create to set up a basic HTML page.

3.   View the new web page in Design View and then make sure that the Properties toolbar is in CSS mode.

4. To create **a CSS style for the main heading**, using the Properties toolbar, create a CSS style named **.main** that includes these properties:
   font: Georgia, Times New Roman, Times, serif;
   size: 36px;
   color: #FF6600;
5. To **create a CSS style for the paragraph headings** using the Properties toolbar, create a CSS Style named **.headings** that includes these properties:
   font: Arial, Helvetica, sans-serif;
   size: 16px;
   color: #FF6600;
   weight: bold;
6. To create **a CSS style for the body text** using the Properties toolbar, create a CSS Style named **.text** that includes these properties:
   font: Verdana, Arial, Helvetica, sans-serif;
   size: 12px;
   color: #330099;
7. Select File, followed by Save from the menu. Enter **lesson1.htm** as the file name.

Enter Text and Position Images on the Web Page

 Now that we have prepared our images as well as creating navigation buttons, drop caps and CSS styles, we can set up the **lesson1.htm** web page. A table is required to display text relating to Systems Software and Applications Software in column format. The navigation buttons are also positioned using a table.

Dreamweaver
Open the lesson1.htm web page if it is not already open. Click the Design View button and set up the web page as shown on page 150. For useful guidelines look at the Remember section that follows.

 Tip: Hold down Shift and press Enter to bring the cursor to a new line without creating a blank line.

Remember:
- Insert the **bigpc.jpg** image at the beginning of the first paragraph, using the image button. To position the image to the right of the paragraph, set the alignment of the image to right. Set the alternative text of this image to Personal Computer.
- Insert the drop cap using the image button. Using the Properties toolbar set the alignment of the drop cap image to left so the text wraps around the drop cap.
- Create a table to display the Systems Software and Applications Software paragraphs in column format. Set the cell padding to 10 in the opening <table> tag to make sure there is spacing between each column of text.

Lesson 1: Your PC

dropcap1.jpg

bigpc.jpg

The first PC was made by IBM in 1981. Back then, PCs weren't very powerful and had limited graphics. Over time PCs gradually became more user-friendly and more powerful. Today millions of people use PCs at work. A huge range of sophisticated software packages can be installed on your PC. Specialised software allows you to use your PC to carry out many different tasks in the workplace. The growth in leisure-related software means that your home PC can be used to watch DVDs, play computer games and listen to music CDs, as well as creating your own CDs and DVDs!

Software that comes with the PC allows you to carry out a variety of tasks with your PC. There are two main types of software: System Software and Applications Software.

Systems Software

Also referred to as the operating system, this software allows the PC to organise and manage important tasks, such as saving and printing files. The most popular operating system is Microsoft Windows. Other operating systems such as Linux and Mac OS are also available. Operating Systems have developed in response to advances in technology. Modern operating systems allow you to link your PC to a network of other PCs in the building. Windows 2000 and Windows XP have sophisticated security and password systems which allow you to protect your PC from unauthorised use.

Applications Software

As the name suggests, applications software relates to a specific application or task. The most popular applications are word processing, spreadsheets, databases, desktop publishing and web design.

You can type a letter using a word processor, create a budget with a spreadsheet, store names and addresses of business contacts using a database, design a birthday card using desktop publishing software or create a web site using web design software. The most popular software package is Microsoft Office, which contains Word (word processing), Excel (spreadsheets), Access (databases), Publisher (desktop publishing) and Frontpage (web design).

- Set the vertical alignment of both table cells to Top.
- Apply the **.main** style to the main heading.
- Apply the **.headings** style to the Systems Software and Applications Software paragraph headings.

 Tip: Adding width="50%" to each opening <td> tag stops Dreamweaver from resizing table cells as you type.

- Apply the **.text** style to all the remaining text. Insert <br /> tags where necessary to retain the paragraph spacing.
- Position the navigation buttons using a table. Set the alignment of each table cell to "center".
- Set the page title to Learn about your PC.
- Check your spelling by selecting Text, followed by Check Spelling from the menu.

- Position the cursor to the left of the **home.gif** navigation button and then click the Comment button. Enter this comment:

```
This table row contains the navigation buttons. Each button is a
hyperlink to a web page. home.gif is a hyperlink to index.htm,
next.gif is a hyperlink to lesson2.htm, test.gif is a hyperlink
to test1.htm.
```

- Save the web page and preview the web page in Internet Explorer.

Create the Lesson 2 Web Page

Now that you have set up your images, navigation buttons, drop caps and CSS styles, creating the remaining lesson web pages is relatively straightforward. Other lesson web pages can be created by copying and editing an existing lesson web page. Some of the lesson web pages will need small adjustments to tables. Additional digital photographs will also be required. You can create the **lesson2.htm** web by copying and editing the **lesson1.htm** web page. When you have finished this section, the **lesson2.htm** web page will look something like Fig. 4.54.

Lesson 2: Using The Mouse

The mouse is an input device that allows you to give commands to your PC. These commands are given by pointing at icons and clicking, or by selecting items from a menu. As you move the mouse across the mouse mat, the mouse pointer, a white arrow, moves around the monitor screen. Each software application is represented by an icon. So, for example, to start Excel, move the mouse across the mouse mat until the mouse pointer is over the Excel icon. Now double click the left mouse button. This gives a command to your PC to start Excel. A double click is two presses of the left mouse button in quick succession.

The introduction of the mouse revolutionised the computer industry because it made PCs more accessible to non-computer experts. Before the mouse was introduced, all commands given to the PC had to be typed. These commands were technical and difficult to learn.

Mouse Buttons

The first mouse had two buttons, a left button and a right button. In general, the left button is for giving commands to the PC and the right button is for displaying menus. Pointing and clicking with the left button will instruct the PC to do something, such as opening a file.

Pointing and clicking with the right button will display a menu of items. Modern mice have a wheel between the two buttons. The wheel can be used in Word and Excel to quickly scroll through a document. As you roll the wheel with your finger, the document scrolls up or down on the screen. In Access, the wheel can be used to scroll through records in a form. Five-button mice are now available. Two additional buttons on the side of the mouse can be used to go to the previous or next slide in a presentation.

How It Works

If you turn your mouse upside down, you will notice a ball in the middle. This ball is exposed so that it rolls as you move the mouse across the mat. The rolling of the ball is converted into a series of commands that instruct the mouse pointer to move across the screen. Over time dirt builds up on the ball, causing the mouse pointer to jump on the screen or to become unresponsive to movements of the mouse across the mat. To ensure that your mouse continues to work efficiently, you should take out the ball every month and remove any dirt from it.

Laser mice have recently been introduced. A laser mouse doesn't have a ball. It works by detecting the movement of a laser beam across the mouse mat. Laser mice are more expensive than standard mice but will require little or no maintenance.

 Home   Previous   Next   Test

Fig. 4.54 The completed **lesson2.htm** web page

Take Pictures with a Digital Camera

1. Using a digital camera, take close up shots of:
   - A mouse viewed from above (make sure that it is a mouse with a wheel).
   - The underside of the mouse, with the roller ball visible.

Sample pictures with file names are shown in Table 4.12.

Project 4
 digital photos

Note: If you do not have access to a digital camera, you can copy these images from the *Step by Step Web Design* CD. Open the **Project 4** folder in the CD. It has a sub-folder named **digital photos**. Copy the **mbutton.jpg** and **mball.jpg** images from the **digital photos** folder to your own **images** folder.

Table 4.12 Digital photographs with their file names

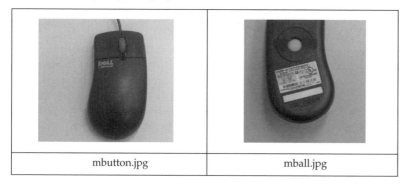

mbutton.jpg	mball.jpg

2. tutorial   images   Save each digital photograph to the **images** sub-folder using the file names in Table 4.12.

3. In Paint Shop Pro, resize each image to 128×96 pixels.

4. Using the JPEG Optimiser, set the compression value to 2 and the file type to Progressive for each image.

5. Save each optimised image using the original file names. (Click Yes when Paint Shop Pro asks if you want to overwrite the original image.)

Set Up the Web Page Structure Using Dreamweaver's Site Panel

 In this section you copy the **lesson1.htm** web page using Dreamweaver's Site Panel.

1. 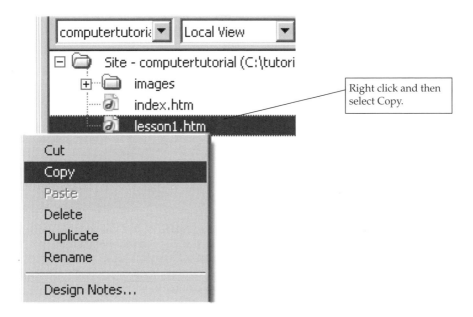 In Dreamweaver, make sure that the **computer-**
Dreamweaver **tutorial** site is active.

2. Copy the **lesson1.htm** web page by right clicking the web page name and then selecting Copy from the menu, as shown in Fig. 4.55.

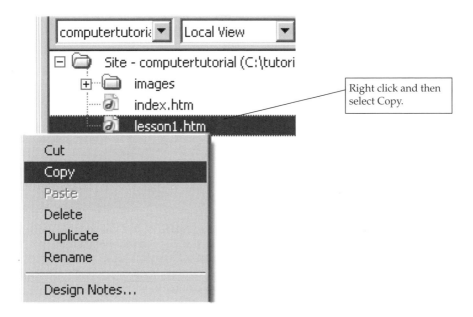

Fig. 4.55   Using the Site Panel to copy and existing web page

3. Now right click anywhere in a blank area of the site panel. Select Paste from the menu. The new web page is pasted into the site panel. It is called **Copy of lesson1.htm**.
4. Rename **Copy of lesson1.htm** by right clicking the file name and selecting Rename from the menu. Enter **lesson2.htm** as the new file name and press Enter.
5. lesson2.htm Open the **lesson2.htm** web page by double clicking the Dreamweaver icon to the left of the file name.
6. Set up the web page as shown on page 154. To replace the existing Lesson 1 text, simply highlight it and type in the new text. For useful guidelines look at the Remember section that follows.

Lesson 2: Using The Mouse

dropcap1.jpg

bigmouse.jpg

T he mouse is an input device that allows you to give commands to your PC. These commands are given by pointing at icons and clicking, or by selecting items from a menu. As you move the mouse across the mouse mat, the mouse pointer, a white arrow, moves around the monitor screen. Each software application is represented by an icon. So, for example, to start Excel, move the mouse across the mouse mat until the mouse pointer is over the Excel icon. Now double click the left mouse button. This gives a command to your PC to start Excel. A double click is two presses of the left mouse button in quick succession.

The introduction of the mouse revolutionised the computer industry because it made PCs more accessible to non-computer experts. Before the mouse was introduced, all commands given to the PC had to be typed. These commands were technical and difficult to learn.

Mouse Buttons

mbutton.jpg

The first mouse had two buttons, a left button and a right button. In general, the left button is for giving commands to the PC and the right button is for displaying menus. Pointing and clicking with the left button will instruct the PC to do something, such as opening a file. Pointing and clicking with the right button will display a menu of items. Modern mice have a wheel between the two buttons. The wheel can be used in Word and Excel to quickly scroll through a document. As you roll the wheel with your finger, the document scrolls up or down on the screen. In Access, the wheel can be used to scroll through records in a form. Five-button mice are now available. Two additional buttons on the side of the mouse can be used to go to the previous or next slide in a presentation.

How It Works

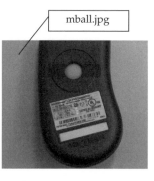

mball.jpg

If you turn your mouse upside down, you will notice a ball in the middle. This ball is exposed so that it rolls as you move the mouse across the mat. The rolling of the ball is converted into a series of commands that instruct the mouse pointer to move across the screen. Over time, dirt builds up on the ball, causing the mouse pointer to jump on the screen or to become unresponsive to movements of the mouse across the mat. To make sure that your mouse continues to work efficiently, you should take out the ball every month and remove any dirt from it.

Laser mice have recently been introduced. A laser mouse doesn't have a ball. It works by detecting the movement of a laser beam across the mouse mat. Laser mice are more expensive than standard mice but require little or no maintenance.

home.gif   previous.gif   next.gif   test.gif

Home   Previous   Next   Test

Remember:
- Insert the images **bigmouse.jpg, mbutton.jpg** and **mball.jpg** as shown above. Set the alignment of each image to right.
- Set alternative text for images as in Table 4.13.

Table 4.13   Alternative text for images in the *lesson2.htm* web page

Image Name	Alternative Text
bigmouse.jpg	The Mouse
mbutton.jpg	left button, wheel and right button
mball.jpg	mouse roller ball

- Insert an additional navigation button for **previous.gif** as shown in Fig. 4.54.

 Tip: Add an extra cell to the table by editing the HTML code.

- Set the page title to Learn about the Mouse.
- Check your spelling by selecting Text, followed by Check Spelling from the menu.
- Edit the comment about the navigation buttons so it reads:

```
This table row contains the navigation buttons. Each button is a
hyperlink to a web page. home.gif is a hyperlink to index.htm,
previous.gif is a hyperlink to lesson1.htm, next.gif is a hyperlink
to lesson3.htm, test.gif is a hyperlink to test2.htm.
```

- Save the web page and preview the web page in Internet Explorer.

Create the Lesson 3 Web Page

 The structure of the **lesson3.htm** page has some small differences to the lesson pages before. You create the **lesson3.htm** web page by copying **lesson2.htm** and editing the HTML code. When you have finished this section, the **lesson3.htm** web page will look something like Fig. 4.56.

Lesson 3: Using The Keyboard

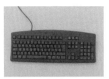

The keyboard is the main device for entering data into the PC. It is primarily for typing text but also has a numeric keypad for entering numbers. Many people who use computers at work or at home don't know how to type properly and only use two or three fingers when they are typing. With this technique you will never break the 25 words per minute barrier. There are lots of computerised typing tutors on the market, Mavis Beacon being the most popular. With a little time and patience, you can teach yourself to type and reach 40 words per minute in as little as two months! Knowing how to type is a very useful and marketable skill, as computers now play a major role in everday life.

The Keys
The way in which the alphabetical keys are arranged on the keyboard is known as the QWERTY layout. Before the computer was invented, typewriters were used to produce printed text. Typewriter keys were arranged in the same order as letters in the alphabet. However, over time the speed of typists improved and the mechanical typewriters jammed because they were not able to cope with the increased speed. To get around this problem, the typewriter designers mixed up the keys to slow down the typists! The layout that they came up with is the QWERTY layout which is still used today.

Num Lock

The numeric keypad has a dual function. It can be used to type numbers and as a directional keypad. When the Num Lock light is off 2, 4, 8 and 6 become the down, left, up and right arrow keys. When the Num Lock light is on, all the keys are for entering numbers. Directional arrow keys were very useful before the mouse was invented but are rarely used today.

Caps Lock

The explanation of the Caps Lock key is much simpler. When the Caps Lock light is on, all the alphabetical characters on the keyboard will produce upper-case letters on the screen. When Caps Lock is off, the letters will be lower-case. A single capital letter can be produced by holding down the Shift key while typing that letter.

Scroll Lock

The Scroll Lock button has very little use these days. Before the introduction of the mouse, turning Scroll Lock on allowed you to scroll through a document without moving the cursor. This function is now performed by the vertical and horizontal scroll bars.

(Home)   (Previous)   (Next)   (Test)

Fig. 4.56   The completed **lesson3.htm web** page

Take Pictures with a Digital Camera

   1. Using a digital camera, take close up shots of:
- The QWERTY section of the keyboard.
- The Numeric Keypad with the Num Lock light on.
- The Numeric Keypad with the Caps Lock light on.
- The Numeric Keypad with the Scroll Lock light on.

Sample pictures file names are shown in Table 4.14.

 Note: If you do not have access to a digital camera, you can copy these images from the *Step by Step Web Design* CD. Open the **Project 4** folder in the CD. It contains a sub-folder named **digital photos.** Copy the **keys.jpg, num.jpg, caps.jpg** and **scroll.jpg** images from the **digital photos** folder to your own **images** folder.

2. Save each digital photograph to the **images** sub-folder using the file names in Table 4.13.

3. In Paint Shop Pro, resize each image to 128 × 96 pixels.

4. Using the JPEG Optimiser, set the compression value to 2 and the file type to Progressive for each image.

5. Save each optimised image using the original file names. (Click Yes when Paint Shop Pro asks if you want to overwrite the original image.)

Table 4.14   Digital photographs with their file names

| keys.jpg | num.jpg |
| caps.jpg | scroll.jpg |

Set up the Web Page Structure

 In this section you copy the **lesson2.htm** web page using Dreamweaver's Site Panel.

1.   In Dreamweaver, make sure that the **computer-tutorial** site is active.
    Dreamweaver

2.   Copy the **lesson2.htm** web page by right clicking the web page name, then selecting Copy from the menu.

3.   Right click anywhere in a blank area of the site panel. Select Paste from the menu.

4.   Rename **Copy of lesson2.htm** by right clicking the file name and selecting Rename from the menu. Enter **lesson3.htm** as the new file name and press Enter.

5.   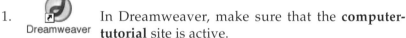 lesson3.htm Open the **lesson3.htm** web page by double clicking the Dreamweaver icon displayed to the left of the file name.

6.   Set up the web page as shown on page 158. For useful guidelines, look at the Remember section that follows.

Remember:
- Insert the images **bigkeyboard.jpg, keys.jpg, num.jpg, caps.jpg** and **scroll.jpg** as shown in on page 158. Set the alignment of **keys.jpg** to left. Set the alignment of all other images to right.
- Set alternative text for images as in Table 4.15 on page 159.
- Display the information relating to Num lock, Caps lock and Scroll lock using a three-column table. Set the cell padding to 10 pixels. Set the vertical alignment of the table cells to top.

Lesson 3: Using The Keyboard

bigkeyboard.jpg

T he keyboard is the main device for entering data into the PC. It is primarily for typing text but also has a numeric keypad for entering numbers. Many people who use computers at work or at home don't know how to type properly and only use two or three fingers when they are typing. With this technique you will never break the 25 words per minute barrier. There are lots of computerised typing tutors on the market, Mavis Beacon being the most popular. With a little time and patience, you can teach yourself to type and reach 40 words per minute in as little as two months! Knowing how to type is a very useful and marketable skill, as computers now play a major role in everyday life.

The Keys

keys.jpg

The way in which the alphabetical keys are arranged on the keyboard is known as the QWERTY layout. Before the computer was invented, typewriters were used to produce printed text. Typewriter keys were arranged in the same order as letters in the alphabet. However, over time the speed of typists improved and the mechanical typewriters jammed because they were not able to cope with the increased speed. To get around this problem, the typewriter designers mixed up the keys to slow down the typists! The layout that they came up with is the QWERTY layout which is still used today.

num.jpg

caps.jpg

scroll.jpg

Num Lock

The numeric keypad has a dual function. It can be used to type numbers and as a directional keypad. When the Num Lock light is off 2, 4, 8 and 6 become the down, left, up and right arrow keys. When the Num Lock light is on, all the keys are for entering numbers.
Directional arrow keys were very useful before the mouse was invented but are rarely used today.

Caps Lock

The explanation of the Caps Lock key is much simpler. When the Caps Lock light is on, all the alphabetical characters on the keyboard will produce upper-case letters on the screen. When Caps Lock is off, the letters will be lower case. A single capital letter can be produced by holding down the Shift key while typing that letter.

Scroll Lock

The Scroll Lock button has very little use these days. Before the introduction of the mouse, turning Scroll Lock on allowed you to scroll through a document without moving the cursor. This function is now performed by vertical and horizontal scroll bars.

home.gif   previous.gif   next.gif   test.gif

Home   Previous   Next   Test

Table 4.15 Alternative text for images in the *lesson3.htm* web page

Image Name	Alternative Text
bigkeyboard.jpg	The Keyboard
keys.jpg	number, letter and function keys
num.jpg	Num Lock light on
caps.jpg	Caps Lock light on
scroll.jpg	Scroll Lock light on

- Set the page title to Learn about the Keyboard.
- Check your spelling by selecting Text, followed by Check Spelling from the menu.
- Edit the comment about the navigation buttons so it reads:

```
This table row contains the navigation buttons. Each button is a
hyperlink to a web page. home.gif is a hyperlink to index.htm,
previous.gif is a hyperlink to lesson2.htm, next.gif is a hyperlink
to lesson4.htm, test.gif is a hyperlink to test3.htm.
```

- Save the web page and preview the web page in Internet Explorer.

Create the Lesson 4 Web Page

When you have finished this section, the **lesson4.htm** web page will look something like Fig. 4.57.

Lesson 4: Using The Monitor

The monitor displays applications that are currently running and files that are currently open. As you type text, it appears on the monitor in the current application. Without a monitor, a PC would be virtually useless. Monitors have greatly improved in quality since the introduction of the first PC in 1981. The original monitors could only display black, white and shades of grey. Modern monitors are capable of displaying 16.7 million different colours! The resolution of the monitor is expressed in pixels. The monitor is divided into an invisible grid which is made up of pixels. The more pixels that are in the grid, the higher the quality or resolution of the image that is displayed on the monitor. Modern monitors have resolutions ranging from 1024 x 768 pixels to 1280 x 1024 pixels.

The graphics card controls the output to your monitor. The graphics card is inside your PC. If you work a lot with graphics, it is important to buy a PC with a powerful graphics card. Graphics cards have memory where the current screen display is stored. If you play games or watch DVDs on your PC, make sure your graphics card has lots of memory.

Desktop Background
The desktop background is displayed on the monitor when no applications are running or when applications are minimised. Windows XP has a number of background themes, which allow you to add a bit of colour and life to your desktop. The underwater theme is displayed above. Other themes such as Jungle and Sport are also available. Changing the desktop background is easy. Firstly, make sure that no applications are open or, if applications are open that they are minimised. Next, point anywhere on the desktop, but not at an icon and right click. Select Properties from the menu, followed by Desktop. A list of available desktop themes is displayed. Simply select the one you want. Additional backgrounds can be downloaded from the Internet.

Screensavers
If the image displayed on the monitor doesn't change over an extended period of time (normally 2 or 3 days) it will eventually burn into the monitor display permanently. If this happens, your monitor is more or less useless. A shadow of the burned image will be constantly displayed on the monitor. Screensavers stop this from happening. A screensaver is simply a moving image that plays over and over again, a bit like a very short animation. The screensaver can be programmed to start after a period of inactivity. For example, you could set the screensaver to start automatically if no keys have been pressed and the mouse hasn't been moved for an hour. You can set this time interval to suit yourself. It depends on how regularly you use your PC during the day.

Fig. 4.57 The completed **lesson4.htm** web page

Take Pictures with a Digital Camera

 1. Using a digital camera, take close up shots of:
   - The monitor with a desktop background displayed.
   - The monitor with the screen saver active.

   Sample pictures with file names are shown in Table 4.16.

 Note: The desktop background and screensaver in Table 4.15 may not be available on your PC. If it is not, take a photo of your favourite desktop background and screensaver.

2. Save each digital photograph to the **images** sub-folder using the file names in Table 4.16.

Table 4.16   Digital photographs with their file names

| desktop.jpg | screensaver.jpg |

 Note: If you do not have access to a digital camera, you can copy these images from the *Step by Step Web Design* CD. Open the **Project 4** folder in the CD. It has a sub-folder named **digital photos**. Copy the **desktop.jpg** and **screensaver.jpg** images from the **digital photos** folder to your own **images** folder.

3. In Paint Shop Pro, resize each image to 128 × 96 pixels.

4. Using the JPEG Optimiser, set the compression value to 2 and the file type to Progressive for each image.

5. Save each optimised image using the original file names. (Click Yes when Paint Shop Pro asks if you want to overwrite the original image.)

6. In Dreamweaver, make sure that the **computertutorial** site is active.

Lesson 4: Using The Monitor

bigmonitor.jpg

The monitor displays applications that are currently running and files that are currently open. As you type text, it appears on the monitor in the current application. Without a monitor, a PC would be virtually useless. Monitors have greatly improved in quality since the introduction of the first PC in 1981. The original monitors could only display black, white and shades of grey. Modern monitors are capable of displaying 16.7 million different colours! The resolution of the monitor is expressed in pixels. The monitor is divided into an invisible grid which is made up of pixels. The more pixels that are in the grid, the higher the quality or resolution of the image that is displayed on the monitor. Modern monitors have resolutions ranging from 1024 × 68 pixels to 1280 × 1024 pixels.

The graphics card controls the output to your monitor. The graphics card is inside your PC. If you work a lot with graphics, it is important to buy a PC with a powerful graphics card. Graphics cards have memory where the current screen display is stored. If you play games or watch DVDs on your PC, make sure your graphics card has lots of memory.

Desktop Background

desktop.jpg

The desktop background is displayed on the monitor when no applications are running or when applications are minimised. Windows XP has a number of background themes, which allows you to add a bit of colour and life to your desktop. The underwater theme is displayed above. Other themes such as Jungle and Sport are also available. Changing the desktop background is easy. Firstly, make sure that no applications are open or, if applications are open, that they are minimised. Next, point anywhere on the desktop, but not at an icon and right click. Select Properties from the menu, followed by Desktop. A list of available desktop backgrounds is displayed. Simply select the one you want. Additional backgrounds can be downloaded from the Internet.

Screensavers

screensaver.jpg

If the image displayed on the monitor doesn't change over an extended period of time (normally 2 or 3 days) it will eventually burn into the monitor display permanently. If this happens, your monitor is more or less useless. A shadow of the burned image will be superimposed over any image currently displayed on the monitor. Screensavers stop this from happening. A screensaver is simply a moving image that plays over and over again, a bit like a very short animation. The screensaver can be programmed to start after a period of inactivity. For example, you could set the screensaver to start automatically if no keys have been pressed and the mouse hasn't been moved for an hour. You can set this time interval to suit yourself. It depends on how regularly you use your PC during the day.

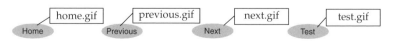

home.gif | previous.gif | next.gif | test.gif

Home | Previous | Next | Test

7. Create the **lesson4.htm** web page by making a copy of **lesson2.htm.**
8. Set up the **lesson4.htm** web page as shown on page 161. For useful guidelines, look at the Remember section that follows.

Remember:
- Insert the images **bigmonitor.jpg, screensaver.jpg** and **desktop.jpg** as shown on page 161. Set the alignment of these images to right.
- Set alternative text for images as in Table 4.17.

Table 4.17   **Alternative text for images in the** *lesson4.htm* **web page**

Image Name	Alternative Text
bigmonitor.jpg	The Monitor
desktop.jpg	desktop background
screensaver.jpg	windows screensaver

- Set the page title to Learn About The Monitor.
- Check your spelling by selecting Text, followed by Check Spelling from the menu.
- Edit the comment about the navigation buttons so it reads:

  This table row contains the navigation buttons. Each button is a hyperlink to a web page. home.gif is a hyperlink to index.htm, previous.gif is a hyperlink to lesson3.htm, next.gif is a hyperlink to lesson5.htm, test.gif is a hyperlink to test4.htm.

- Save the web page and preview the web page in Internet Explorer.

Create the Lesson 5 Web Page

When you have finished this section, the **lesson5.htm** web page will look something like Fig. 4.58.

Lesson 5: The CPU

The CPU, or central processing unit, is the brain of the computer. Every time you carry out a task such as formatting in a document or calculating in a spreadsheet, the CPU carries out instructions that it receives from the applications software. The result of the processing is then displayed on the monitor. Tasks such as formatting and calculating may seem relatively simple to us but often require the CPU to carry out millions of instructions! The speed at which the CPU carries out instructions is measured in gigahertz (Ghz). Modern processors such as Intel's Pentium and AMD's Athlon can achieve speeds ranging from 2.0 to 3.0 Ghz. A 2.0 Ghz processor can carry out roughly 2000 million instructions per second.

The CD Drive

The CD drive can be used to install software from CDs and also to play audio CDs. If you have a CDr or CDrw drive you can also copy data onto a CD. CDs can store between 600 Mb and 800 Mb of data. The speed at which you can write data to a CD depends on the speed of the CD drive. Modern drives have a write speed of 32X. Despite this, it can still take up to 30 minutes to fill up a CD with data. For this reason, CDs are not generally used for work in progress and are more suitable for storing completed work.

The Floppy Disk Drive

The floppy disk is the original "portable" disk for storing data. Floppy disks are made from flexible plastic that is magnetically coated, which gives it its name. The disk is housed in a protective case that is inserted into the floppy disk drive. A floppy disk can store 1.44 Mb of data. It is useful for work in progress as new data can be quickly saved onto the disk. However, if you work a lot with graphics, a floppy disk will not be big enough to store all of your files. In this case, it would be best to store your work on a zip disk.

(Home)   (Previous)   (Next)   (Test)

Fig. 4.58 The completed **lesson5.htm** web page

Take Pictures with a Digital Camera

1. Using a digital camera, take close up shots of:
   - The PC with the CD tray open with a CD inserted.
   - The floppy disk drive with a disk partly inserted.

   Sample pictures with file names are shown in Table 4.18.

Table 4.18 Digital photographs with their file names

| cd.jpg | disk.jpg |

Note: If you do not have access to a digital camera, you can copy these images from the *Step By Step Web Design* CD. Open the **Project 4** folder on the CD. It contains a sub-folder named **digital photos.** Copy the **cd.jpg** and **disk.jpg** images from the **digital photos** folder to your own **images** folder.

NOTE

📁 Project 4
📁 digital photos

2. 📁 tutorial 💾 Save each digital photograph to the images sub-folder using the
    📁 images   file names displayed in Table 4.18.

3. ✂ In Paint Shop Pro, resize each image to 128 × 96 pixels.

4. 🔲 Using the JPEG Optimiser, set the compression value to 2 and the file type
    to Progressive for each image.

5. 💾 Save each optimised image using the original file names. (Click Yes when
    Paint Shop Pro asks if you want to overwrite the original image.)

6. ⬛ In Dreamweaver, make sure that the **computertutorial** site is active.
    Dreamweaver

7. Create the **lesson5.htm** web page by making a copy of **lesson4.htm.**

8. Set up the **lesson5.htm** web page as shown below. For useful guidelines, look
    at the Remember section that follows.

Lesson 5: The CPU

bigcpu.jpg

The CPU, or central processing unit, is the brain of the computer. Every time you carry out a task such as formatting in a document or calculating in a spreadsheet, the CPU carries out instructions that it receives from the applications software. The result of the processing is then displayed on the monitor. Tasks such as formatting and calculating may seem relatively simple to us but often require the CPU to carry out millions of instructions! The speed at which the CPU carrries out instructions is measured in gigahertz (Ghz). Modern processors such as Intel's Pentium and AMD's Athlon can achieve speeds ranging from 2.0 Ghz to 3.0 Ghz. A 2.0 Ghz processor can carry out roughly 2000 million instructions per second.

The CD Drive

cd.jpg

The CD drive can be used to install software from CDs and also to play audio CDs. If you have a CDr or CDrw drive you can also copy data onto a CD. CDs can store between 600 Mb and 800 Mb of data. The speed at which you can write data to a CD depends on the speed of the CD drive. Modern drives have a write speed of 32X. Despite this, it can still take up to 30 minutes to fill up a CD with data. For this reason, CDs are not generally used for work in progress and are more suitable for storing completed work.

The Floppy Disk Drive

disk.jpg

The floppy disk is the original "portable" disk for storing data. Floppy disks are made from flexible plastic that is magnetically coated, which gives it its name. The disk is housed in a protective case that is inserted into the floppy disk drive. A floppy disk can store 1.44 Mb of data. It is useful for work in progress as new data can be quickly saved onto the disk. However, if you work a lot with graphics, a floppy disk will not be big enough to store all of your files. In this case, it would be best to store your work on a zip disk.

home.gif   previous.gif   next.gif   test.gif
Home   Previous   Next   Test

Remember:
- Insert the images **bigcpu.jpg, cd.jpg** and **disk.jpg** as shown on page 164. Set the alignment of these images to right.
- Set alternative text for images as in Table 4.19.

Table 4.19   Alternative text for images in the *lesson5.htm* web page

Image Name	Alternative Text
bigcpu.jpg	The CPU or System Unit
cd.jpg	CD drive
disk.jpg	floppy disk drive

- Set the page title to Learn About The CPU.
- Check your spelling by selecting Text, followed by Check Spelling from the menu.
- [💬] Edit the comment about the navigation buttons so it reads:

```
This table row contains the navigation buttons. Each button is a
hyperlink to a web page. home.gif is a hyperlink to index.htm,
previous.gif is a hyperlink to lesson4.htm, next.gif is a hyperlink
to lesson6.htm, test.gif is a hyperlink to test5.htm.
```

- [💾] [🌐] Save the web page and preview the web page in Internet Explorer. Check your spelling and spacing.

Create the Lesson 6 Web Page

When you have finished this section, the **lesson6.htm** web page will look something like Fig. 4.59.

Lesson 6: Using Your Printer

While the monitor is useful for viewing your work on the screen, this output can only be viewed while the PC is turned on. A printer can produce a paper version of any document or file that you create with your PC. Using a printer, you can print out your Excel spreadsheets, Word documents, Access reports and any other documents or images. There are two main types of printer:- Laserjet printers and Deskjet printers. Laserjet printers are more expensive than deskjet printers but produce higher quality output and are cheaper to run. A deskjet printer, as shown in the image opposite, produces printed output by spraying ink at the page. Colour deskjets can produce relatively cheap high quality colour printouts. Deskjet printers are very popular with home PC users but are not so popular in the workplace because they are very expensive to run.

Test Page
Before you can use your printer, you must install the printer software on your PC. Once the printer software is installed you should check that the printer is working properly by printing a test page.

Black Ink
The printer uses black ink mainly for producing printed text but also mixes black ink with colour ink to produce a range of different colours. The price of the ink cartridge depends on the model of your printer.

Colour Ink
If you have a colour deskjet printer, you will also need to buy a colour ink cartridge. It is best to set the quality of print to draft to save ink. The quality can be set to best for important printouts.

(Home)   (Previous)   (Test)

Fig. 4.59   The completed **lesson6.htm** web page

Take Pictures with a Digital Camera

1. Using a digital camera, take close up shots of:
    - The printer as a test page is being printed.
    - A black ink cartridge.
    - A colour ink cartridge.

    Sample pictures with file names are shown in Table 4.20.

Table 4.20   Digital photographs with their file names

| testprint.jpg | blacking.jpg | colourink.jpg |

Note: If you do not have access to a digital camera, you can copy these images from the *Step by Step Web Design* CD. Open the **Project 4** folder in the CD. It contains a sub-folder named **digital photos.** Copy the **testprint.jpg, blackink.jpg** and **colourink.jpg** images from the **digital photos** folder to your own **images** folder.

2. Save each digital photograph to the **images** sub-folder using the file names in Table 4.20.

3. In Paint Shop Pro, resize each image to 128×96 pixels.

4. 🖼 Using the JPEG Optimiser, set the compression value to 2 and the file type to Progressive for each image.

5. 💾 Save each optimised image using the original file names. (Click Yes when Paint Shop Pro asks if you want to overwrite the original image.)

6. 🅳 In Dreamweaver, make sure that the **computertutorial** site is active.
Dreamweaver

7. Create the **lesson6.htm** web page by making a copy of **lesson3.htm.**

8. Set up the **lesson6.htm** web page as shown below. For useful guidelines, look at the Remember section that follows.

Lesson 6: Using Your Printer

dropcap2.jpg

bigprinter.jpg

W hile the monitor is useful for viewing your work on the screen, this output can only be viewed while the PC is turned on. A printer can produce a paper version of any document or file that you create with your PC. Using a printer, you can print out your Excel spreadsheets, Word documents, Access reports and any other documents or images. There are two main types of printer: laserjet printers and deskjet printers. Laserjet printers are more expensive than deskjet printers but produce higher quality output and are cheaper to run.

A deskjet printer, as shown in the image opposite, produces printed output by spraying ink at the page. Colour deskjets can produce relatively cheap high quality colour printouts. Deskjet printers are very popular with home PC users but are not so popular in the workplace because they are very expensive to run.

testprint.jpg

blackink.jpg

colourink.jpg

Test Page
Before you can use your printer, you must install the printer software on your PC. Once the printer software is installed you should check that the printer is working properly by printing a test page.

Black Ink
The printer uses black ink mainly for producing printed text but also mixes black ink with colour ink to produce a range of different colours. The price of the ink cartridge depends on the model of your printer.

Colour Ink
If you have a colour deskjet printer, you will also need to buy a colour ink cartridge. It is best to set the quality of print to draft to save ink. The quality can be set to best for important printouts

 home.gif

 previous.gif

 test.gif

Remember:

- Display the correct drop cap by changing the image source to **dropcap2.jpg** in the HTML code.
- Insert the images **bigprinter.jpg, testprint.jpg, blackink.jpg** and **colourink.jpg** as shown. Set the alignment of these images to right.
- Set alternative text for images as in Table. 4.21.

Table 4.21 Alternative text for images in the *lesson6.htm* **web page**

Image Name	Alternative Text
bigprinter.jpg	Deskjet Printer
testprint.jpg	printer test page
blackink.jpg	black ink cartridge
colourink.jpg	colour ink cartridge

- Set the page title to Learn about the Printer.
- Adjust the table so that it contains three navigation buttons, as in Fig. 4.59 on page 166.
- Check your spelling by selecting Text, followed by Check Spelling from the menu.
- Edit the comment about the navigation buttons so it reads:

```
This table row contains the navigation buttons. Each button is a
hyperlink to a web page. home.gif is a hyperlink to index.htm,
previous.gif is a hyperlink to lesson5.htm, test.gif is a hyperlink
to test6.htm.
```

- Save the web page and preview the web page in Internet Explorer.

Create Test and Solution Web Pages

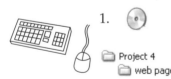

1. Open the **Project 4** folder on the *Step by Step Web Design* CD. It contains a **web pages** sub-folder. Copy all of the web pages from the **web pages** folder to the **tutorial** folder on your own disk.

Project 4
web pages

2.
Dreamweaver

Add navigation buttons at the bottom of each of the **test1.htm, test2.htm, test3.htm, test4.htm, test5.htm** and **test6.htm** web pages, as shown in Fig. 4.60.

Tip: Position the buttons on the web page, using a table. Once you have inserted the navigation buttons in the table, copy this table to the remaining test web pages.

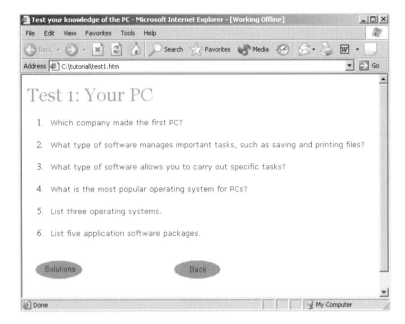

Fig. 4.60   Navigation buttons added to the **test1.htm** web page

3. Add navigation buttons at the bottom of the **solution1.htm** web page, as shown in Fig. 4.61.

Fig. 4.61   Navigation buttons to be added to the **solution1.htm** web page

4. Add navigation buttons at the bottom of the **solution2.htm** web page, as shown in Fig. 4.62.

Fig. 4.62   Navigation buttons to be added to the **solution2.htm** web page

   Tip: Copy and edit the table containing the navigation buttons from **solution1.htm.**

5. Add navigation buttons at the bottom of the **solution3.htm, solution4.htm** and **solution5.htm** web pages in the same way.
    *   In **solution3.htm,** replace **lesson3.gif** with **lesson4.gif.**
    *   In **solution 4.htm,** replace **lesson4.gif** with **lesson5.gif.**
    *   In **solution 5.htm,** replace **lesson5.gif** with **lesson6.gif.**

6. Add navigation buttons at the bottom of the **solution6.htm** web page, as shown in Fig. 4.63.

Fig. 4.63   Navigation buttons to be added to the **solution6.htm** web page

Set Up Text Hyperlinks

   Rather than setting up text hyperlinks by typing the HTML code, you can use Dreamweaver's Hyperlink button instead.

1.   Open **index.htm** in Dreamweaver.

Dreamweaver

2.   Highlight the text Start Lesson 1 and delete it. Click the Hyperlink button. The Hyperlink dialog box is displayed. Re-enter the text Start Lesson 1 as in Fig. 4.64. Click the folder icon and select **lesson1.htm** from the list of web pages. Click OK to set up the hyperlink.

Note: Using the Hyperlink button can be a little confusing as Dreamweaver assumes that you have not typed the hyperlink text on the web page. This is why we need to delete the text Start Lesson 1 and then re-enter it in the Hyperlink dialog box.

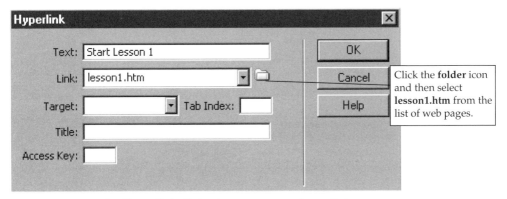

Fig. 4.64   Using the Hyperlink dialog box to set up a hyperlink

3. Using the Hyperlink button, set up hyperlinks to the remaining lesson pages as in Table 4.22.

Table 4.22   Hyperlinks from the home page to the lesson pages

Text	Hyperlink to:
Start Lesson 2	lesson2.htm
Start Lesson 3	lesson3.htm
Start Lesson 4	lesson4.htm
Start Lesson 5	lesson5.htm
Start Lesson 6	lesson6.htm

4. ▣ ◉. Save the web page and preview the web page in Internet Explorer. Test all hyperlinks.

Set Up Image Hyperlinks

Setting up an image as a hyperlink is more straightforward.

1. Open **lesson1.htm** in Dreamweaver. The navigation buttons are shown in Fig. 4.65.

Dreamweaver

Fig. 4.65   Navigation buttons on the **lesson1.htm** web page

2. Click the **home.gif** navigation button to select it. The Properties toolbar now shows information relating to **home.gif.**
3. In the Properties toolbar, set up a hyperlink to the home page by clicking the Link folder icon and then selecting **index.htm** from the Select File dialog box.

Click the **folder** icon and then select **index.htm** from the list of web pages.

Fig. 4.66 Using the Properties toolbar to create an image hyperlink

4. Using the Properties toolbar set up hyperlinks from the remaining images as in Table 4.23.

Table 4.23 Hyperlinks from the *lesson1.htm* web page

Button	Hyperlink to:
Next	lesson2.htm
Test	test1.htm

5. Open **lesson2.htm.** The navigation buttons are shown in Fig. 4.67.

Fig. 4.67 Navigation buttons on the **lesson2.htm** web page

6. Using the Properties toolbar, set up hyperlinks as in Table 4.24.

Table 4.24 Hyperlinks from the *lesson2.htm* web page

Button	Hyperlink to:
Home	index.htm
Previous	lesson1.htm
Next	lesson3.htm
Test	test2.htm

7. Set up hyperlinks in the **lesson3, lesson4, lesson5** and **lesson6** web pages in the same way.
8. Open **test1.htm.** The navigation buttons are shown in Fig. 4.68.

Fig. 4.68 Navigation buttons on the **test1.htm** web page

9. Using the Properties toolbar, set up hyperlinks as in Table 4.25.

Table 4.25 **Hyperlinks from the** *test1.htm* **web page**

Button	Hyperlink to:
Solutions	solution1.htm
Back	lesson1.htm

10. Open **test2.htm.** Using the Properties toolbar, set up hyperlinks as in Table 4.26.

Table 4.26 **Hyperlinks from the** *test2.htm* **web page**

Button	Hyperlink to:
Solutions	solution2.htm
Back	lesson2.htm

11. Set up hyperlinks in the **test3, test4, test5** and **test6** web pages in the same way.
12. Open **solution1.htm.** The navigation buttons are shown in Fig. 4.69.

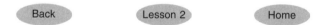

Fig. 4.69 Navigation buttons on the *solution1.htm* web page

13. Using the Properties toolbar, set up hyperlinks as in Table 4.27.

Table 4.27 **Hyperlinks from the** *solution1.htm* **web page**

Button	Hyperlink to:
Back	test1.htm
Lesson 2	lesson2.htm
Home	index.htm

14. Set up hyperlinks in the **solution2, solution3, solution4, solution5** and **solution6** web pages in the same way.
15. Preview all web pages in Internet Explorer and test all hyperlinks.

Check your work

To view the completed Online Computer Tutorial web site log on to **www.gillmacmillan.ie.**

CSS Styles Revision Exercise 1

1. Create a new folder named **project4review** on a floppy disk, zip disk, USB storage device or hard disk.

2. Create an **images** sub-folder inside the **project4review** folder

3. Find the **google.jpg** image in the **Project 4 Revision Exercises** folder on the *Step by Step Web Design* CD. Copy this file to your own **project4review\images** sub-folder.

4. Set up a new site named **project4review** linked to the **project4review** folder. (See Define a Site in Dreamweaver on page 119 for a detailed description of how to set up a new site.)

5. Create a new web page named **search.htm** in the **project4review** web site.

6. Open the **search.htm** web page.

7. Create a style named **.text** that includes the formatting instructions: 12px Verdana with a colour of #616161.

8. Create a style named **.title** that includes the formatting instructions: 24px Georgia with a colour of #006B84.

9. Create a style named **.keywords** that includes the formatting instructions: 12px Verdana in bold print with a colour of #CE007B.

10. Set the page title to Web Pages and Search Engines.

11. Set up the web page and enter text as displayed in Fig. 4.70. Position the **google.jpg** image as shown. (Formatting will be applied after the text has been entered).

What is a Web Page?

A web page is not like a printed page. Web pages are designed to appear on computer screens. They can contain a mixture of text, images, animated graphics, sound and videos. A web page, unlike an A4 page, doesn't have a set length. A web page might be very short or it might require lots of vertical scrolling until you get to the end of the page. The example below shows the Google home page.

The Google web page doesn't contain a lot of text or images so the entire web page fits on one computer screen. The Google search engine is one of the most popular search engines in the World Wide Web. It gets its name from the mathematical term "Googol", a number followed by one hundred zeros!

Search engines have become more important because of the huge growth in the number of web sites. The more web sites there are, the more difficult it becomes to find the information that you are looking for. Using a search engine, you can find all the web sites containing a specific word or a key phrase in less than one second!

Google can also be used to search for images and can be customised so that it only searches web pages from your own country.

Web pages are created using a language called HTML (Hypertext Markup Language). HTML is a page positioning language. Using HTML, the web page designer can specify where text and graphics are positioned on a web page. Most web pages are designed for viewing on a computer screen. The text and static content of web pages can be printed. Obviously animated graphics, sound and video cannot be recreated on a printed page.

Fig. 4.70 The completed **search.htm** web page

Remember:
- Apply the **.title** style to the text What is a Web Page?
- Apply the **.keywords** style to the text Google, search engine and HTML as shown in Fig. 4.70.
- Apply the **.text** style to the rest of the text on the web page.
- 💾 Save the **search.htm** web page.

CSS Styles Revision Exercise 2

1. ⊙ Find the **accessdesk.jpg, accessmenu.jpg, dbwindow.jpg, design.jpg, open.jpg, programs.jpg** and **start.jpg** images in the **Project 4 Revision Exercises** folder on the *Step by Step Web Design* CD. Copy these files to your own **project4review\images** sub-folder.

2. 🟠 Create a new web page named **database.htm** in the **project4review**
   Dreamweaver   web site.

3. Open the **database.htm** web page.

4. Create a style named **.text** that includes the formatting instructions: 12px Arial.

5. Create a style named **.mainheading** that includes the formatting instructions: 32px bold print Georgia with a colour of #3152A5.

6. Create a style named **.paraheadings** that includes the formatting instructions: 14px bold print Georgia with a colour of #3152A5.

7. Set the page title to Learn about Databases.

8. Set up the web page and enter text as displayed in Fig. 4.71. Position images as shown. (Formatting will be applied after the text has been entered. Remember: The main title, first paragraph and **dbwindow.jpg** can be positioned using a table.)

Remember:
- Apply the **.mainheading** style to the heading Structure of a Database.
- Apply the **.paraheadings** style to the headings Using Database Objects and How Do I Start Using Access?
- Apply the **.text** style to all the remaining text displayed on the web page.
- 💾 Save the **search.htm** web page.

Structure of a database

A database contains objects. There are seven different types of objects that can be used in an Access database. These are Tables, Queries, Forms, Reports, Pages, Macros and Modules. Each object carries out a different function within the database and should be given a unique name. The database itself must also have a name. A database must have, at the very least, a Table to enable it to store data. The number of objects in a database depends on the complexity of the database. More complex databases will have more objects.

Using Database Objects

There are two ways that you can view an object

open.jpg

Firstly, you can open an object. Use this option when you want to use the object for a particular purpose. For example, opening a Form allows you to enter and edit data. Opening a Report displays the data contained in the Report. Opening a Query displays the records found by that Query.

design.jpg

Secondly, you can look at how an object is designed. Use this option if you want to change the way in which a Table, Form, Query, Report or Macro is designed.

How do I start using Access?

To start Access double click the Access icon on the desktop.

accessdesk.jpg

Alternatively click the Start button, select Programs or All Programs and then select Microsoft Access.

start.jpg   programs.jpg   accessmenu.jpg

Fig. 4.71   The completed **database.htm** web page

Progress Test 4

Finish the review of Web Project 4 by answering these questions.

1. A JPEG image can display a maximum of _____ colours.
2. A GIF image can display a maximum of _____ colours.
3. What is an interlaced image? _____
   _____
4. Why is it normally necessary to resize a digital photograph before it will fit on the computer screen?
   _____
5. As a web designer, you must reach a compromise between image _____ and _____ time.
6. In XHTML, _____ have replaced the <font> tag.
7. In Dreamweaver, you can view your web pages in three different ways. These are:
   a. _____
   b. _____
   c. _____

8. CSS code is written between opening and closing _____ tags in the _____ section of the HTML file.

9. Each CSS style is made up of a number of _____ / _____ pairs.

10. Identify the errors in this CSS code:

```
.text{
font-family: Verdana
font-size: 12px
}
```

11. When working in Design View in Dreamweaver, holding down the shift key and pressing Enter is equivalent to typing a _____ tag in HTML.

12. When you press the Enter key without holding down the shift key, Dreamweaver inserts opening and closing _____ tags in the HTML code.

13. In Dreamweaver, which of the following buttons should you click to insert a comment in a web page?

   a.

   b.

   c.

   d.

14. A navigation button image would normally be saved as a:

   a. GIF.
   b. JPEG.

15. The effect of ticking the Make Document XHTML Compliant check box is that Dreamweaver will insert _____ instead of <br>, _____ instead of <hr> and that the _____ symbol will be inserted at the end of all <img> tags.

Check Your Work

 To view the answers to the progress test together with the solutions to the CSS styles review exercises, log on to **www.gillmacmillan.ie.**

New in Web Project 4

Dreamweaver Toolbar Buttons

 **The Design View button**   Click this button to create your web page in Design View. Working in design view is very similar to using a word processing package. Web page text can be typed in directly. Images and tables can be positioned on the web page using toolbar buttons or menu options.

 **The Code View button**   Clicking the Code View button shows the HTML code used to create the web page currently open in Dreamweaver. Click this button if you want to edit existing HTML code or if you want to create your web page by entering HTML code directly.

The Insert Table button   Click this button to insert a table on your web page. When the Insert Table button is clicked, Dreamweaver displays the Insert Table dialog box where you can specify the number of rows and columns in the table and the table width and border size. Dreamweaver sets up the HTML table code based on the values you enter in the Insert Table dialog box.

The Merge button   This button is available on the Properties toolbar when two or more table cells are selected in Design View. Click the Merge button to merge the selected table cells into one big cell.

The Image button   Click this button to specify the name and location of an image that you want to display on your web page. When you click the Image button, Dreamweaver displays the Select Image Source dialog box where you can browse for the image. The image may be stored on the hard disk of your PC, or on a floppy disk, zip disk or CD.

The Preview/Debug in Browser button   To see how your web page will appear in Internet Explorer, click this button and select Preview in iexplore from the menu.

The Comment button   When working in Design View, click this button to enter comments in your HTML code. The comment is entered in the Comment dialog box and Dreamweaver inserts the comment in the HTML code.

For example, if you type:

```
This is a comment
```

in the Comment dialog box, HTML code becomes:

```
<!-- This is a comment -->
```

The Hyperlink button   When working in Design View, you can quickly set up a text hyperlink with the hyperlink button. Simply click the hyperlink button, enter the hyperlink text and select the web page you want to link to.

The Email Link button   When working in Design View, click this button to set up an email hyperlink. Dreamweaver will prompt you to enter hyperlink text and an email address. When the hyperlink text is clicked, the web page viewer's email software will open with the email address entered in the To: box.

Paint Shop Pro Toolbar Buttons

The Preset Shapes button   Click this button and drag to create a preset shape, such as a circle, square, triangle or ellipse, which can be used as buttons or symbols in a web page.

The Text button   Click this button to insert text in an image. Use the Text Entry dialog box to specify the size, style and colour for the text.

The Copy button   Click this button to copy a selected image or part of an image. Once you copy an image or part of an image, it can be pasted as many times as you want into other images.

The Export JPEG button   Click this button to optimise a JPEG image for the web. Optimising an image reduces the file size and results in the image being loaded quicker in Internet Explorer, although reducing the file size to increase download speed reduces image quality.

Web Project 5

Online Database Web Site

Scenario

With the growth in popularity of the Internet and the increase in modem speeds and bandwidth, more and more newly published books either have their own web site or are listed on the publisher's web site. Other resources, such as assignment solutions, are often given on these web sites. Because updating a web site is much easier and cheaper than updating printed matter, updates to a book can be published on a web site between printed editions.

In this project, you create an online version of the *Step by Step Databases* book. The web site will include a mixture of database theory and self-tests. Hyperlinks will be used to access various sections of the book.

Project Objectives

By completing this web project, you will learn how to:
- Scan an image for the web.
- Test download times.

In **Dreamweaver**, you will learn how to:
- Control hyperlink text with CSS styles.
- Create a rollover image.
- Create anchors.
- Create a site map.
- Add meta tags to web pages.
- Test a web page at different screen resolutions.
- Test web pages in Internet Explorer and Netscape Navigator.

In **Paint Shop Pro**, you will learn how to:
- Edit images.
- Create a web page background image.
- Create graphics and bullet symbols.

To complete the Online Database Web Site, you need:

 Paint Shop Pro

 Dreamweaver

Dreamweaver

 Internet Explorer

 Scanner

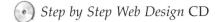 *Step by Step Web Design* CD

Colour Palette

In the Online Database web site, we will use a white background with purple body text in the home page and a white background with black body text in all other web pages. The page headings and section headings in the navigation menu are purple. In this project you will also learn how to change the colours of hyperlink text. The colour scheme is summarised in Table 5.1.

Table 5.1   Online Database web site colour scheme

Item	Colour	Hex Code
Page headings	Purple	#7B52A5
Paragraph headings	Wine	#990000
Menu Section headings	Purple	#7B52A5
Body text in home page	Purple	#7B52A5
Body text in all other pages	Black	#000000
Hyperlink in link state	Red	#CC0000
Hyperlink in active state	Orange	#FF6600
Hyperlink in visited state	Black	#000000
Hyperlink in hover state	Green	#330099

Fonts

In any web project, a little planning will always improve the end result. Planning helps to make sure pages in a web site are consistent. In a well-designed web site, all the web pages will have a similar structure and colour scheme. As a web designer, you must also decide what fonts to use for web page main titles, paragraph headings, body text and hyperlink text. Once you have decided on a set of fonts, this must be applied consistently across all the web pages. Tables 5.2 and 5.3 show the fonts to be used in the Online Database web site.

Table 5.2   **Fonts to be used in the home page of the Online Database web site**

HOME PAGE	
Web Page Text	**Font**
Main heading	Arial, 36px
Navigation Menu headings	Verdana, 16px, bold
Body text	Verdana, 12px, bold
Hyperlinks	Verdana, 12px, bold

Table 5.3   **Fonts to be used in all the other web pages of the Online Database web site**

ALL OTHER WEB PAGES	
Web Page Text	**Font**
Main heading	Arial, 36px
Navigation Menu headings	Verdana, 16px, bold
Table headings	Arial, 16px, bold
Paragraph headings	Arial, 16px, bold
Emphasis	Verdana, 14px
Body text	Verdana, 12px
Hyperlinks	Verdana, 12px, bold

The advantage of controlling web page formatting with CSS styles is that a CSS style with a format, for example paragraph headings, is only specified once but can be applied many times.

Site Structure

In this web project, you create the **index.htm, abouttables.htm, fieldtypes.htm, createtable.htm, tsolution1.htm, tsolution2.htm** and **sitemap.htm** web pages. All the other web pages are provided on the *Step by StepWeb Design* CD. The site structure for the Online Database web site is in Fig. 5.1.

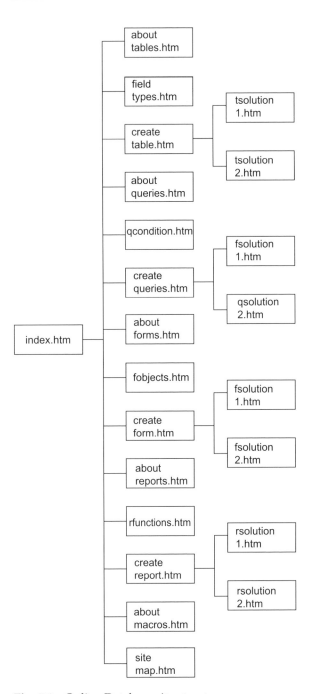

Fig. 5.1   Online Database site structure

Create a New Web Site

 1.
My Computer
Create a new folder named **database** on a floppy disk, zip disk, USB storage device or hard disk.

2. 🗁 database Create an **images** sub-folder inside the **database** folder
   🗁 images

3.
Dreamweaver
In Dreamweaver, set up a new site named **onlinedatabase** linked to the **database** folder, using the following information:
   1. Server Technology: No
   2. Edit local copies on my machine
   3. Connect to remote server: None
4. Create a new web page named **index.htm** in the **onlinedatabase** site.
5. Set the page title to Welcome to Step by Step Databases Online.

   💾 Save the **index.htm** web page.

Create the Home Page

In the next section you create the home page. When you have finished this section, you will have created a web page that looks something like Fig. 5.2.

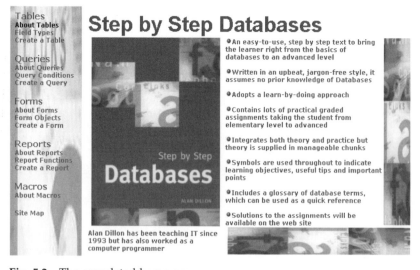

Fig. 5.2   The completed home page

Create the home page in four stages:
1. Prepare the images.
2. Set up the CSS styles.
3. Plan the web page layout.
4. Enter the text and position the images.

Stage 1: Prepare the Images

In this section, you scan the front and back cover of the *Step by Step Databases* book. If you do not have this book, skip the section on using a scanner. You will find the scanned images on the *Step by Step Web Design* CD.

Using a Scanner

 Each scanner comes with its own software to guide you through the process of converting a printed image into a digital image. Fig. 5.3 shows a typical example of the steps in the scanner software. The options on your scanner software will not necessarily be the same as those in Fig. 5.3.

Whatever the type of scanner, there are four basic steps to scanning an image. These are:
1. Start a new scan.
2. Select the section of the image that you want to scan.
3. Specify the file format to be used when saving the image. When scanning images for the web, save your images as JPEGs or GIFs. JPEG (16.7 million colours) is best for images with lots of colours where there are subtle transitions between colours. GIF (256 colours) is best for images with limited colours where there are large areas of solid colour.
4. Save the scanned image to your **images** folder.

Follow these steps to scan the front and back cover of the book:
(If you do not have a copy of the *Step by Step Databases* book, skip to the next section to copy the scanned images from CD.)

1. Start your scanner software. There should be an icon for the scanner on the desktop. Alternatively, select Start followed by Programs, and then select the scanner from the list of available programs.
2. Open the cover of the scanner and place the *Step by Step Databases* book face down on the glass.
3. Start a new scan. Your scanner will give you a message that it is 'warming up the lamp'.
4. Click and drag with the mouse to select the book cover, as in Fig. 5.3.
5. Select the output type. Normally, the scanner software will give you a range of options, as in Fig. 5.4. This image is best saved as a JPEG (16.7 million colours).

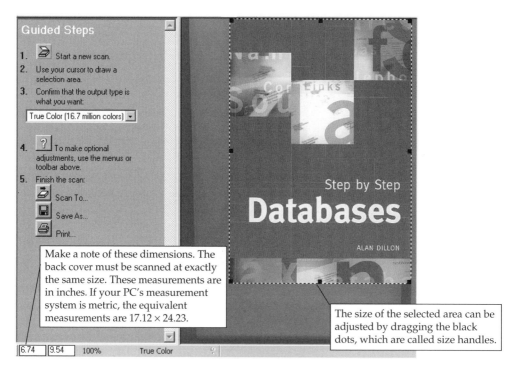

Fig. 5.3 The book cover has been selected using the scanner software

Fig. 5.4 A scanned image can be saved using a range of output types

6. Click the Save button. Save the image as **front.jpg** in the images folder.

7. Using steps 1 to 6, scan the back cover of the book. Make sure that the dimensions are exactly the same as the front cover. Examples of the scanned images with their file names are shown in Table 5.4.

8. database Check that each image scanned has been saved to the **images** sub-
   images folder using the file names in Table 5.4.

Table 5.4   Scanned images with their file names

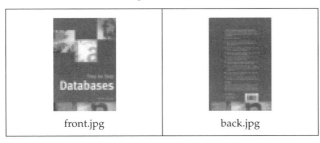

front.jpg	back.jpg

 Open **front.jpg** in Paint Shop Pro, select Image followed by Image Information from the menu. The details should look like those in Table 5.5.

Table 5.5   Details of the *front.jpg* image

Dimensions	1348 × 1909 pixels 6.740 × 9.545 inches (17.12 × 24.23 centimetres)
Pixels per inch	200
Pixel depth/colours	24/16 million

Note:

* When you scanned the front cover of the book, you selected an area of 6.74 × 9.54 inches (17.12 × 24.23 centimetres) using the scanning software. This corresponds to the dimensions displayed in Table 5.5.
* A resolution of 200 pixels per inch is too high for web design because most monitors have a resolution of either 72 or 96 pixels per inch.
* The pixel depth/colours reflects the fact you saved the scanned image as a JPEG file. In a JPEG image, each pixel is represented by 24 bits in memory, which gives a total 16.7 million possible colours (2^{24} = 16.7 million).

 Follow these steps if you do not have the *Step by Step Databases* book:

1. 🔘 📁 Project 5   Open the **Project 5** folder and then open
   📁 Scanned Images   the **Scanned Images** folder on the *Step by Step Web Design* CD

2. 📁 database   Copy **front.jpg** and **back.jpg** from this folder to the your own
   📁 images **images** folder.

 Resize Scanned Images in Paint Shop Pro

At 1348 × 1909 pixels, both scanned images are far too big to fit on a monitor with a resolution of 800 × 600. In this exercise, you will resize both images.

1. Open **front.jpg** in Paint Shop Pro, if it is not already open.
2. Select Image, followed by Resize from the menu.
3. Select Pixel Size and then enter a width of 247 and a height of 350.
4. 📁 database   Select File, followed by Save As from the menu. Save the resized
   📁 images   image as **smallfront.jpg** in the **images** folder.
5. Resize **back.jpg** by repeating steps 1 to 4. Save the resized image as **smallback.jpg** in the **images** folder.
6. 📷 Using the JPEG Optimiser, reduce the file size of **smallfront.jpg** and **smallback.jpg,** using a compression value of 2. Click the Format tab and select a Progressive file type. Save each compressed image using the original file name.

More About Web Image File Types

It is important to select the correct file type when you are saving a scanned image. The file type that you choose will affect both the quality of the image and the size of the image in kilobytes. Fig. 5.5 shows how GIF and JPEG produce very different results. In this case, JPEG is the best file type because it produces better quality and a smaller file size.

GIF

29Kb file size
247 × 350 pixel size
(after resizing and compression)

JPEG

17Kb file size
247 × 350 pixel size
(after resizing and compression)

Fig 5.5   Different quality is produced by the GIF and JPG formats

Edit Images in Paint Shop Pro

 In this exercise we cut out three sections of the front book cover, saving each section as a separate image. These images will later become part of the home page.

1. Open **smallfront.jpg** in Paint Shop Pro, if it is not already open. If necessary, zoom the image by selecting View, followed by Zoom In By 1 from the menu.

Tip: If you have a wheel mouse, you can zoom in or out by rolling the wheel with your finger.

2. ⬚ Click the Selection button in the Tool Palette.
3. Click and drag to select the first of the three squares, as in Fig. 5.6.
4. 🖺 Click the Copy button on the toolbar.

Fig. 5.6 smallfront.jpg with part of the image selected

5. Select Edit, followed by Paste from the menu. Now select As New Image.

6. Save this image as **pattern1.jpg** in the **images** folder.

> **Note:**
> Paint Shop Pro displays this message when the image is saved as a JPEG file:
>
> *Because of the limitations of the specified file format (and possibly the save options you have selected), the saved file will be limited to a merged image. Would you like to continue?*

This is because the JPEG file format uses compression to reduce the file size. This compression removes some of the original data from the image by taking out specific colours. You should click the Yes button to continue saving the file.

7. Select Image, followed by Image Information from the menu. Write down the dimensions of the image. It is important that all three images have the same dimensions.

8. Using steps 2 to 7, select the second of the three squares and create a new image named **pattern2.jpg.** Make sure that **pattern2.jpg** has the same width and height as **pattern1.jpg.**

9. Select the third of the three squares and make a new image named **pattern3.jpg.**

> **Tip:** If you are finding it difficult to copy the three images with exactly the same dimensions, adjust the dimensions of the images using the Resize dialog box.

Merging Images

 In this exercise we merge **pattern1.jpg, pattern2.jpg** and **pattern3.jpg** into one vertical image.

1. Make sure that **pattern1.jpg, pattern2.jpg** and **pattern3.jpg** are all open.

2. Create a new image in Paint Shop Pro using these dimensions:
   Width: Same as the width used for **pattern1.jpg, pattern2.jpg** and **pattern3.jpg**
   Height: Three times the height of **pattern1.jpg**
   Background Colour: Transparent
   Image Type: 16.7 million colours

3. Save the new image as **sidebar.jpg**.

4. Activate **pattern1.jpg** by clicking the title bar of this image.

4. Select Selections, followed by Select All from the menu.

5. Click the Copy button on the toolbar.

6. Activate **sidebar.jpg** by clicking the title bar of this image.

7. Select Edit followed by Paste and then As New Layer.

8. Point at the layer. When the mouse pointer changes to ✥, click and drag and move the layer to the top of the window, as in Fig. 5.7a.

10. Now activate **pattern2.jpg.** Copy this image and paste as a new layer into **sidebar.jpg** by following steps 4 to 8.
11. Position the layer so that it looks as in Fig. 5.7b.
12. Activate **pattern3.jpg.** Copy and paste as a new layer into **sidebar.jpg.** Position the layer as in Fig. 5.7c.
13. Select Layers, followed by Merge and then Merge All (Flatten) from the menu.
14. Resize the image by selecting Image, followed by Resize from the menu. First, make sure that the Maintain Aspect Ratio check box is not ticked. Now select Pixel Size and enter 48 as the width and 330 as the height. Click OK to resize the image.
15. 🖫 Save the changes to **sidebar.jpg** by clicking the Save button.

Fig. 5.7a

Fig. 5.7b

Fig. 5.7c

Rotating An Image

1. 🎨 Open **sidebar.jpg** in Paint Shop Pro, if it is not already open.
2. Select Image, followed by Rotate from the menu.
3. Rotate the image 90 degrees to the right by selecting the options shown in Fig. 5.8 and then clicking OK.
4. Select File, followed by Save As from the menu. Enter **bottombar.jpg** as the name for the new image.

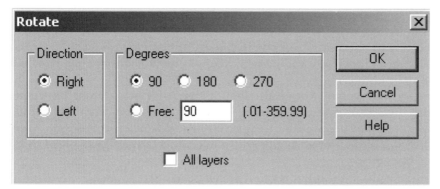

Fig. 5.8 Use the Rotate dialog box to specify the amount and direction of rotation

Create a Web Page Background Image

1. Create a new image in Paint Shop Pro using these settings:
   Width: 1600 pixels
   Height: 900 pixels
   Background Colour: White
   Image Type: 16.7 million colours

2. 🖫 Save this image as **homeback.jpg**.

> **Note:** The highest screen resolution setting is currently 1600 × 1200. At this resolution, a web page can be approximately 900 pixels high, when you allow for the menu bar, toolbars, status bar and start menu. Creating a background image with a width of 1600 and a height of 900 means the image will not be repeated on the screen.

3. Open **pattern2.jpg.**
4. Select Image, followed by Resize from the menu and make sure that the Maintain Aspect Ratio check box is not ticked. Select Pixel Size and enter 140 as the width and 900 as the height. Click OK to resize the image.
5. Select File, followed by Save As from the menu. Enter **pattern21.jpg** as the name for the new image.
6. Make sure that **pattern21.jpg** is the active image by clicking its title bar and that **homeback.jpg** is open. Select Selections, followed by Select All from the menu. Click the Copy button on the toolbar.
7. Activate **homeback.jpg** by clicking its title bar. Now select Edit, followed by Paste and then As New Layer from the menu.
8. Point at the layer. When the mouse pointer changes to ✛, click and drag and move the layer to the left of the window, as in Fig. 5.9.
9. 🖫 Save the changes to **homeback.jpg.**

Fig. 5.9 **pattern1.jpg** has been pasted into **homeback.jpg** as a new layer

Make Your Own Bullet Symbols

  1. Create a new image in Paint Shop Pro using these settings:
   Width: 12 pixels
   Height: 12 pixels
   Background Colour: Transparent
   Image Type: 16.7 million colours

2. Increase the on-screen size of the image by selecting View, followed by Zoom In By 5 from the menu.

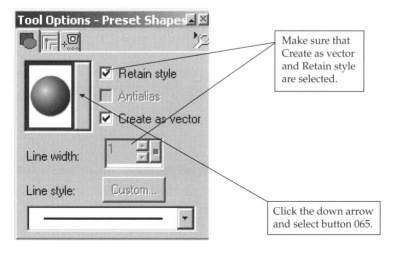

Fig. 5.10 Preset Shapes with Button 065 selected

3.   Click the Preset Shapes button.
4. In the Tool Options dialog box, select Button 065 from the list of preset shapes, as in Fig. 5.10. Make sure that the Retain style and Create as vector check boxes are selected.
5. Click and drag to draw the button as in Fig. 5.11.

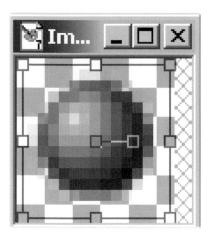

Fig. 5.11 Click and drag to draw a button.

6.   Save this image as **bullet.jpg**

Organise Your Images

Table 5.6 shows the images you have created so far. These images will be displayed in the Online Database home page. Confirm that each of these images is stored in your images folder by ticking the boxes.

NOTE

Note: As **front.jpg, back.jpg, pattern1.jpg, pattern2.jpg, pattern3.jpg** and **pattern21.jpg** are no longer needed, these images can be deleted from the **images** folder. Removing unnecessary files makes it easier to manage your web site.

Stage 2: Set Up CSS Styles

In Web Project 4, we learned how to specify the style, size, colour and weight of text using CSS styles. An example of a typical CSS style is:

```
.main{
font-family: Arial;
font-size: 30px;
font-weight: bold;
color: #330099;
}
```

Table 5.6   Summary of images in the Online Web Design site

Image Name		Dimensions	Created √
smallfront.jpg		247×350	
smallback.jpg		247×350	
sidebar.jpg		*defined by you*	
bottombar.jpg		width=330 *height defined by you*	
homeback.jpg		1600×900	
bullet.jpg		12×12	

This set of formatting instructions (specified in the Head section) is picked up in the Body section of the web page and applied to all the text between opening and closing paragraph tags where the class of the opening paragraph tag is "main".

Example:

```
<p class= "main">Online Computer Tutorial</p>
```

CSS styles can also be linked to specific HTML tags, so the formatting instructions are picked up each time a specific tag is used in the Body section.

In this project you learn how to remove the underline from a hyperlink using CSS styles and how to specify a background image for a web page. In the next section, you will set up CSS styles to control hyperlinks. Later on in this project you will set up CSS styles to specify a background image.

Use CSS Styles to Control Hyperlink Text

 In Internet Explorer, hyperlink text is underlined by default and can be in one of three possible states. In HTML these are referred to as the 'link', 'active' and 'visited' states.

Hyperlink in Link State

This is how the hyperlink text looks on a web page **before it is clicked.** The default colour for a hyperlink in link state is **blue.**

Hyperlink in Active State

This is how the hyperlink text looks on a web page **while it is in the process of being clicked.** The default colour for a hyperlink in active state is **red.** The hyperlink will only be in active state for a split second, so it is often difficult to see the active state colour.

Hyperlink in Visited State

This is how the hyperlink text looks on a web page **after it has been clicked.** The default colour for a hyperlink in visited state is **purple.**

Many web site designers are beginning to move away from the tradition of underlining hyperlink text. By creating CSS styles linked to the anchor tag, we can remove the hyperlink underline and control the colour of hyperlinks.

CSS styles also offer an extra hyperlink state, called 'hover'. The hover state controls the behaviour of hyperlink text as the mouse pointer hovers over it. Many web designers use the hover state so that either the font colour or the background colour changes as the mouse pointer hovers over the hyperlink text.

Create CSS Styles for the Link State

 The hyperlink text can be in one of four states:
- link state
- active state
- visited state
- hover state.

In the following worked example, you will specify properties of hyperlink text in the link state using the Properties toolbar in CSS mode. Set the properties of hyperlink text in link state as follows:

font-family: Verdana, Arial, Helvetica, sans-serif;
font-size: 12px;
font-weight: bold;
color: #CC0000;
text-decoration: none;

This means that any text enclosed in anchor tags will be displayed in 12px bold Verdana with a colour of #CC0000. Unlike traditional hyperlink text, it will not be underlined.

Note: text-decoration: none; removes the underline from the hyperlink text.

1. Open **index.htm** in Dreamweaver. Click the Design View button.
   Dreamweaver
2. Make sure that the Properties toolbar is in CSS mode and then select New CSS Style, as in Fig. 5.12.

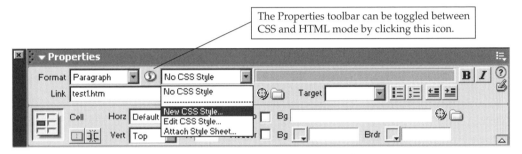

The Properties toolbar can be toggled between CSS and HTML mode by clicking this icon.

Fig. 5.12 The Properties toolbar in CSS mode

Tip: If the Properties toolbar is not displayed, select Window followed by Properties from the menu. Alternatively, hold down the CTRL key and then press F3.

3. Click the Use CSS Selector radio button and then select **a:link** from the list of selectors, as in Fig. 5.13. Select the This Document Only radio button to make sure that the CSS code is added to the Head section of the web page.
4. Click OK to set up the new CSS style. The CSS Style definition for a:link dialog box is displayed (see Fig. 5.13).

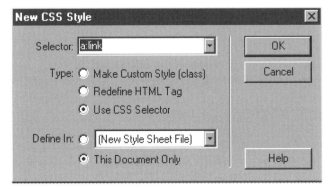

Fig. 5.13 The New CSS Style dialog box

5. Select properties for the Font, Size, Weight, Decoration and Color from the CSS Style definition dialog box as shown in Fig. 5.14 and then click OK.

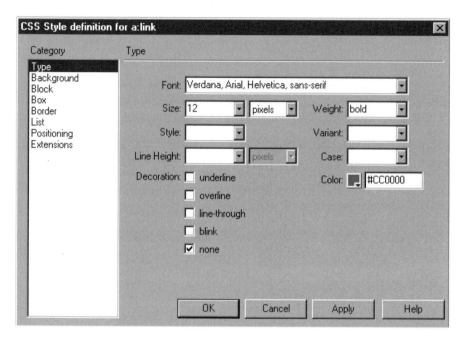

Fig. 5.14 Create a style CSS using the CSS Style definition dialog box

Switch to code view to see the CSS code for the new style. This will be in the Head section and should appear as in Fig. 5.15.

```
a: link {
    font-family: Verdana, Arial, Helvetica, sans-serif;
    font-size: 12px;
    font-weight: bold;
    color: #CC0000;
    text-decoration: none;
}
```

Fig. 5.15 A CSS Style with formatting instructions that control hyperlinks in link state

6. 💾 Save the changes to your web page.

As with all CSS styles, property-value pairs are listed between the opening and closing curly brackets. These property-value pairs will only affect text that has been enclosed in anchor tags. In the next section you will create CSS styles for the visited, hover and active states.

Towards the end of this project, you will set up hyperlinks. As soon as you do this, the hyperlink text will automatically pick up the styles defined for the link, visited, hover and active states.

Create CSS Styles for the Visited, Hover and Active States

1. Open **index.htm** in Dreamweaver, if it is not already open. Click the Design View button.
   Dreamweaver

2. Using the Properties toolbar in CSS mode, create styles for the visited, hover and active states, using the information in Table 5.7.

Table 5.7   CSS hyperlinks styles

	a:visited	a:hover	a:active
font-family	Verdana	Verdana	Verdana
font-size	12px	12px	12px
font-weight	bold	bold	bold
color	#000000	#339900	#FF6600
text-decoration	none	none	none

Create CSS Styles to Format Web Page Text

1. Create a custom CSS style named **.title** that includes these formatting instructions: 36px Arial in bold print with a colour of #7B52A5.
2. Create a custom CSS style named **.tabletext** that includes these formatting instructions:
   12px Verdana in bold print with a colour of #7B52A5.
3. Create a custom CSS style named **.menutext** that includes these formatting instructions:
   16px Verdana in bold print with a colour of #7B52A5.
4. 🖫 Save the changes to your web page.

Stage 3: Plan Web Page Layout

Up to now the web page layout has been made by creating tables that expand and contract depending on screen resolution by adding width="100%" in the opening table tag. The effect of this is that elements on the web page will always occupy the full width of the screen whatever the screen resolution.

In this project, we design the home page to fit in an 800 × 600 screen. At this resolution the home page will occupy all the available space on the screen. At higher resolutions, there will be unused space on the web page.

Use a table to position text and images on the home page. Fig. 5.16 is a rough sketch of this table. You should always plan the layout of a web page on paper before trying to create it in Dreamweaver. Time spent planning greatly reduces the amount of time spent editing and revising web page layout.

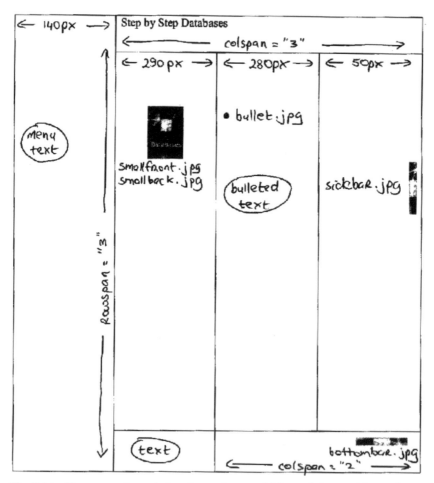

Fig. 5.16 Homepage layout showing column widths and the positions of text and images

At a resolution of 800 × 600, the web page can have a maximum width of 760 pixels (allowing roughly 40 pixels for the vertical scroll bar in Internet Explorer.) Notice how the column widths of 140, 290, 280 and 50 all add up to 760. This means that you do not have to do any horizontal scrolling because the width in pixels will never be more than the pixel width of the lowest resolution screen.

Stage 4: Enter Text and Position Images

1.   Open **index.htm** in Dreamweaver. Click the Design View button.
   Dreamweaver

2.   Create a table using these settings:

   Rows: 3
   Columns: 4
   Width: 760 pixels
   Border: 0
   Cell Padding: 0
   Cell Spacing: 5

3.   Using the Merge button in the Properties toolbar, merge cells 2, 3 and 4
   in Row 1 of the table and then enter the text *Step by Step Databases*, as in Table
   5.8.

Table 5.8   **Merge three cells in Row1, then enter the main heading**

	Step by Step Databases		

4. Using the Properties toolbar, apply the **.title** style to the text *Step by Step Databases*.

5.   Merge cells in Column 1 of the table, as in Table 5.9.

Table 5.9   **The table with cells in Column 1 merged**

	Step by Step Databases		

6.   Click the Code View button and enter column widths as:

   Column 1: 140 pixels
   Column 2: 290 pixels
   Column 3: 280 pixels
   Column 4: 50 pixels

Specify column widths by adding the width attribute to each opening <td> tag in the top row of the table. Where table cells have been merged in the top row, enter the widths in the second row. The HTML code for your table should look something like Fig. 5.17.

```
<table width="760" border="0" cellspacing="5" cellpadding="0">
   <tr>
      <td rowspan="3" width="140"> </td>
      <td colspan="3">Step by Step Databases</td>
   </tr>
   <tr>
      <td width="290"> </td>
      <td width="280"> </td>
      <td width="50"> </td>
   </tr>
   <tr>
      <td> </td>
      <td> </td>
      <td> </td>
   </tr>
</table>
```

Fig. 5.17 HTML code for the table, with column widths entered

7.   Click the Design View button and enter the text in Column 1 of the table, as in Table 5.10.

 Tip: Hold down the Shift key and press Enter to move to a new line. This inserts a <br /> tag. To insert a blank line at the end of each group of items, press the Enter key without holding down the Shift key.

8.   Set the vertical alignment of the table cell with the navigation menu to Top.
9.   Apply the **.menutext** style to the titles Tables, Queries, Forms, Reports and Macros.
10.   With the cursor to the left of the title Tables in Column 1, click the Comment button and enter this comment:

```
This table cell contains the navigation menu. Menu items are
hyperlinks to web pages.
```

Table 5.10 The table with the navigation menu entered in Column 1

Tables About Tables Field Types Create a Table Queries About Queries Query Conditions Create a Query Forms About Forms Form Objects Create a Form Reports About Reports Report Functions Create a Report Macros About Macros Site Map	Step by Step Databases		

11. ⟨⟩ ▦ ▦ Click the Code View button and then position the cursor before the opening <table> tag. If necessary, press the Enter key to create a blank line.

12. 💬 Click the Comment button and then enter this comment:

```
Table width is 760 pixels so that it will fit in a monitor with
a resolution of 800 × 600.
Column 1 of the table is 140 pixels wide.
Column 2 of the table is 290 pixels wide.
Column 3 of the table is 280 pixels wide.
Column 4 of the table is 50 pixels wide.
```

13. 💾 Save the changes to your web page.

Rollover Images

 A rollover image is an image that changes when mouse pointer moves over the image. As the mouse pointer moves away from the image, the original image is shown again. Use **smallfront.jpg** and **smallback.jpg** to create a rollover image.

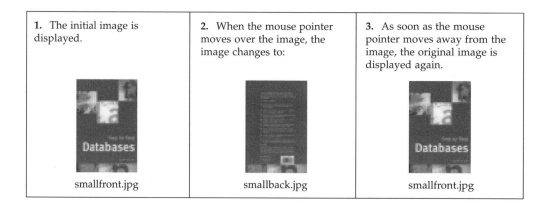

| 1. The initial image is displayed. | 2. When the mouse pointer moves over the image, the image changes to: | 3. As soon as the mouse pointer moves away from the image, the original image is displayed again. |
| smallfront.jpg | smallback.jpg | smallfront.jpg |

Create a Rollover Image

Before you begin, look back at Fig. 5.16 to make sure that you put the rollover image in the correct table cell.

1. Open **index.htm** in Dreamweaver, if it is not already open. Click **Dreamweaver** the Design View button.

2. Put the cursor in the second column of the table and in the second row. Click the ⬚ Rollover Image button.

3. Specify **smallfront.jpg** as the original image and **smallback.jpg** as the rollover image as in Fig. 5.18. Enter this alternate text:

    `An easy-to-use guide to databases - From beginners to advanced`

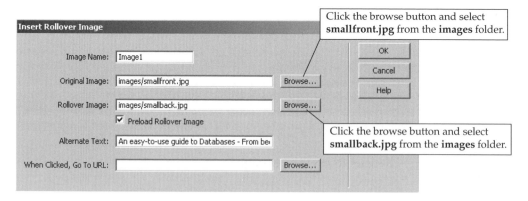

Fig. 5.18   The Insert Rollover Image dialog box

4. Click OK to insert the rollover image.
5. Set the horizontal alignment of the table cell with the rollover image to Center and the vertical alignment to Top.

6. [icon] Select the rollover image and then add this comment:

Initial image is smallfront.jpg. Rollover image is smallback.jpg.

7. [icon] Save the changes and preview the web page in Internet Explorer. Test the rollover image by moving the mouse pointer over the image.

Enter Bulleted Text

Use **bullet.jpg** as a bullet symbol for each sentence of descriptive text on the home page.

1. Position the cursor in the third column of the table and in the second row, as shown in Fig. 5.19.

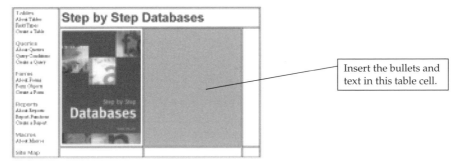

Insert the bullets and text in this table cell.

Fig. 5.19 Bullets and text will be entered in the highlighted cell

2. Enter text and bullets shown here. Click the [icon] Image button each time you want to insert a bullet symbol. Insert a blank line after each bulleted point.

⚫ An easy-to-use, step by step text to bring the learner right from the basics of databases to an advanced level

⚫ Written in an upbeat, jargon-free style, it assumes no prior knowledge of databases

⚫ Adopts a learn-by-doing approach

⚫ Contains lots of practical graded assignments taking the student from elementary to advanced level

⚫ Integrates theory and practice but theory comes in manageable chunks

⚫ Symbols are used throughout to indicate learning objectives, useful tips and important points

⚫ Includes a glossary of database terms, which can be used for quick reference.

⚫ Solutions to the assignments will be available on the web site

3. Apply the **.tabletext** style to each line of bulleted text on page 205.
4. Set the vertical alignment of this table cell to Top.
5.   Put the cursor to the left of the first bullet and then enter this comment:

    ```
    Bulleted text using bullet.jpg as the bullet image.
    ```

6. Save the changes and preview the web page in Internet Explorer.

Tip: Dreamweaver applies the **.tabletext** style to the bulleted text by enclosing each line of bulleted text in <p> and <span> tags, as in Example 5.1.

```
<td width= "280" valign="top">
<p>
<img src="images/bullet.jpg" width="12" height="12" />
    <span class= "tabletext">An easy-to-use step by step text to
    bring the learner right from the basics of databases to an
    advanced level</span>
</p>

<p class="tabletext">
<img src="images/bullet.jpg" width="12" height= "12" />
    <span class= "tabletext">Written in an upbeat, jargon-free
    style, it assumes no prior knowledge of databases

</p>

<p class="tabletext">
<img src="images/bullet.jpg" width="12" height="12" />
    Adopts a learn-by-doing approach</

</p>
```

Example 5.1 The .tabletext style is applied to each line using <span> or <p> tags. This creates two problems:

*   There is unnecessary code. Instead of enclosing every line of bulleted text in <p> and <span> tags, it is much more efficient to use <span class="tabletext"> **once** before the first line of bulleted text together with </span> after the last line of bulleted text.
*   Because each closing </p> tag includes a blank line, this spaces out the bulleted text and makes it continue below the image of the book cover.

*   Click the Code View button and then edit the HTML code so that the bulleted text is enclosed in one set of <span> tags. Link the opening <span> tag to the **.tabletext** style.

- Delete the <p class="tabletext"> </p> tags that enclose each line of bulleted text.
- Insert two <br /> tags at the end of each line of bulleted text. Your code should now look something like Example 5.2.

```
<td width="280" valign="top">
<span class="tabletext">
<img src="images/bullet.jpg" width="12" height= "12" />
    An easy-to-use step by step text to bring the learner right from
    the basics of databases to an advanced level
<br /><br />

<img src="images/bullet.jpg" width="12" height="12" />
    Written  in an upbeat, jargon-free style, it assumes no prior
    knowledge of databases
<br /><br />
↓
<img src="images/bullet.jpg" width="12" height="12" />
  Solutions to the assignments will be available on the web site
</span>
</td>
```

Example 5.2 *The edited HTML code*

Position Remaining Images

 Position the **sidebar.jpg** and **bottombar.jpg** images on the web page. Fig. 5.20 shows where these images should be positioned on the web page.

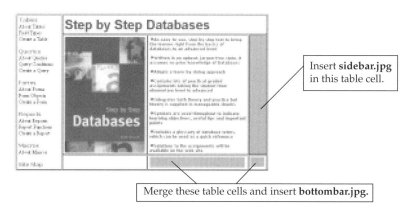

Insert **sidebar.jpg** in this table cell.

Merge these table cells and insert **bottombar.jpg**.

Fig. 5.20

1. Insert **sidebar.jpg** in the appropriate table cell, as in Fig. 5.20.
2. Set the vertical alignment of table cell with this image to Top.
3. 🔲 Merge the two table cells as shown in Fig. 5.20.
4. Insert **bottombar.jpg** in this merged cell.
5. Set the alignment of this image to Right.

Enter the Rest of the Text

1. Put the cursor in the second column of the table and in the third row, as in Fig. 5.21.

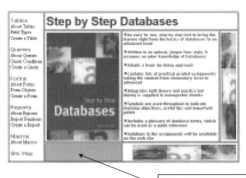

Insert text in this table cell.

Fig. 5.21

2. Enter this text:

   ```
   Alan Dillon has been teaching IT since 1993 but has also worked
   as a computer programmer.
   ```

3. Apply the **.tabletext** style to this text.

Use CSS Styles to Specify a Background Image

To finish the web page, use **homeback.jpg** as a background image. A background image is specified by setting up a CSS style for the body tag.

1. 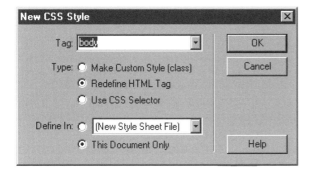 Open **index.htm** in Dreamweaver. Click the Design View button.

2. Select New CSS Style in the Properties toolbar.
3. In the New CSS Style dialog box, click the Redefine HTML tag radio button and then select the body tag, as in Fig. 5.22.

Fig. 5.22 Creating a CSS Style for the body tag

4. Click OK to display the CSS Style definition for body dialog box (see Fig. 5.23).
5. Select Background from the list of categories and specify **homeback.jpg** as the Background Image, as in Fig. 5.23.

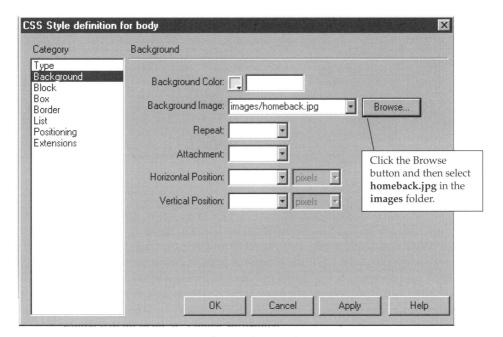

Fig. 5.23 Using a CSS Style to specify a background image

6.   Click OK to set up the new CSS style.

Note: Some of your menu text may be wider than the sidebar image on the left of the web page. Later on in this project, this text is used for hyperlinks. Once this happens, the styles defined for the link, active, visited and hover states will be picked up and the text will become small enough to fit into the sidebar.

About Screen Resolutions

The monitor on your PC has an invisible grid, made up of columns and rows, a bit like a sheet of graph paper. Each square in the grid is a pixel. The resolution of your monitor specifies how many pixels your monitor can display.

Most monitors have a resolution of 1024×768, meaning that 1024 pixels can be displayed horizontally and 768 pixels can be displayed vertically (a bit like a spreadsheet with 1024 columns and 768 rows). Laptop computers tend to have higher resolutions, typically 1280×1024, while many older monitors have a resolution of 800×600.

As the resolution increases, the pixels are closer together, making the items on the screen look smaller and sharper. At higher resolutions, more of a web page will be visible on the screen and at lower resolutions less of the same web page can be seen. Look at Fig. 5.24, which shows the same web page viewed at resolutions of 800×600, 1024×768 and 1280×1024.

800×600 1024×768 1280×1024

Fig. 5.24   A web page viewed at three different resolutions

Fig. 5.24 clearly shows at higher resolutions more of a web page appears on the screen. In Fig. 5.24, a table is used to position text and images on the web page. The width of the table has been set to 100 per cent in the opening <table> tag. Notice how the web page 'stretches' to fit the screen at higher resolutions. The paragraphs become wider and shorter. If table widths are specified in pixels, as in the case of the Online Database home page, there will be unused space on the web page at higher resolutions. This is shown in Fig. 5.25.

The web page in Fig. 5.25 was designed to fit on a screen with a resolution of 800×600. The table used to position text and images on the web page is 760 pixels wide. At a resolution of 800×600, this fits the screen exactly.

At a resolution of 1024×768, there are roughly 264 pixels (1,024 minus the table

| 800 × 600 | 1024 × 768 | 1280 × 1024 |

Fig. 5.25 Specifying table width in pixels has different effects at higher resolutions

width of 760) of blank space on the right of the screen. Blank space also appears at the bottom of the screen because the text and images are smaller at this resolution. At a resolution of 1280 × 1024, the amount of blank space becomes even more obvious.

Most web designers allow for this by designing web pages to fit in a screen with a resolution of 800 × 600. Specifying widths in percentages means that the web page will expand to fit higher screen resolutions. Specifying widths in pixels means that there will be unused areas on the web page at higher resolutions. The approach you take depends on the web page and your own style of web design.

Vertical Display Space at Different Resolutions

Fig. 5.26 shows a web page displayed in Internet Explorer with the monitor resolution set to 800 × 600.

Fig. 5.26 Internet Explorer displays a web page in 800 × 600

At a resolution of 800 × 600, 125 pixels are needed to display the title bar, the menu, the toolbars and the address bar. To display the status bar and the taskbar 50 pixels are needed. This leaves 425 pixels available to display the web page.

This has two important implications.
- Any web pages that are longer than 425 pixels will require scrolling.
- Images with a height of more than 425 pixels will not fit on the screen.
  Fig. 5.27 shows the same web page in Internet Explorer, with the screen resolution set to 1024 × 768. More of the web page is visible on the screen at this resolution.

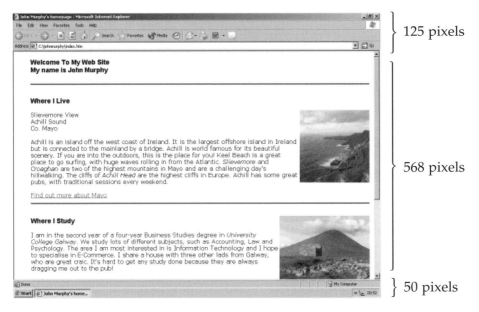

125 pixels

568 pixels

50 pixels

Fig. 5.27   Internet Explorer displays the same web page in 1024 × 768

Although the toolbars and status bar each still take up 125 pixels and 50 pixels, the pixels are closer together so they take up less space on the screen. At this resolution, more of the web page can be seen vertically and horizontally. As a web page designer, you should test your web pages at resolutions of 800 × 600 and 1024 × 768. It is also important to test your web pages at a resolution of 1280 × 1024, as this resolution is often used for laptop computer screens.

Remember:
- The most common screen resolutions are 800 × 600, 1024 × 768 and 1280 × 1024. At higher resolutions, you will see more of the web page on the screen. Test your web pages at each of these resolutions.
- As a web designer, you must decide whether your web pages will stretch at higher resolutions or take up less than the whole screen at higher resolutions.
- The toolbars and scroll bars take approximately 175 pixels of vertical space.
- Design the home page to fit on an 800 × 600 screen, with either no scrolling or a minimal amount of scrolling.

For You To Do

Test the home pages of five of your favourite web sites at resolutions of 800 × 600, 1024 × 768 and 1280 × 1024. For each web site make a note of the differences at each resolution. Has the web designer chosen a fixed or variable page width?

Test the Home Page at Different Resolutions

 1. Open **index.htm** in Dreamweaver. Click the Design View
Dreamweaver button.

2. Click the web page's Restore Down button (see Fig. 5.28) at the top right of the screen. (Clicking the Restore Down reduces the size of the window. Make sure that you click the lower of the two Restore Down buttons, as this is the one that controls the size of your web page's window.)

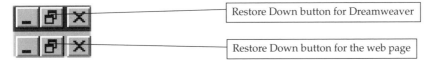

Fig. 5.28 Minimize, Restore Down and Close buttons for Dreamweaver and the web page

3. Click the window size setting in the status bar (bottom right of the screen) and then select (800 × 600, Maximized), as shown below in Fig. 5.29. Your web page appears in the window as it would on a monitor with a resolution of 800 × 600.

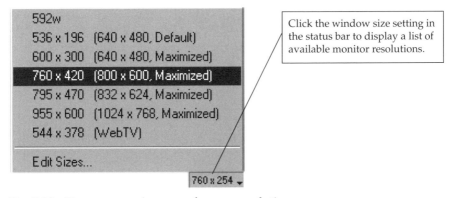

Fig. 5.29 Dreamweaver's range of screen resolutions

4. Click the window size setting again and then select 1024 × 768, Maximized. Your web page appears in the window as it would on a monitor with a resolution of 1024 × 768 (the most popular monitor resolution).

5. To get a more accurate representation of what your web page will look like at different resolutions, change the screen resolution in the display properties of your monitor. I prefer to use this method.
    • Close or minimise all programs that are running.
    • Right click on a blank area of the desktop.
    • Select Properties from the menu. The Display Properties dialog box is displayed (see Fig. 5.30).

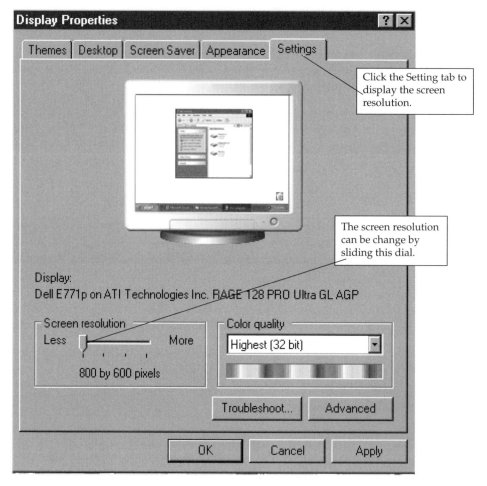

Fig. 5.30 Using the Display Properties dialog box to change the screen resolution

• To display the screen resolution of your monitor, click the Settings tab. Select 800 × 600, as in Fig. 5.30.
• If your screen resolution was not already set to 800 × 600, click the Apply button to apply the new settings. The monitor will go blank for a few seconds while the new settings are applied. Click OK to accept the new screen resolution.

- Open or maximise **index.htm** in Dreamweaver and preview the web page in Internet Explorer.
- Change the screen resolution to 1024 × 768 (see steps 1 to 4 page 213).
- Preview **index.htm** in Internet Explorer again. Notice how the text and images are smaller and that there is blank space at the right of the screen and at the bottom of the screen.

Create the Lesson Pages

We will create the first lesson page in four stages:
1. Copy and edit the home page.
2. Prepare the images.
3. Set up CSS styles.
4. Enter the text and position images.
Because all the lesson pages have the same format and structure, the other lesson pages will be created by copying and editing.

Stage 1: Copy and Edit the Home Page

1. In Dreamweaver make sure that the **onlinedatabase** site is active.
2. Using the Site Panel, create a new web page by copying **index.htm.**
3. Rename **Copy of index.htm** as **abouttables.htm.**
4. Open **abouttables.htm** in Design View. Replace the main heading *Step by Step Databases* with About Tables.
5. Delete data from all the other table cells, except for the cells with the menu text. Merge cells so that the table looks like Fig. 5.31.
6. Save the changes to **abouttables.htm.**

NOTE

Note:
The formats specified for the link, active, visited and hover states will be picked up when each menu item becomes a hyperlink.

Stage 2: Prepare Images

In this section, you create a background image to be used in all of the lesson pages. You also create an image of an arrow pointing upwards. Later on you will display

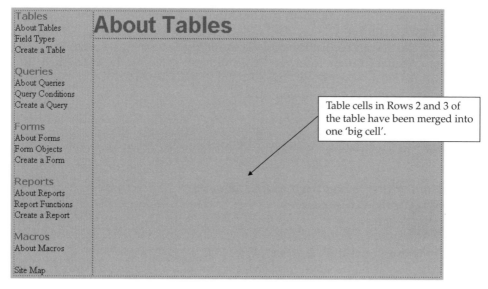

Fig. 5.31 The basic structure of the lesson web pages

this image on the **abouttables.htm** web page and use it as a hyperlink to a named anchor at the top of the page. You create two additional images:

- a right arrow
- a correct symbol

to be used in the lesson pages.

 Create a Background Image for the Lesson Pages

1. Create a new image in Paint Shop Pro using these settings:
   Width: 1600 pixels
   Height: 20 pixels
   Background Colour: White
   Image Type: 256 colours (8 bit)
   Save this image as **lessonback.gif** in the **images** folder.
2. ▢ Click the Selection button in the Tool Palette. Starting from the top left of the image, click and drag to select an area that is 140 pixels wide and 20 pixels high (see Fig. 5.33).
3. ◈ Click the Flood Fill button and then change the foreground colour to light grey (#CCCCCC) in the colour palette as in Fig. 5.32.
4. Point anywhere inside the selected area and click once to fill the selection with grey (#CCCCCC), as in Fig. 5.33.
5. 🖫 Click the Save button to save the changes to **lessonback.gif**.
6. 🌀 Dreamweaver ⟨⟩ ▦ ▦ Open **abouttables.htm** in Dreamweaver. Display the HTML code by clicking the Code View button.

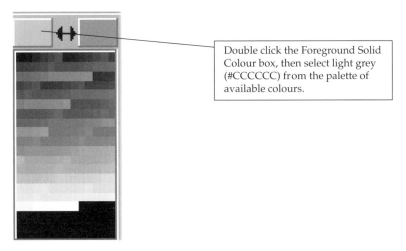

Double click the Foreground Solid Colour box, then select light grey (#CCCCCC) from the palette of available colours.

Fig. 5.32   The colour palette for a GIF image displays 256 possible colours

Fig. 5.33   A selection area of 140 × 20 pixels has been filled with light grey (#CCCCCC)

7. In the Head section, find the code for the background image for the web page. This code reads as:

    ```
    body{
    background-image: url(images/homeback.jpg)
    }
    ```

8. Change the background image to **lessonback.gif.**

9. 🖫 Save the changes and then preview the web page. It should appear as shown in Fig. 5.34.

    Tip: If the sidebar has white gaps and is not continuous grey, it means that the selection area of 140 × 20 pixels that you filled with grey is not in exactly the right position. Do the Create A Background Image For The Lesson Pages section again.

  Make Your Own Return To Top Symbol

1. 🖌 Create a new image in Paint Shop Pro using these settings:

Width: 40 pixels
Height: 40 pixels
Background Colour: White
Image Type: 256 colours (8 bit)

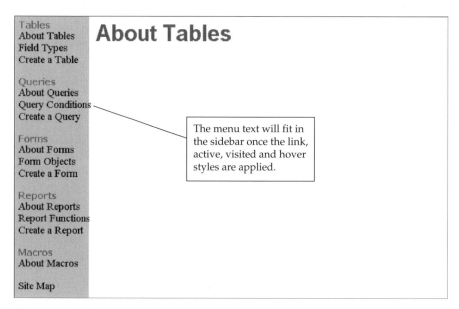

Fig. 5.34 The **lessonback.gif** will be used as a background for all lesson web pages

2. [icon] Click the Preset Shapes button.
3. In the Tool Options dialog box, select Arrow 23 from the list of preset shapes, as in Fig. 5.35. Make sure that the Retain style and Create as vector check boxes are selected.

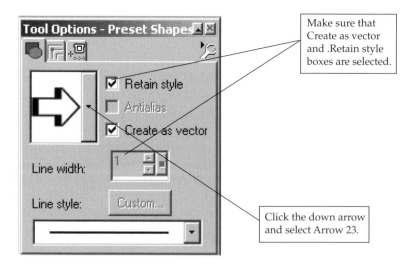

Fig. 5.35 Preset Shapes with Arrow 23 selected

4. Click and drag to draw the arrow as in Fig. 5.36.
5. Select Image, followed by Rotate from the menu. Rotate the image 90 degrees to the left. Your image should now look like Fig. 5.37.

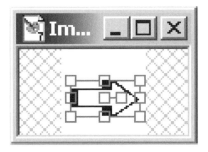

Fig. 5.36 Click and drag to draw an arrow in your new image.

Fig. 5.37 The arrow has been rotated 90 degrees to the left.

6. Select Selections, followed by Select All from the menu.

7. Click the Copy button on the toolbar.

8. In the Colour Palette change the background solid colour to white. Select Edit, followed by Paste from the menu. Now select As New Image.

9. Save the new image as **up.gif** in your **images** folder.

Create a Pointer Symbol

1. In Paint Shop Pro, set the background solid colour to #CCCCCC in the colour palette (see Fig. 5.38).

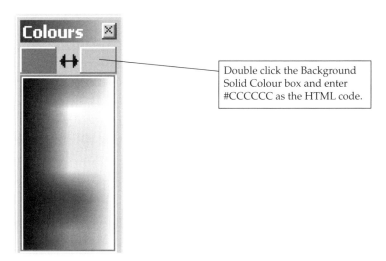

Double click the Background Solid Colour box and enter #CCCCCC as the HTML code.

Fig. 5.38 Use the colour palette to select a background colour

2. Create a new image using these settings:

    Width: 15 pixels
    Height: 10 pixels
    Background Colour: Background Colour
    Image Type: 256 colours (8 bit)

 Note: Setting the background colour of the image to 'background colour' picks up the background colour that is currently selected in the colour palette.

3. Zoom the image by selecting View, followed by Zoom In By 5.

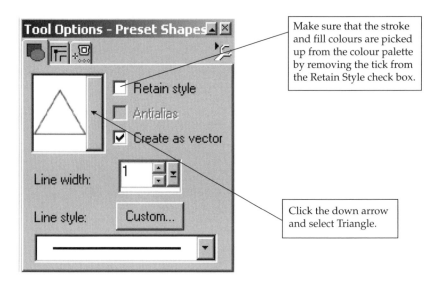

Fig. 5.39   Preset shapes with the triangle selected

4. 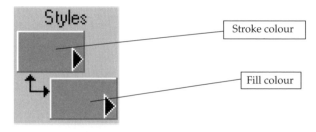 Click the Preset Shapes button and select the Triangle image from the Tool Options dialog box (see Fig. 5.39).
5. In the colour palette set the stroke colour to #FF6600 and the fill colour to #FF6600.

Fig. 5.40   Using the colour palette to select the stroke and fill colour

6. Click and drag to draw a triangle, as in Fig. 5.41.

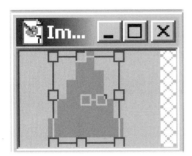

Fig. 5.41

7. Rotate the image 90 degrees to the right so that it looks as in Fig. 5.42

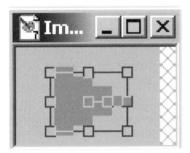

Fig. 5.42   The image has been rotated 90 degrees to the right

8. ▣ Save the image as **arrow.gif**.

 Create a Correct Symbol

1. Create a new image using these settings:
   Width: 18 pixels
   Height: 20 pixels
   Background Colour: White
   Image Type: 256 colours (8 bit)

2. Zoom the image by selecting View, followed by Zoom In by 5.

3. Click the Preset Shapes button and select the Check 2 image from the Tool Options dialog box.

4. In the colour palette set the Stroke Colour to #FF6600 and the Fill Colour to #FF6600.

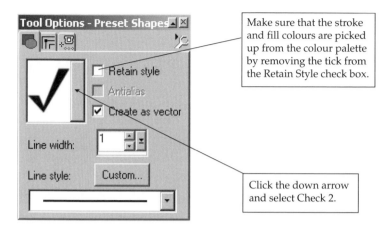

Fig. 5.43 Preset shapes with the check 2 selected

5.   Click and drag to draw a correct symbol, as in Fig. 5.44.
6.   ▣ Save the image as **answer.gif**.

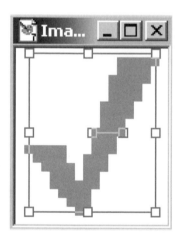

Fig. 5.44

 Copy Images

The other image files for the lesson web pages are on the *Step by Step Web Design* CD. Follow these steps to copy the image files to your **images** folder:

1.   Open the **Project 5** folder and then open the **Images** folder on the *Step by Step Web Design* CD.

2.   Copy all the image files from this folder to your **images** folder.

Stage 3: Set Up CSS Styles

In this section, you will set up CSS styles for text formats in the **abouttables.htm** web page. The link, active, visited, hover, title and menu text styles have already been created and copied from the home page. Delete the **tabletext** style, as it will not be used in any of the lesson web pages.

1. Open **abouttables.htm** in Dreamweaver. Click the Code View button to display the HTML code.

2. Locate the **.tabletext** style in the <head> section of the HTML code. It should read:

```
.tabletext{
   font-family: Verdana, Arial, Helvetica, sans-serif;
   font-size: 12px;
   font-weight: bold;
   color: #7B52A5;
}
```

3. Highlight the CSS code for the **.tabletext** style and press the Delete key to delete this CSS style.
4. Click the Design View button and, using the Properties toolbar in CSS mode, set up five new styles named **.tableheadings**, **.paraheadings**, **.emphasis**, **.text** and **.currentlink**, using the properties and values in Table 5.11.

Table 5.11   Summary of CSS Styles

	.tableheadings	.paraheadings	.emphasis	.text	.currentlink
font-family	Arial	Arial	Verdana	Verdana	Arial
font-size	16px	16px	14px	14px	12px
font-weight	bold	bold	bold		bold
color	#FFFFFF	#990000	#000000	#000000	#FF6600

5. Save the changes to your web page.

Stage 4: Enter Text and Position Images

 Open the **abouttables.htm** web page, if it is not already open. Click the Design View button and set up the web page as shown on page 224. Allow the text to wrap naturally. For useful guidelines, look at the Remember section on page 225.

About Tables

Creating a Table   Setting a Field's Data Type

Tables are the most important part of any database. The table stores data. A database must have at least a table. Before we can store data in a table we must organise the data so that each record has the same structure. To store data in a table, it must be divided into sections, which are called fields. The fields are in the top row of the table. In the example below, the fields are Member No, Firstname, Surname, Gender, Phone and Date of Birth.

Member No	Firstname	Surname	Gender	Phone	Date of Birth
1	Paul	Moore	Male	2036558	20/06/1982
2	Deirdre	O'Connell	Female	5440291	15/10/1988
3	Seamus	Horgan	Male	8795412	03/01/1987
4	Ross	Mooney	Male	4590298	28/02/1986
5	Cathy	Duffy	Female	8701593	21/08/1985
6	Geraldine	Abbey	Female	3390217	12/12/1989

Creating a Table
Select Tables from the list of objects and then click the New button.

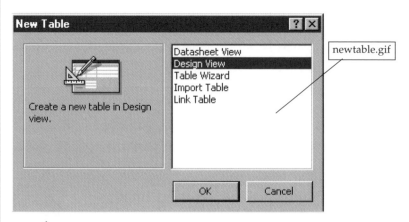

Select Design View from the New Table dialog box, as shown above, and then click OK.

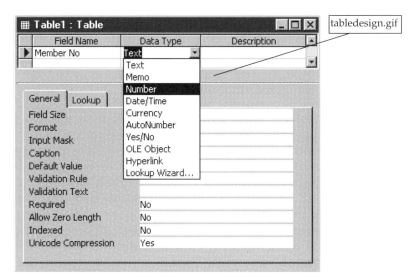

A field is created by entering the field name, then selecting the data type. In the example above, a Member No field has been set up and the data type has been set to Text.

Setting a Field's Data Type
The field type should match the data that is stored in the field. There are many different field types, but to keep things simple use these rules:

Rule 1: Any field that stores text entries will have a data type of text.
Rule 2: Any field that stores dates will have a data type of date/time.
Rule 3: Any field that stores numbers will have a data type of number.

Remember:
- Add **Home** as an extra menu item at the top of the navigation menu.
- Insert the images **arrow.gif, newtable.gif, tabledesign.gif** and **up.gif** in the positions indicated.
- Set the alternative text of both up arrow images to Click to Return to Top.

- Use the Non-Breaking Space button (in the Characters menu) to insert spaces between the text items on the second line of the web page:
  Creating a Table Setting a Field's Data Type
- Apply the **.text** style to all text in the web page except for the headings, the first row of the table and Rule 1, Rule 2 and Rule 3.
- Set the width of the table to 100% and the width of the border to 1. Set the cellspacing and the cellpadding to 0.
- Set the border colour of the table to #CCCCCC.
- Apply the **.tableheadings** style to each cell in the first row of the table. (The text will be temporarily invisible until you set the background colour.)
- Set the background colour of the table row containing the headings to #990000.
- Apply the **.tabletext** style to all the other remaining cells in the table.
- Apply the **.paraheadings** style to the paragraph headings Creating a Table and Setting a Field's Data Type. (Do not apply this CSS style to the text that comes immediately below the main heading.)
- Apply the **.emphasis** style to the text Rule 1:, Rule 2: and Rule 3:.
- In the navigation menu, apply the **.currentlink** style to the text About Tables. Make sure that the **arrow.gif** image has been inserted to the left of this text.
- Insert appropriate comments in your web page.
- Set the page title to Lesson 1 – About Tables.
- Check your spelling by selecting Text, followed by Check Spelling from the menu.
-  Save the web page and preview the web page in Internet Explorer.

Create a Hyperlink to a Named Anchor

Create a named anchor at the top of the page and use each up arrow image as a hyperlink to this anchor. Clicking either up arrow will bring the web page viewer to the top of the web page.

1. **Dreamweaver** Open **abouttables.htm** in Dreamweaver, if it is not already open.
    Click the Design View button.

2. Put the cursor at the top of the web page by clicking to the left of the letter A in About Tables.

3. Click the Named Anchor button. The Named Anchor dialog box is in Fig. 5.45. Enter Top as the anchor name, as in Fig. 5.45. Click OK to set up the anchor tag.

4. Select the up arrow image, which appears immediately below the New Table dialog box on page 224. The properties of the **up.gif** are shown in the Properties toolbar in Fig. 5.46.

5. Make the **up.gif** image a hyperlink to the anchor named "top" by entering **#top** as the Link in the Properties toolbar, as in Fig. 5.46.

Fig. 5.45 The Named Anchor dialog box

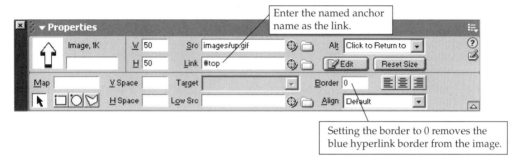

Fig. 5.46 Use the Properties toolbar to set up an image hyperlink to a named anchor

6. Set the border of the image to 0 to remove the blue hyperlink border (see Fig. 5.46).
7. In same way, make the second up arrow image a hyperlink to the anchor named "top".
8. 💾 🌐. Save and then preview the web page in Internet Explorer. Test both hyperlinks by clicking each up arrow in turn. Clicking an up arrow should bring you to the top of the web page.

Create Additional Anchors

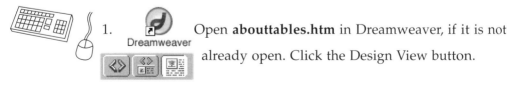

1. Open **abouttables.htm** in Dreamweaver, if it is not already open. Click the Design View button.
2. Position the cursor to the left of the letter C in the paragraph heading Creating a Table.
3. ⚓ Click the Named Anchor button. Enter **createtable** as the anchor name.
4. Put the cursor to the left of the letter S in the paragraph heading Setting a Field's Data Type and create a second anchor named **datatype.**

5. This line of text appears immediately below the web page heading:

Creating a Table   Setting a Field's Data Type

Highlight the text `Creating a Table` and delete it.

6. Click the Hyperlink button.

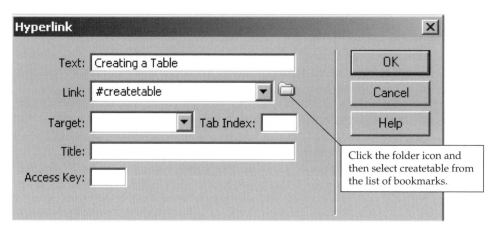

Fig. 5.47   Using the Hyperlink dialog box to set up an text hyperlink to a bookmark

7. In the Hyperlink dialog box, enter the text `Creating a Table` and link to the **createtable** bookmark (see Fig. 5.47) The hyperlink text automatically picks up the styles that you defined for the link, active, visited and hover states.

Tip: Highlight the text `Creating a Table`. Select Edit followed by Cut from the menu. Now click the Hyperlink button and paste the text back into the Hyperlink dialog box.

8. In the same way, set up the text `Setting a Field's Data Type` as a hyperlink to the anchor named **datatype.**

9. 🖫 ⊙, Save and preview the web page in Internet Explorer. Test all the hyperlinks.

Create The fieldtypes.htm Web Page

1. In Dreamweaver make sure that the **onlinedatabase** site is active.

2. Using the Site Panel, create a new web page by copying **abouttables.htm.**

3. Rename **Copy of abouttables.htm** as **fieldtypes.htm.**
4.   fieldtypes.htm Open **fieldtypes.htm** in Design View. Set up the web page as shown on pages 230. Allow the text to wrap naturally. For useful guidelines, refer to the Remember section that follows.

Remember:

*   ⬇ Use the Non-Breaking Space button to insert spaces between the text items that appear on the second line of the web page: Text, Date and Time, Currency, Yes/No, Number, Summary.
*   Display text in italics as shown.
*   Insert the images **arrow.gif, text.gif, datetime.gif, currency.gif, up.gif** and **yesno.gif** in the positions indicated.
*   Set the hspace to 10 pixels and the vspace to 10 pixels for the **text.gif, datetime.gif, currency.gif** and **yesno.gif** images.

> NOTE
>
> **Note:** Your web page will have a cramped and cluttered look, if the text is wrapping very close to an image. Text can be 'pushed away' from an image by specifying the hspace (horizontal space) and vspace (vertical space) in pixels for each image. Horizontal space is the amount of space to the left and right of the image. Vertical space is the amount of space above and below the image.

*   Format text using the **.paraheadings** and **.text** styles.
*   Set the width of both tables to 100%. Set the border to 1 and the cellpadding/cellspacing to 0.
*   Apply styles and formatting to tables as before.
*   In the navigation menu, apply the **.currentlink** style to the text Field Types. Make sure that the **arrow.gif** image has been inserted to the left of this text.
*   Set the page title to Lesson 2 – Field Types.
*   ⚓ Set up named anchors for each of the paragraph headings in Table 5.12 on page 232.
*   This line of text appears immediately below the web page heading:

    Text   Date and Time   Currency   Yes/No   Number   Summary

    ✎ Set up each item as a hyperlink to the appropriate anchor. For example, *Text* should be a hyperlink to the anchor named **textfield.**
*   💬 Delete and/or edit comments so that they are specific to the **fieldtypes.htm** web page.
*   Check your spelling.
*   💾 🔍 Save the web page and preview the web page in Internet Explorer. Test all hyperlinks.

Field Types

Text   Date and Time   Currency   Yes/No   Number   Summary

Each record in a table is divided into a number of sections. Each section is referred to as a field. A field stores a unit of data. The field type of a given field must be set to match the type of data that will be stored in that field. For example, a field that stores a person's name should have a field type of text. A field that stores a person's age should have a field type of number. Each field type is discussed in detail below.

Text

Set the field type to *Text* for any field that stores data consisting of:

  (i) letters: e.g. names, addresses, product names, descriptions etc.

  (ii) letters and numbers: e.g. car registration numbers, social security numbers

  (iii) numbers and characters: e.g. phone numbers that include a prefix or area code.

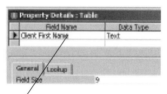

The field size of a text field must be specified by the database designer. For each character stored, one byte of storage is required. The maximum number of characters that can be stored in a text field is 255. The example shows a text field with a field size set to 9. The field size that you set should be long enough to accommodate any data that may be entered in that field in the future. If the field size is too small, you may not be able to enter all the data in the field.

text.gif

Date and Time

datetime.gif

If you want to store a date or a time in a field, the field type must be set to *Date/Time*. Date/Time fields require eight bytes of storage per field entry. Having set the data type to *Date/Time*, you must then choose an

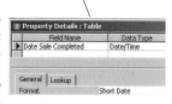

appropriate format. The format affects how the date or time is displayed. For example, the date 25/08/04 could be displayed as 25-Aug-2004, 25/08/2004 or Wednesday, August 25 2004. The time 08:07 could be displayed as 08:07:00 AM, 08:07 AM or 08:07. The example shows a *Date/Time* field with the format set to Short Date.

Currency

Set the field type to *Currency* if you want to store money amounts

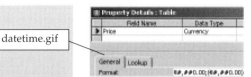

in a field. Once the field type is set to *Currency*, the currency symbol is automatically added to each number entered in the field. The currency symbol used depends on how the Regional Settings on your computer are set up. For example, if you had identified the USA as the country, a dollar sign will be added each time you enter a number in a currency field. The field size of a currency field is eight bytes. The example shows a currency field with the format set to show the euro sign.

Yes/No

A *Yes/No* field type should be used where one of two possible data items can be entered in a particular field. These will normally be either 'yes' and 'no', 'true' and 'false', or 'on' and 'off'. The classic example of a field requiring a Yes/No data type is a paid field. The field size of a Yes/No field is one byte. The example shows a field which will accept 'yes' and 'no'.

Number

There are four main types of number. These are Byte, Integer, Long Integer and Single. Depending on which number type you select, the range of values and number of decimals allowed will be affected.

Number Type	Range of Values	No. of Decimals
Byte	0–255	none
Integer	–32,768 to +32,767	none
Long Integer	–2,147,483,648 to +2,147,483,647	none
Single	Numbers with fractions	7

Summary

The most common field types and the effect of selecting a particular field type are summarised in the table below.

Field Type	Field Size
Text	Variable – depends on the number of characters entered
Date and Time	8 bytes
Currency	8 bytes
Yes/No	1 byte
Number – Byte	1 byte
Number – Integer	2 bytes
Number – Long Integer	4 bytes
Number – Single	4 bytes

up.gif

Table 5.12   Positions of named anchors on the *fieldtypes.htm* web page

Paragraph Heading	Anchor Name
Text	textfield
Date and Time	datetimefield
Currency	currencyfield
Yes/No	yesnofield
Number	numberfield
Summary	summarypara

Create the createtable.htm Web Page

1. In Dreamweaver make sure that the **onlinedatabase** site is active.
2. Using the Site Panel, create a new web page by copying **abouttables.htm.**
3. Rename **Copy of abouttables.htm** as **createtable.htm.**
4. createtable.htm Open **createtable.htm** in Design View. Set up the web page as shown on page 233. Allow the text to wrap naturally. For useful guidelines, refer to the Remember section that follows on page 234.

Home

arrow.gif

Tables
About Tables
Field Types
Create a Table ▶

Queries
About Queries
Query Conditions
Create a Query

Forms
About Forms
Form Objects
Create a Form

Reports
About Reports
Report Functions
Create a Report

Macros
About Macros

Site Map

Create a Table

Question 1   Question 2

A database table will be created to store the data below:

Order Number	Date	Pizza Type	Customer Name	Address	Total Due
1	03/11/2004	Spicy Cheese	Harry O'Leary	15 Main Street	€8.95
2	03/11/2004	Pesto Pizza	Margaret Kenna	10 Cremore Lawns	€10.50
3	03/11/2004	Mozzarella	Chris Duggan	12 Gledswood Park	€10.00
4	03/11/2004	Ham and Mushroom	Noel Mc Donald	15 Grange Park	€10.95
5	03/11/2004	Vegetarian	Diane O'Connor	101 Kings Road	€11.50
6	03/11/2004	Four Seasons	Mary Smith	15 Woodpark	€10.95
7	03/11/2004	Pepperoni	Eamonn Buckley	27 The Pines	€10.50
8	03/11/2004	Vegetarian	John Murphy	5 The Gallops	€11.50
9	03/11/2004	Spicy Cheese	Declan Keane	33 Meadowvale	€8.95
10	03/11/2004	Pepperoni	Emma Daly	Glenview Drive	€10.50

Q1. What is the most appropriate field type for each of the fields listed below?

bullet.jpg

● Order Number
● Date
● Pizza Type
● Customer Name
● Address
● Total Due

answer.gif

✓ View Solutions

Q2. What is the most appropriate field size, in bytes, for each of the fields listed below?

● Order Number
● Date
● Pizza Type
● Customer Name
● Address
● Total Due

✓ View Solutions

up.gif

Remember:

- 🔱 Set up named anchors for each of the headings in Table 5.13.

Table 5.13   Positions of named anchors on the *createtable.htm* web page

Heading	Anchor Name
Q1	firstquestion
Q2	secondquestion

- This line of text appears immediately below the web page heading:

Question 1   Question 2

  🔗 Set up each item as a hyperlink to the appropriate anchor. For example, Question 1 should be a hyperlink to the anchor named **firstquestion.**
- Set the width of the table to 620 pixels. Set the border to 1 and the cellpadding/ cellspacing to 0.
- Set appropriate column widths in the opening <td> tags in the top row of the table to 'best fit' the data. Suggested column widths are: 70, 95, 135, 125, 145 and 50.
- Apply formatting to text and tables as before.
- In the navigation menu, apply the **.currentlink** style to the text `Create a Table`. Make sure that the **arrow.gif** image has been inserted to the left of this text.
- Set the page title to Test 1 – Create a Table.
- 💬 Delete and/or edit comments so that they are specific to the **fieldtypes.htm** web page.
- Check your spelling.
- 💾 🌐 Save the web page and preview the web page in Internet Explorer.

Create the First Solution Web Page

1. In Dreamweaver make sure that the **onlinedatabase** Dreamweaver site is active.
2. Using the Site Panel, create a new web page by copying **createtable.htm.**
3. Rename **Copy of createtable.htm** as **tsolution1.htm.**
4. 📄 tsolution1.htm Open **tsolution1.htm** in Design View. Select the table cell containing the navigation menu and then delete it.
5. Set up the web page as shown on page 235.

Field Type Solutions

Field Name	Field Type
Order Number	Number, Integer
Date	Date/Time
Pizza Type	Text
Customer Name	Text
Address	Text
Total Due	Currency

Return to Create a Table

Fig. 5.48

Remember:
- Remove the background image from this web page by deleting the body style from the <head> section in the HTML code.
- Delete all comments from the web page.
- Apply the **.title** style to the heading Field Type Solutions.
- Set the table width to 400 pixels and the width of each column to 200 pixels.
- Set the table border to 1 and the cellpaddding/cellspacing to 0.
- Apply formats to the table and text as before.
- Set the page title to Solution to Field Types.
- Check your spelling.

- 💾 🌐. Save the web page and preview the web page in Internet Explorer.

Create the Second Solution Web Page

1. 　In Dreamweaver make sure that the **onlinedatabase**
   Dreamweaver　site is active.
2. Using the Site Panel, create the second solution web page by copying **tsolution1.htm.**
3. Rename **Copy of tsolution1.htm** as **tsolution2.htm.**
4. 　tsolution2.htm Set up the web page as shown.

Field Size Solutions

Field Name	Field Size
Order Number	4
Date	8
Pizza Type	17
Customer Name	14
Address	17
Total Due	8

Return to Create a Table

Fig. 5.49

Remember:
* Apply formats to the heading and the table as before. Centre the data in the second column of the table.
* Set the page title to Solution to Field Sizes.
* Check your spelling.
* Save the web page and preview the web page in Internet Explorer.

Copy Web Pages

 The remaining web pages in the Online Database web site are on the *Step by Step Web Design* CD. Follow the steps below to copy these web pages to your **database** folder.

1.  Open the **Project 5** folder and then the **Web Pages** folder on the *Step by Step Web Design* CD.

2. Copy all the web pages from this folder to your own **database** folder.

Set Up Hyperlinks

 In this section you set up hyperlinks in the **index.htm, abouttables.htm, fieldtypes.htm, createtable.htm, tsolution1.htm** and **tsolution2.htm** web pages. Once the hyperlinks have been applied, the menu text will pick up the styles for the link, active, visited and hover states that you defined earlier in this project.

1.
   Dreamweaver
   Open **index.htm** in Dreamweaver. The navigation menu looks like Fig. 5.50.

Tables
About Tables
Field Types
Create a Table

Queries
About Queries
Query Conditions
Create a Query

Forms
About Forms
Form Objects
Create a Form

Reports
About Reports
Report Functions
Create a Report

Macros
About Macros

Site Map

Fig. 5.50

2. Set up the text `About Tables` as a hyperlink to **abouttables.htm.** (Highlight the text `About Tables`, then select Modify followed by Make Link from the menu. In the Select File dialog box, select **abouttables.htm** and then click OK.)

3. Set up the text `Field Types` as a hyperlink to **fieldtypes.htm.**

4. Set up all the other menu items as hyperlinks to the appropriate web pages, using the file names in Table 5.14.

 Tip: A quick way of setting up a hyperlink is to highlight the menu text and then hold down the CTRL key and type L. This brings you directly to the Select File dialog box.

Table 5.14   Navigation menu hyperlinks in the home page

Text	Hyperlink to:
Create a Table	createtable.htm
About Queries	aboutqueries.htm
Query Conditions	qcondition.htm
Create a Query	createquery.htm
About Forms	aboutforms.htm
Form Objects	fobjects.htm
Create a Form	createform.htm
About Reports	aboutreports.htm
Report Functions	rfunctions.htm
Create a Report	createreport.htm
About Macros	aboutmacros.htm

5. Open **abouttables.htm** in Dreamweaver. The navigation menu looks like Fig. 5.49.

6. Set up the text Home as a hyperlink to **index.htm.**

7. Set up the text `Field Types` as a hyperlink to **fieldtypes.htm.**

8. Set up all the other menu items as hyperlinks to the appropriate web pages, using the file names in Table 5.15.

9. Open **fieldtypes.htm.** Set up hyperlinks to each of the web pages in the navigation menu (except for the site map).

10. Open **createtable.htm.** Set up hyperlinks to each of the web pages in the navigation menu (except for the site map).

Home

Tables
▶ About Tables
Field Types
Create a Table

Queries
About Queries
Query Conditions
Create a Query

Forms
About Forms
Form Objects
Create a Form

Reports
About Reports
Report Functions
Create a Report

Macros
About Macros

Site Map

Fig. 5.51

11. In **createtable.htm** set up the text `View Solutions` that appears at the end of Question 1 as a hyperlink to **tsolution1.htm.**
12. In **createtable.htm** set up the text `View Solutions` that appears at the end of Question 2 as a hyperlink to **tsolution2.htm.**
13. Open **tsolution1.htm.** Set up the text `Return to Create a Table` as a hyperlink to **createtable.htm.** Set up a similar hyperlink from **tsolution2.htm.**
14. ◉ Preview each web page in Internet Explorer and test all the hyperlinks.

Table 5.15   Navigation menu hyperlinks in the
abouttables.htm **web page**

Text	Hyperlink to
Create a Table	createtable.htm
About Queries	aboutqueries.htm
Query Conditions	qcondition.htm
Create a Query	createquery.htm
About Forms	aboutforms.htm
Form Objects	fobjects.htm
Create a Form	createform.htm
About Reports	aboutreports.htm
Report Functions	rfunctions.htm
Create a Report	createreport.htm
About Macros	aboutmacros.htm

Create a Site Map

A site map is a web page that includes a hyperlink to every other web page in your web site. By viewing the site map, the web page viewer should get an overall idea of the structure of the web site and the number of web pages it contains. Web page viewers often access the site map if they are not sure how to get to a specific page in your web site in the same way that a reader looks up the index at the back of a book to find the page with information on a particular topic.

Just as a geographical map shows you how to go from one place to another, a site map should show you which hyperlinks to access to move from one web page to another. The site map shows the layout of your web site and the routes to follow as web page viewers navigate their way through the web pages in the site.

Most site maps are text-based. A site map can also be represented as a graphic image.

1. **Dreamweaver** Create a new web page by copying **tsolution1.htm.** Save the new web page as **sitemap.htm.**

2. sitemap.htm With **sitemap.htm** open in Design View, select the table with field names/field types and the hyperlink text and then delete it so that you are left with a blank web page.

3. Set up the **sitemap.htm** web page as shown below:

Site Map

Home

Tables
About Tables
Field Types
Create a Table
Solution to Question 1
Solution to Question 2

Queries
About Queries
Query Conditions
Create a Query
Solution to Question 1
Solution to Question 2

Forms
About Forms
Form Objects
Create a Form
Solution to Question 1
Solution to Question 2

Reports
About Reports
Report Functions
Create a Report
Solution to Question 1
Solution to Question 2

Macros
About Macros

Remember:
- Set the page title to Site Map.
- Apply the **.title** style to the main heading Site Map.
- Apply the **.menutext** style to the subheadings Tables, Queries, Forms, Reports and Macros.
- Set up the text Home as a hyperlink to **index.htm.**
- Set up the text About Tables as a hyperlink to **abouttables.htm.**
- Set up all the other menu items as hyperlinks to the appropriate web pages, using the file names in Table 5.16.

Table 5.16   **Hyperlinks in the *sitemap.htm* web page**

Text	Hyperlink to:
Home	index.htm
About Tables	abouttables.htm
Field Types	fieldtypes.htm
Create a Table	createtable.htm
Solution to Question 1	tsolution1.htm
Solution to Question 2	tsolution2.htm
About Queries	aboutqueries.htm
Query Conditions	qcondition.htm
Create a Query	createquery.htm
Solution to Question 1	qsolution1.htm
Solution to Question 2	qsolution2.htm
About Forms	aboutforms.htm
Form Objects	fobjects.htm
Create a Form	createform.htm
Solution to Question 1	fsolution1.htm
Solution to Question 2	fsolution2.htm
About Reports	aboutreports.htm
Report Functions	rfunctions.htm
Create a Report	createreport.htm
Solution to Question 1	rsolution1.htm
Solution to Question 2	rsolution2.htm
About Macros	aboutmacros.htm

- 🖫 Save the **sitemap.htm** web page.
- Open **index.htm.** Set up the text `Site Map` as a hyperlink to sitemap.htm.
- In the same way, set up the text `Site Map` as a hyperlink to **sitemap.htm** in the **abouttables.htm, fieldtypes.htm** and **createtable.htm** web pages.
- 🖫 🌐. Save **index.htm** and preview in Internet Explorer. Click the Site Map hyperlink and test all the hyperlinks in the site map web page.

Meta Tags

 There are millions of web sites published on the World Wide Web. New web sites appear every day. The chances of somebody finding your site is a bit like finding a needle in a haystack! At least, it would be if we did not have search engines. People who surf the web use search engines, such as Google, Yahoo, Lycos and Alta Vista, to find web sites with information on specific topics.

Using a search engine, you can enter any search term. The search engine searches through millions of web sites and displays a list of web sites with references to your search term. For example, you could enter 'estate agent' in a search engine's search box and click the Search button. The search engine would then display a list of web sites with references to the term 'estate agent'. A search engine can find thousands of web sites matching your search term in less than a second.

How Do Search Engines Find Web Sites?

Most search engines use complex algorithms to find web sites matching a given search term. These algorithms take many factors into account, including meta tags that the web designer has included in the <head> section of the web page.

What is a Meta Tag?

A meta tag is a HTML tag that gives important information about your web site to a search engine. Meta tags are entered in the <head> section of a HTML file and do not appear on the web page when it is viewed in a web browser, such as Internet Explorer. For this reason, the majority of web page viewers do not know about meta tags.

The most important meta tags to include in a web page are the Keywords meta tag and the Description meta tag. The Keywords and Description meta tags are the main tags that search engines look for when they are compiling a list of web sites matching a search term.

Keywords Meta Tag

The function of the Keywords meta tag is to store a list of words or phrases relevant to your web site. If a web surfer enters one of these words or phrases in a search engine, there is a greater chance that the search engine will find your web site and rank it higher in its list of web sites matching the search term. Table 5.17 shows how to create a Keywords meta tag in HTML.

Table 5.17 The Keywords meta tag

Tag Name	Keywords Meta Tag
HTML Code	`<meta name="Keywords" content="keyword1, keyword2, …" />`
Effect	If the search term entered in a search engine matches one of the keywords specified in the Keywords meta tag, the search engine will find your web site.

Example:

<meta name="Keywords" content="database, Microsoft Access, data, data entry, sort, table, query, report, macro, module, data entry form" />

The importance of the keyword has diminished over time. In the early days of Internet searching, keywords played a very important role in getting your web site found by a search engine. Over time, however, web site designers began to abuse the system by repeating keywords a number of times. This repetition meant that the web site would be ranked higher up on the list of sites found by a search engine. To get around this, search engines began to use additional factors to rank search results. Today, keywords are still an important method of getting your web site noticed by search engines but they are not the only factor that search engines take into account.

Guidelines for Using the Keywords Meta Tag

- Choose keywords relevant to your site.
- Avoid excessive repetition of keywords, as some search engines will penalise you for this.
- Try to think of all the search terms that people are likely to enter in a search engine when looking for your web site. Include all of these search terms in the Keywords meta tag.
- Include some keywords spelled incorrectly, in case some people misspell them when searching for a web site.

Description Meta Tag

The function of the Description meta tag is to give a brief description of your web site and what it does. Some search engines display text stored in the Description meta tag in the search results. Table 5.18 shows you how to create a Description meta tag in HTML.

Table 5.18 The Description meta tag

Tag Name	Description Meta Tag
HTML Code	`<meta name="Description" content=" " />`
Effect	Some search engines will display text contained in the content in the search results.

Example:

> <meta name="Description" content= "Access the Step by Step Databases book online – all you need to start using databases" />

It is important to write your description well. If your description is not more interesting than other descriptions on the search results page, people will not visit your site. Because there is a limited amount of space where the description can be displayed in the search results, web designers should keep descriptions as short as possible. It is also useful to know that some search engines ignore the Description meta tag and simply display the first few lines of text found on the home page. You may need to register your web site with a particular search engine before it will recognise your description.

Create a Keywords Meta Tag

 We will use the Head section of Dreamweaver's Insert Toolbar (see Fig. 5.52) to insert meta tags in the home page of the Online Database web site.

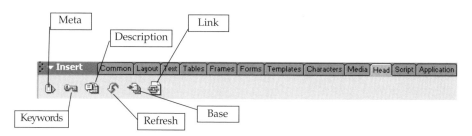

Fig. 5.52   The Insert Toolbar with the Head tab selected

1.   Make sure that the **onlinedatabase** site is active, then open
   Dreamweaver   **index.htm** in Dreamweaver.
2.   Click the Head tab in the Insert toolbar and then click the Keywords button. The Keywords dialog box is displayed.
3.   Enter keywords separated by commas, as shown in Fig. 5.53.
4.   Click OK and then click the Code View button. Check the HTML code entered by Dreamweaver in the Head section. It should read:

```
<meta name="Keywords" content="database, Microsoft Access, data,
data entry, sort, table, query, report, macro, module, data entry
form" />
```

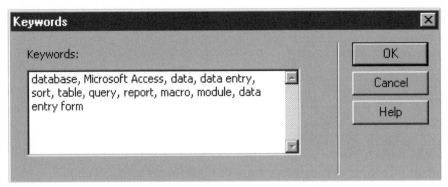

Fig. 5.53 Enter keywords using Dreamweaver's keywords dialog box

5. 🖫 Save the changes to **index.htm**.

Create a Description Meta Tag

1. 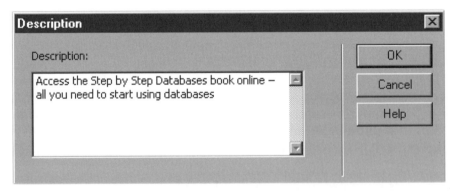 Open **index.htm**, if it is not already open.
   Dreamweaver

2. 🗐 Click the Head tab if the Head section of the toolbar is not already displayed.

3. 🗐 Click the Description button. The Description dialog box is displayed.

4. Enter the description, as in Fig. 5.54.

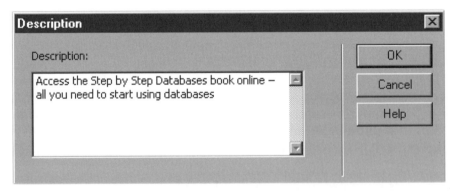

Fig. 5.54 Enter a description using Dreamweaver's Description dialog box

5. ⟨⟩ ⊞ ⊞ Click OK and then click the Code View button. Examine the HTML code entered by Dreamweaver in the Head section. It should read:

```
<meta name= "Description" content= "Access the Step by Step
Databases book online - all you need to start using databases"
/>
```

6. Save the changes to **index.htm.**

Meta Tags in Action

Because meta tags do not actually appear on a web page, it can be difficult to get to grips with exactly how they work. The following example shows the importance of the Keywords and Description meta tags in getting your web site recognised by a search engine. The example also illustrates the importance of the title tag.

Example: How meta tags are interpreted by a search engine

Step 1: The search term, in this case 'estate agent' is entered in a search engine, such as Google. The Google search engine then searches through all web sites that it knows to exist for the term 'estate agent'. This is shown in Fig. 5.55.

Fig. 5.55   Use the Google search engine to find web sites with information about 'estate agent'

Step 2: The search engine lists web sites containing the search term (see Fig. 5.54). The search engine looks for the search term in the keywords and description meta tag as well as the page title. Most search engines also look for the search term in the web page itself. In the example in Fig. 5.56, the search term was found in the page title, in the description, in the keywords and in the web page. The more times a search engine finds the search term, the higher up your web site will be ranked in the search results. Notice how the search term 'estate agent' is highlighted in bold in the search results.

Fig. 5.56 The top three web sites matching the search term 'estate agent'

Test Your Web Site in Different Web Browsers

 A web browser is an application software package that allows you to view web pages on your PC. Internet Explorer is the most popular web browser. Consequently, it is very important that your web site looks good and works well in Internet Explorer. Up to now, you have tested and debugged each of the five web design projects in this book using Internet Explorer. A good web designer will allow for that fact that some people do not use Internet Explorer. After Internet Explorer, the next most popular web browser is Netscape Navigator. In this section you will test the Online Database Web Site in Internet Explorer and Netscape Navigator.

Note: You will need to have Netscape Navigator on your PC to complete this section. If Netscape Navigator is not already loaded on your PC, it can be downloaded free from www.netscape.com. Alternatively, Netscape Navigator is often included in free CDs that come with computer magazines.

 Add Netscape Navigator to the Browser List

1. In Dreamweaver, click the Preview/Debug in Browser button and then select Edit Browser List.

Fig. 5.57 Editing the Browser List

2. The Preferences dialog box is displayed (see Fig. 5.58). Select 'Preview in Browse'.

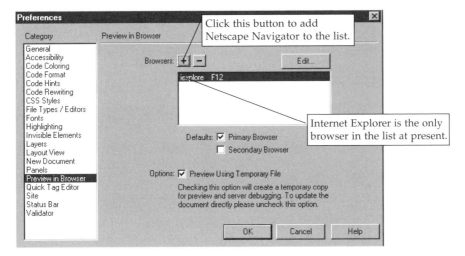

Fig. 5.58 The Preferences dialog box

The Preferences dialog box shows that Dreamweaver can only preview web pages in Internet Explorer at present.

3. To add Netscape Navigator to the list of browsers, click the + button, as in Fig. 5.58. The Edit Browser dialog box is displayed (see Fig. 5.59).

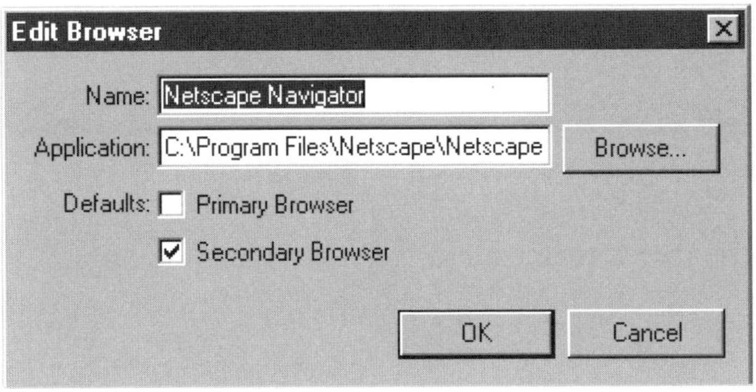

Fig. 5.59 The Edit Browser dialog box

4. Click the Browse button and search for the file that runs Netscape Navigator. This will normally be located at C:\Program Files\Netscape and will probably be called netscp.exe.
5. Enter *Netscape Navigator* in the Name box, as in Fig. 5.59 and then identify Netscape Navigator as the secondary web browser by ticking the Secondary Browser check box.
6. Check that Netscape Navigator has been added to the list of web browsers by clicking the Preview/Debug in Browser button. Netscape Navigator should appear second in the list, as shown in Fig. 5.60.

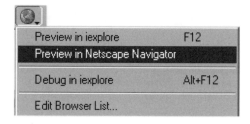

Fig. 5.60 Netscape Navigator now appears in the list

Preview the Home Page in Netscape Navigator and Internet Explorer

1. Dreamweaver Open **index.htm**, if it is not already open.
2. Click the Preview/Debug in Browser button and select Preview in Netscape Navigator from the list. Your web page should open in Netscape Navigator, as in Fig. 5.61.

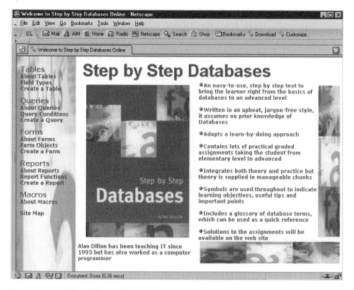

Fig. 5.61 The Home Page previewed in Netscape Navigator

3. 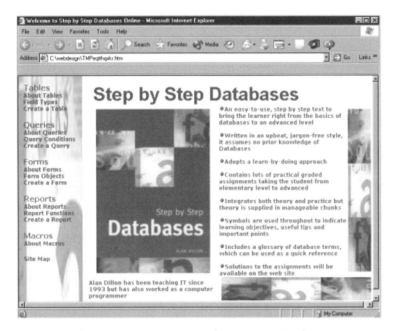 Activate Dreamweaver and then click the Preview/Debug in Browser again. This time select Internet Explorer as the browser. Your web page should open in Internet Explorer, as in Fig. 5.62.

Fig. 5.62 The Home Page previewed in Internet Explorer

4. Identify inconsistencies (if there are any) between the way that Netscape Navigator and Internet Explorer display this web page by filling out a checklist like the one in Table 5.19.

Table 5.19 Checklist of items to highlight differences between Netscape Navigator and Internet Explorer

Item	Internet Explorer √	Netscape Navigator √
Images displayed properly		
Formatting correct		
Hyperlinks working correctly		
Rollover image working		

Things to Watch Out for

1. Make sure that your code is in the correct location. <title> and <meta> tags should be in the Head section together with CSS styles. All other HTML code

should be in the Body section. Make sure that your code is not in 'no man's land' – somewhere in between the closing </head> tag and the opening <body> tag.

2. Check that all references to files and images are spelled correctly. If Internet Explorer displays a red X instead of an image, this could be for one of the following reasons:
   - The image name is spelled incorrectly.
   - An incorrect file extension has been used, e.g. gif instead of jpg.
   - The path to the image is incorrectly specified.
   - The image is stored in the wrong folder.

   Netscape Navigator displays either a question mark or a broken image icon if it encounters a problem with one of your images.

3. Check that each tag is closed properly and that the closing tag is in the correct position.

For You To Do

Test each web page in the Online Database web site in Internet Explorer and Netscape Navigator, paying close attention to:
- images
- formatting
- hyperlinks.

Test Download Times

When people view web pages, they expect them to appear on the monitor relatively quickly. The amount of a time it takes for a web page to be fully displayed is called the download time.

Each web page that you view on your PC has been downloaded from a server and transmitted across the telecommunications network. Before you can view the web page on the monitor, your PCs modem has to translate the web page data that was sent down the phone line into digital signals that your PC can understand.

The speed at which the modem does this is measured in kilobits per second (Kbps). Most modems operate at 56.6 Kbps. If you have a really old modem, its speed is probably 28.8 Kbps. The speed of your modem determines how quickly you can download a web page and view it on your PC. The faster your modem, the less time you wait for a web page to download.

Dreamweaver can give you an approximate calculation of download time for each web page in your web site based on the modem speed that you specify. Download time is measured in seconds. As a web page designer you must try to keep the download time as low as possible. Most web page viewers will not wait more than eight seconds for a web page to download. If the page has not fully downloaded by then, they will simply go to another web site.

Most people are in Ireland surf the net with 56.6 Kbps modems. In 2002, 7 per cent of Americans and 2.3 per cent of web surfers from Britain were surfing the net using broadband connections. If you have a broadband connection, web pages will download almost instantly. Broadband connection speeds range from 256 kilobits to 2 megabits. As broadband becomes more popular, the percentage of people with broadband connections will increase. For the moment, it is best to test your web pages at 56.6 Kbps.

Test the Download Time of the Home Page

1.  Open **index.htm** in Design View, if it is not already open.

2. Select Edit, followed by Preferences from the menu.
3. In the Preferences dialog box, select Status Bar from the list of categories. The Preferences dialog box is shown in Fig. 5.63.

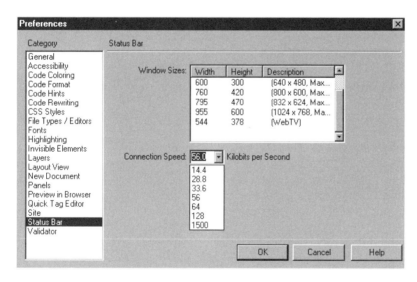

Fig. 5.63   Before testing download times, use the Preferences dialog box to set the connection speed

4. Select 56.0 as the connection speed to calculate the download time of your web pages and then click OK.
5. The download time appears in the status bar at the bottom right of the screen, as shown in Fig. 5.64.

Fig. 5.64   Download time of **index.htm**

Dreamweaver has calculated that the file size of the **index.htm** web page is 59 kilobytes and that this will take nine seconds to download. The homepage has a longer download time than other pages in the web site because it has a rollover image.

For You To Do

Test the download times for every other web page in the Online Database web site.

Guidelines for Reducing Download Times

To keep your download times as low as possible, follow the guidelines below.

- Use the GIF or JPEG optimiser to reduce file size of images. As you reduce the file size of an image, two things happen; the download time drops and the quality of the image deteriorates. You will have to reach a compromise between image quality and download time.
- You can also reduce the file size of an image by making it physically smaller. Images can be resized in using graphics software, such as Paint Shop Pro.
- If you want to display high quality images on a web page, display the image as a thumbnail, which will download quickly. A thumbnail image is created by resizing the original image to roughly passport-photo size. The thumbnail image is then set up as a hyperlink to the full-sized image. In effect, you allow web page viewers to decide whether they want to download the full image. This is much better than including the full size image without giving people the option of viewing it by clicking the thumbnail image.
- Limit the amount of data on a web page. The more data there is on the web page, the longer it will take to download. Rather than having a very long web page where the web page viewer accesses information by scrolling, try having two or three web pages where that the information is accessed by hyperlinks.
- Clean up your HTML code. Dreamweaver often leaves unused paragraph tags when text is deleted in design view. These should be removed. Dreamweaver also adds height and width attributes to <img> tags. If you have created your images in a graphics package, you will already have specified the height and the width of the image. Remove any unnecessary height and width attributes from <img> tags.
- Keep your web page and image names as short as possible. The length of file names also affects download time.

Revision Exercise

1. 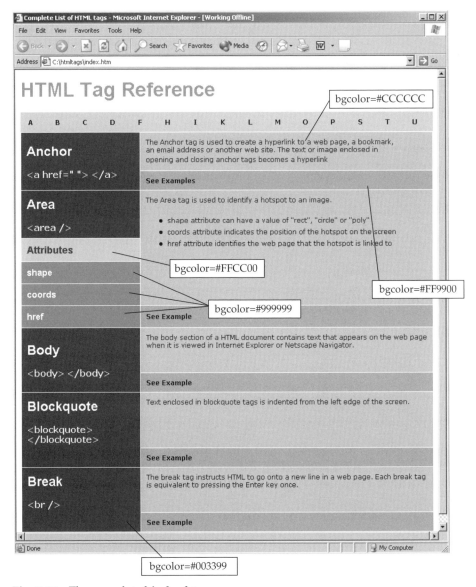 Create a new folder named **htmltags** on a floppy disk, zip disk, USB
   My Computer storage device or hard disk.

2. Set up a new site named **htmlguide** linked to the **htmltags** folder.
   Dreamweaver

3. Using appropriate table layout, styles and colours, set up the **index.htm** web
   page like Fig. 5.65. For useful guidelines, refer to the Remember section that
   follows.

Fig. 5.65 The completed **index.htm** page

Remember:
- Set the cellspacing of the table to 1 and the cellpadding to 10.
- Set up CSS styles for hyperlinks in link, visited, active and hover states, using the information in Table 5.20.

Table 5.20   CSS Hyperlink styles

	a:link	a:visited	a:hover	a:active
font-family	Verdana	Verdana	Verdana	Verdana
font-size	12px	12px	12px	12px
font-weight	bold	bold	bold	bold
color	#000099	#000000	#330099	#CC0000
text-decoration	none	none	none	none

- Set up CSS styles to format text on the web page, using the information in Table 5.21.

Table 5.21   Summary of CSS styles

	.mainheading	.tagnames	.tagcode
font-family	Arial	Arial	Verdana
font-size	36px	24px	16px
font-weight	bold	bold	bold
color	#FF6600	#FFFFFF	#FFCC00

	.tagattributes	.attributenames	.text
font-family	Arial	Arial	Verdana
font-size	18px	16px	12px
font-weight	bold	bold	–
color	#003399	#FFCC00	#000000

- Using the information in Fig. 5.65, set the background colours of the table cells.
- Apply CSS styles to text displayed on the web page.
- Set the page title to Complete List of HTML Tags.

Note: Special codes are needed to display < and > on a web page. This is because web browsers interpret these symbols as the opening and closing brackets of a HTML tag and will not display them on a web page unless instructed otherwise.
The code for < is **<**
The code for > is **>**

To display <a> </a> in the title bar of the web browser, the HTML code is:

```
<title>
&lt;a&gt; &lt;/a&gt;
</title>
```

Fortunately, Dreamweaver looks after all these codes when you enter < or > in Design View.

- Create a new web page named **anchor.htm** in the **htmlguide** web site.
- Using appropriate table layout, styles and colours, set up the **anchor.htm** web page like Fig. 5.66.

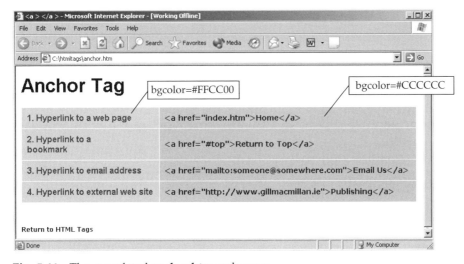

Fig. 5.66   The completed **anchor.htm** web page

- Set up CSS styles to format text on the **anchor.htm** web page, using the information in Table 5.22.

Table 5.22   Summary of CSS styles

	.mainheading	**.tagfunction**	**.example**
font-family	Arial	Arial	Verdana
font-size	36px	16px	14px
font-weight	bold	bold	bold
color	#000000	#003399	#FF3333

- Format hyperlink text using CSS styles as before.
- Set the page title to <a> </a>
- Create a new web page named **area.htm** in the **htmlguide** web site.

- Using appropriate table layout, styles and colours, set up the **area.htm** web page like Fig. 5.67.

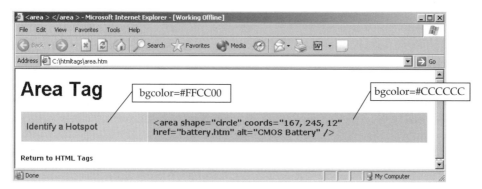

Fig. 5.67 The completed **area.htm** web page

- Set the page title to <area> </area>.
- Create a new web page named **body.htm** in the **htmlguide** web site.
- Using appropriate table layout, styles and colours, set up the **body.htm** web page like Fig. 5.68.

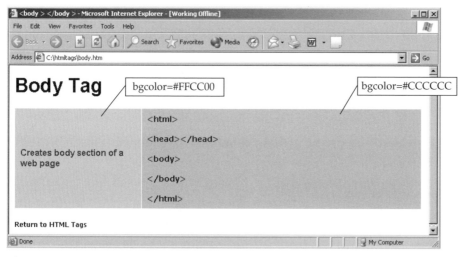

Fig. 5.68 The completed **body.htm** web page

- Set the page title to <body> </body>.
- Create a new web page named **blockq.htm** in the **htmlguide** web site.
- Using appropriate table layout, styles and colours, set up the **blockq.htm** web page like Fig. 5.69.
- Set the page title to <blockquote> </blockquote>.
- Create a new web page named **break.htm** in the **htmlguide** web site.
- Using appropriate table layout, styles and colours, set up the **break.htm** web page like Fig. 5.70.
- Set the page title to <br />.

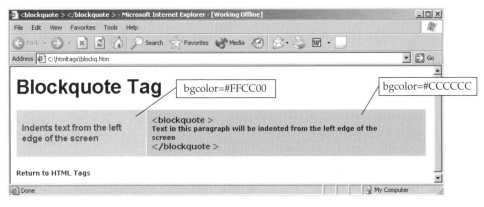

Fig. 5.69   The completed **blockq.htm** web page

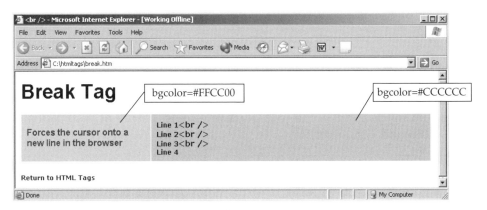

Fig. 5.70   The completed **break.htm** web page

- Open index.htm. Using the text See Example(s), set up hyperlinks to **anchor.htm, area.htm, body.htm, blockq.htm** and **break.htm.**
- In the **anchor.htm, area.htm, body.htm, blockq.htm** and **break.htm** web pages, set up the text Return to HTML Tags as a hyperlink to **index.htm.**
- Preview the homepage in both Internet Explorer and Netscape Navigator. Test all the hyperlinks.

Independent Project

Adding all the HTML tags to the **index.htm** web page is a useful and interesting group project. You will find all the information you need in the HTML Tag Glossary at the end of this book. The completed web site could be shared across a network in your college, providing a useful online reference for web design students.

Progress Test 5

Finish the review of Web Project 3 by answering these questions.

1. Hyperlink text can be in one of four different states.

    a. _____ state
    b. _____ state
    c. _____ state
    d. _____ state

2. What is the default colour for hyperlink text that has not been clicked?
    _____

3. Internet Explorer and Netscape Navigator display hyperlink text underlined by default. How can this underline be removed?
    _____
    _____

4. A table has been used to position text and images on a web page. The width of the table has been set to 760 pixels. The screen resolution is set to 800 × 600. Assuming that the alignment of the table has been set to 'center', what differences will you see in the web page when it is viewed at resolutions of 1024 × 768 and 1280 × 1024?
    _____
    _____

5. If you are using a table to position text and images on a web page, you can make the web page 'stretch' at higher resolutions by specifying the table width in _____ instead of pixels.

6. The background image of a web page can be specified by creating a CSS style for the _____ tag.

7. Web graphics, such as arrows and navigation buttons, are normally saved using the _____ file format.

8. In Dreamweaver, which of the following buttons should you click to insert a non-breaking space?

    a.
    b.
    c.
    d.

9. A _____ map is a web page that includes a hyperlink to every other web page in your web site.

10. The Description and Keywords meta tags give important information about your web site to a _____ _____.

11. Meta tags are entered in the _____ section of the HTML code.

12. In Dreamweaver, which of the following buttons should you click to insert a description meta tag?

    a.

    b. 🖼

    c. 🖼

    d. ⚓

13. In Internet Explorer, an incorrectly specified image is indicated by a _____. Netscape Navigator displays a _____ or a _____ to indicate a problem with an image.

14. Although broadband offers much faster download times, most people are still using modems with a speed of _____ Kbps.

15. List three ways of reducing the download time of a web page.

    a. _____

    b. _____

    c. _____

Check Your Work

To see the completed version of the **htmlguide** web site and the answers to Progress Test 5, log on to **www.gillmacmillan.ie.**

New in Web Project 5

Dreamweaver Toolbar Buttons

🖼 **The Rollover Image button**   Click this button to create a rollover image effect. This is where an image on a web page changes to another image when the mouse pointer moves over the image. Click the Rollover Image button to display the Insert Rollover Image dialog box where you can specify the original image and the rollover image.

⬇ **The Non-Breaking Space button**   Click this button to insert a non-breaking space in your web page. This is useful if you want to insert more than one space between words or images, as Internet Explorer and Netscape Navigator will only allow you to insert one space using the spacebar.

The Named Anchor button   When working in Design View, click this button to identify a specific position on a web page with a named anchor. When the Named Anchor button is clicked, Dreamweaver displays the Named Anchor dialog box where you can enter the anchor name. Hyperlinks can then be created to allow the web page viewer to 'jump' to that position on the web page. The most common example of this is the Return to Top hyperlink.

The Keywords button   To help search engines find your web site, click the Keywords button and then enter important words or phrases from your web site. If one of these words or phrases is entered in a search engine, there is a greater chance that the search engine will find your web site and rank it higher in its list of web sites matching the search term.

The Description button   To create a short description of your web site's function, click the Description button and then enter a one-sentence description in the Description dialog box. Some search engines will display this description in the search results.

Paint Shop Pro Toolbar Buttons

The Selection button   Click this button and, while holding down the left mouse button, drag to select a specific section of an image.

The Flood Fill button   Click this button and then click on an image to fill a specific section of an image with a colour selected from the colour palette. The Flood Fill button can also be used to set the background colour of an image.

Web Assignment 1

Insert Multimedia Files in a Web Page

 In this web assignment, you will learn how to play back sounds on a web page, using hyperlinks.

 To complete this assignment, you need:

 Dreamweaver

 Internet Explorer

 Sound Card

 Speakers

 Step by Step Web Design CD

Using Sound on Web Pages

 What makes web pages different from pages in a book or magazine is the way they present information using a variety of different media (text, sound, video, animated graphics). Because multimedia files tend to be larger than other web site files (web pages and images), they can increase the download time of your web page. With the introduction of broadband, this is becoming less of a problem. If you have a broadband connection, multimedia files will download much quicker.

HTML handles the text that appears on a web page. All other items (images, sound, video) are stored as additional files on disk and then inserted on the web page using tags (anchor tags or img tags). This is shown in Fig. 6.1.

Fig. 6.1 shows how a simple web page with only a page heading and an image is created. Notice how the page heading is created in HTML, but the image is a JPEG file external to HTML and is stored in an images folder on the hard disk of the PC. The image was created using a digital camera, then edited using a graphics package. To position the image on the web page, HTML refers to the image by name and location using the following code:

```
<img src= "images/backdrop.jpg" />
```

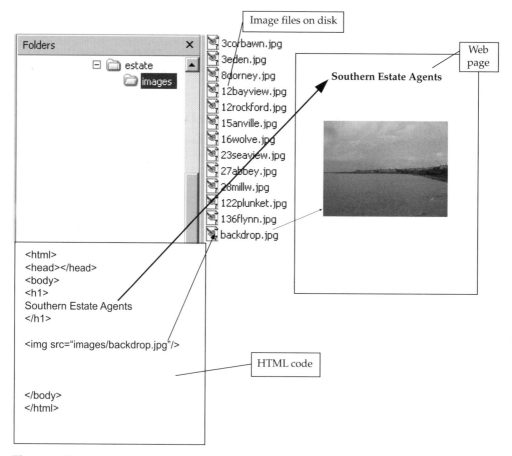

Fig. 6.1 How text and images are placed on a web page

This code instructs the web browser to look for an image called **backdrop.jpg** in the **images** sub-folder and display it on the web page. What it is important to note is that the image was not created in HTML. It was simply referred to by HTML using the <img> tag.

HTML treats sound in a similar way. Each sound that you want to play on your web page must be stored as a separate sound file. To make the sound available on the web page, each sound file is referred to in HTML, using an anchor tag.

Using Microsoft Windows to Record Sounds

Before you can record your own sounds, you must have three essential items of hardware.

1. Your PC must have a sound card.

Fig. 6.2   A typical sound card

The sound card enables the PC to record and play back sounds. Check the back of your PC. If it has a sound card, you will see sockets like those in Fig. 6.2. The microphone socket usually has a picture of a microphone next to it.

2.   You will need a microphone to record sounds.

Fig. 6.3   If your PC has a sound card, a microphone is also included

The microphone is plugged into the microphone socket of the sound card.

3.   To be able to play back sounds, you need speakers. The speakers are plugged into the speaker socket of the sound card.

Fig. 6.4   Speakers are included with your PC if your PC has a sound card

Once you have the necessary hardware, you can record your own sounds using sound recording software. This software, which is called Sound Recorder, is included in the Windows operating system.

Making a Recording

1.   **Sound Recorder** To start Sound Recorder, click the Start button and then select Programs or All Programs. Now select Accessories followed by Entertainment. Sound Recorder is listed in the Entertainment category. When Sound Recorder is launched, it looks like Fig. 6.5.

2. ⟋‑⊪ Make sure your microphone is turned on and plugged into the microphone socket in the sound card and that the volume is turned up.

Fig. 6.5 The Sound Recorder interface

3. ▪ Click the Record button to record a new sound. Sound Recorder starts recording immediately.
4. ▪ When you have finished recording, click the Stop button.
5. Save your sound file by selecting File, followed by Save. It is best to save all your sound files in a separate **sounds** folder. The sounds folder should be a sub-folder of the folder that stores your web pages.

Each sound that you record using Sound Recorder is saved as a Waveform Audio File. Windows gives each sound file a .wav file extension. It is important to remember this when you are creating a hyperlink to a sound file. So for example, to create a hyperlink to a file called **greeting.wav** stored in the sounds folder, you would need this HTML code:

```
<a href="sounds/greeting.wav">Welcome Message</a>
```

When the web page is viewed in a browser, such as Internet Explorer, the text Welcome Message will appear as a hyperlink. Clicking this text will play the **greeting.wav** sound file. Before the sound file can play, it needs to be transferred from the server to your own computer (assuming that the web page is live on the World Wide Web). A dialog box similar to the one in Fig. 6.6 will appear.

Whether you select Open or Save, the sound file is downloaded from the server onto your hard disk before it is played on your PC by Windows Media Player.

Common Sound File Types

A sound file can be saved using a number of different formats.

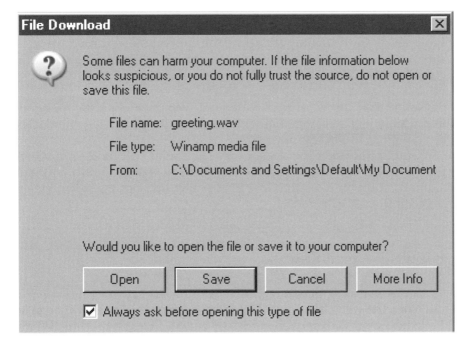

Fig. 6.6 The File Download dialog box appears before the sound is played

WAV Sound Files

Wav files tend to take up a lot of disk space and must be downloaded from the server before being played. For these reasons, the wav format is only suitable for sound files with a short duration such as a greeting. When large wav files are compressed, there is a significant loss of sound quality.

MP3 Sound Files

MP3 files have become very popular and have overtaken wav files on the World Wide Web. The MP3 sound file format is very suitable for sharing sound over the web because of its ability to compress sound files to one tenth of their original file size without significant loss of quality. Smaller file size means faster download time. MP3 files can be either downloaded or streamed. Streaming allows sound files to be played as they download and is much more efficient as long as you have a broadband connection. MP3 files are often used on the web as a cheap method of publishing music, with many unsigned bands making their recordings available on the web. Wav files can be converted to MP3 files using special conversion software, such as Music Match.

Summary of Steps for Using Sound Files

This is a summary of the steps to follow if you want to include sound files in your web pages:

1. Record the sound that you want to play on your web page. Save the sound as a wav file and store it on disk together with your web pages. Larger sound files should be converted to MP3 format.
2. Refer to the sound file using the anchor tag. The sound will be played when the web page viewer clicks the hyperlink text or image. (If your web page includes sound, you will have to allow for the fact that not everyone views web pages with their speakers on.)

Include Sounds in a Web Page

 In this web assignment, you will create a web page of Irish proverbs. When the web page is completed, the web page viewer will be able to hear a proverb spoken in Irish by clicking a text hyperlink. When you have completed this exercise, your web page will look something like Fig. 6.7.

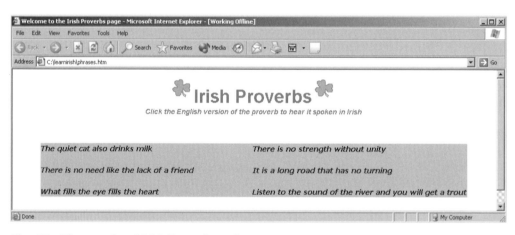

Fig. 6.7 The completed Irish Proverbs web page

1. Create a new folder named **learnirish** on a floppy disk, zip disk, USB storage device or hard disk.
2. learnirish   Create an **images** sub-folder and a **sounds** sub-folder inside the **learnirish** folder
    images
    sounds
3. Multimedia Open the **Multimedia** folder on the *Step by Step Web Design* CD.
4. Copy the **shamrock.gif** file to the **images** sub-folder.

5. Copy **friend.wav, greeting.wav, heart.wav, river.wav, road.wav** and **strength.wav** to the **sounds** sub-folder.

6. In Dreamweaver, set up a new site named **irishproverbs** linked to the **learnirish** folder, using the following information:

   Dreamweaver

   1. Server Technology: No
   2. Edit local copies on my machine
   3. Connect to remote server: None

7. Create a new web page named **index.htm** in the **irishproverbs** site.
8. Set the page title to Welcome to the Irish Proverbs web site.
9. Using the Properties toolbar in CSS mode, create styles for the link, visited, hover and active states, using the information in Table 6.1.

Table 6.1   CSS Hyperlink styles

	a:link	a:visited	a:hover	a:active
font-family	Verdana	Verdana	Verdana	Verdana
font-size	14px	14px	14px	14px
font-weight	bold	bold	bold	bold
font-style	italic	italic	italic	italic
color	#000000	#000099	#990033	#FF6600
text-decoration	none	none	none	none

10. Create a custom CSS style named **.title** that includes these formatting instructions:
    36px Arial in bold print with a colour of #009900

11. Create a custom CSS style named **.subtitle** that includes these formatting instructions:
    14px Arial in bold italics with a colour of #009900

12. Set up the web page as shown below. For useful guidelines, refer to the Remember section that follows.

🍀 **Irish Proverbs** 🍀

Click the English version of the proverb to hear it spoken in Irish

The quiet cat also drinks milk	There is no strength without unity
There is no need like the lack of a friend	It is a long road that has no turning
What fills the eye fills the heart	Listen to the sound of the river and you will get a trout

Tip: The blank table rows will not be displayed unless you use non-breaking spaces.

Remember:

- Position the proverb text using a table. Set the border of the table to 0, the cellspacing to 0 and the cellpadding to 0.
- Set the bgcolor of the table to #CCCCCC.
- Apply the **.title** style to the main heading Irish Proverbs.
- Insert the **shamrock.gif** image to the left and right of the main heading.
- Apply the **.subtitle** style to the sub-heading Click the English version of the proverb to hear it spoken in Irish.
- Set up text hyperlinks as in Table 6.2.

Table 6.2

Text	Hyperlink to:
The quiet cat also drinks milk	greeting.wav
There is no need like the lack of a friend	friend.wav
What fills the eye fills the heart	heart.wav
There is no strength without unity	strength.wav
It is a long road that has no turning	road.wav
Listen to the sound of the river and you will get a trout	river.wav

- Save the web page and preview the web page in both Internet Explorer and Netscape Navigator.
- Turn on your speakers and test all the hyperlinks.

Check Your Work

 To see the completed version of the Irish Proverbs web site log on to **www.gillmacmillan.ie.**

Web Assignment 2

Create an Image Map

 In this web assignment you will learn how to divide an image into clickable regions, each of which is a hyperlink to a separate web page.

 To complete this assignment, you need:

 Dreamweaver

 Internet Explorer

 Step by Step Web Design CD

Web designers often use images as hyperlinks. In Web Project 4 (Online Computer Tutorial), we used button images as hyperlinks. Each button image was a hyperlink to a specific web page. In Web Project 5 (Online Database), we used an up arrow image as a hyperlink to a named anchor to allow the web page viewer to scroll quickly up a web page.

In this assignment you will learn how to divide an image into clickable areas, allowing a single image with multiple hyperlinks to be used as a navigation device. A common example of this where a single image of a map of Ireland has 32 clickable regions (for each county). Each clickable region is a hyperlink to a specific file. These clickable regions are called hotspots.

Create an Image Map

 In this assignment, you use an image of a computer motherboard to create hotspot hyperlinks to seven different web pages. As the web page viewer moves the mouse pointer over the motherboard image on the completed web page, the mouse pointer changes from a pointing arrow to a pointing hand when it comes to a hotspot. By clicking on a hotspot, the web page viewer will be able to jump to a different web page. The motherboard image serves as a navigation device. When you have completed this exercise, your web page will look something like Fig. 7.1.

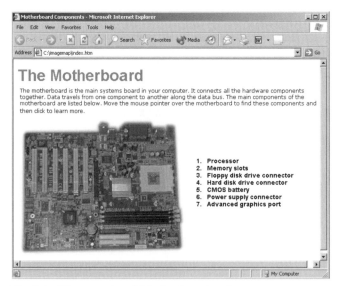

Fig. 7.1 The completed Motherboard web page

1.  Create a new folder named **imagemap** on a floppy disk, zip disk, USB storage device or hard disk.

2. 🗀 imagemap Create an **images** sub-folder inside the **imagemap** folder.

   🗀 images

3. 💿 🗀 Image Map   Open the **Image Map** folder on the *Step by Step Web*
   🗀 Web Pages   *Design* CD. It contains two sub-folders. Copy all the
   🗀 Images   files from the Web Pages folder to the **imagemap** folder on your own disk.

4. Copy all the files from the **Images** folder on the CD to the **images** folder on your own disk.

5. 🎵 In Dreamweaver, set up a new site named **motherboard** linked to
   Dreamweaver the **imagemap** folder, using this information:
   1. Server Technology: No
   2. Edit local copies on my machine
   3. Connect to remote server: None

6. Create a new web page named **index.htm** in the motherboard site.

7. In the index.htm web page set the page title to Motherboard Components.

8. Create a CSS style named **.title** that includes these formatting instructions: 36px Arial in bold print with a colour of #339900

9. Create a CSS style named **.headings** that includes these formatting instructions: 14px Arial in bold print with a colour of #990033

10. Create a CSS style named **.text** that includes these instructions: 12px Verdana with a colour of #990033

11. Set up the web page as shown below. For useful guidelines, refer to the Remember section that follows.

The Motherboard

The motherboard is the main systems board in your computer. It connects all the hardware components together. Data travels from one component to another along the data bus. The main components of the motherboard are listed below. Move the mouse pointer over the motherboard to find these components and then click to learn more.

1. Processor
2. Memory slots
3. Floppy disk drive connector
4. Hard disk drive connector
5. CMOS battery
6. Power supply connector
7. Advanced graphics port

Remember:
- Position the **motherboard.jpg** image and the points numbered 1 to 7 by using a table.

 Tip: The table should have one row and two columns

- Apply the **.title** style to the main heading The Motherboard.
- Σ :≡ Insert the numbers in the numbered list using the Ordered List button. (The Ordered List button is in the Properties toolbar. Click the Ordered List button **before** you type the first item in the list.)

| NOTE | The Dreamweaver Properties toolbar has two buttons for creating lists. The Ordered List button :≡ numbers each item in the list. The Unordered List button ≔ places a bullet symbol before each item in the list. In HTML, the difference between an ordered and an unordered list is small. This is shown in the example. |

Example:

Ordered List	Unordered List

`<ol>`
    `<li>Item 1</li>`
    `<li>Item 2</li>`
    `<li>Item 3</li>`
`</ol>`
	`<ul>`
	    `<li>Item 1</li>`
	    `<li>Item 2</li>`
	    `<li>Item 3</li>`
	`</ul>`

Enclosing list items in <ol> </ol> numbers each item in the list, whereas enclosing list items in <ul> </ul> tags puts a bullet symbol before each item in the list.

- Apply the **.headings** style to each of the seven items in the list.
- Apply the **.text** style to the paragraph of text `The motherboard is the main....`

Creating a Hotspot

 Dreamweaver offers three ways of creating a hotspot. The one you choose depends on the shape of the area you need to select.

Rectangular Hotspot Tool
Use this hotspot tool to select a section of an image that is a rectangle shape.

Oval Hotspot Tool
Use this hotspot tool to select a section of an image that is a circle shape.

Polygon Hotspot Tool
Use this hotspot tool to select an image that is an irregular shape. Click once at each corner and then click the arrow tool to close the shape.

1.   Open the **index.htm** web page, if it is not already open
2. Click the motherboard image to select it.
3. ⬚ In the Properties toolbar, click the Rectangular Hotspot Tool button.
4. Click and drag to draw a rectangle above the processor socket on the motherboard image, as in Fig. 7.2.
5. In the Properties toolbar, click the Browse for File icon and then select **processor.htm** from the list of web pages. Enter `Central Processing Unit` as the alternative text for this hotspot (see Fig. 7.3).

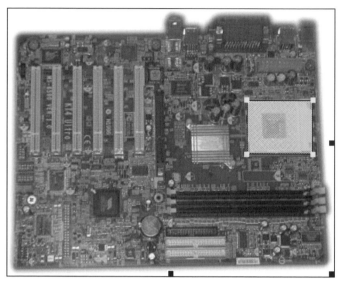

Fig. 7.2   The motherboard image with the processor hotspot

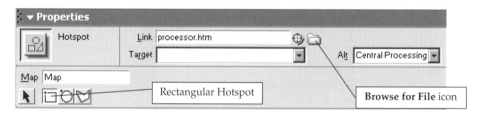

Fig. 7.3   Use the Properties toolbar to create a hotspot hyperlink

6. Using the motherboard image, set up the remaining hotspots (see Fig. 7.4).

Tip: Use the Oval Hotspot tool to create the hyperlink to **battery.htm.**

7. Set up alternative text for the hotspots using the information in Table 7.1.

Table 7.1   Alternative text for the hotspots hyperlinks

Hotspot Hyperlink	Alternative Text
memory.htm	Memory slots
floppydrive.htm	Floppy disk drive connector
harddisk.htm	Hard disk drive connector
battery.htm	CMOS battery
power.htm	Power supply connector
graphics.htm	Advanced graphics port

8. Save the web page and preview the web page in both Internet Explorer and Netscape Navigator. In each case, test all the hotspot hyperlinks.

NOTE
Note: Netscape does not support the **alt** attribute in an image map.

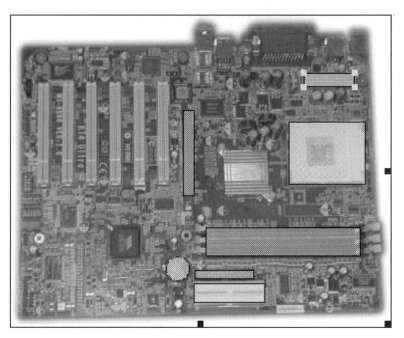

Fig. 7.4   The motherboard image with **seven** hotspots

Check Your Work

 To see the completed version of the Motherboard web site log on to **www.gillmacmillan.ie.**

SECTION 3

Web Design Project Guidelines

Web Design Project Guidelines

As part of the FETAC Level 2 Web Authoring Module you are required to design and create a fully functional web site. The project tests if you can apply what you have learned about web design to a given scenario and then design and create a web site to suit that scenario. The scenario may be real or imaginary.

As in any web design project, you must generate all web site content yourself – text, digital images, graphics, sounds and page layouts. For this reason it is much better to choose a scenario for your web authoring project based on a local topic, as this will allow easy access to the subject matter and enable you to generate any digital images yourself. The list of possible topics for a web site project is endless. You could create a web site on practically anything.

As a very broad guideline, I have listed three subject areas:
- Personal interests or hobbies
- Local interests or clubs
- Local schools or small businesses.

Your web site may not necessarily fall into one of these subject areas, but they are a useful guide. The completed web site should have at least six web pages.

The Web Authoring Project must be completed in four phases:

Phase 1: Research of subject area (10%)
Phase 2: Design and layout (30%)
Phase 3: Web site creation (50%)
Phase 4: Critical evaluation (10%)

The project must be completed in this order. You must research your subject area, specify your site and navigation structure and decide on web page layouts and colour schemes before you begin to create your web pages. It is worth noting that the same number of marks are allocated for researching, designing and evaluating your web site as for the actual creation of the web site. Many students spend too much time creating web pages and not enough time on research, design and evaluation.

Phase 1 – Research of Subject Area (10%)

Once you have decided on the subject matter for your web site project, you must research that subject under a number of headings.

Target Audience

It is important to have a clear idea of the type of people who will access your web site. Once you know who your target audience is, you should design your web site to match their needs and preferences. For example, a web site aimed at teenagers would look very different to a web site designed for older adults. Indicate who you expect to access your web site and what their characteristics are.

- What age category do they fall into – children, teenagers, young adults, older adults?
- Do you expect your web site to be accessed mainly by males, females or both?
- Will the target audience be local, national or international?

Objectives of Web Site

Outline the reasons for developing the web site. For example, in the case of a club, a web site may be needed to promote the club among the local community as well as making information related to the club more available to its members.

Identify the main function of your web site. The function of your web site may be to share information or to educate. Alternatively, your web site may have a commercial focus. Once you have identified the function of the web site, describe how the web site will carry out this function.

Gather Information

Web design is a form of publishing. Just as in newspaper, magazine or book publishing a lot of work is put into gathering information and then summarising, editing and revising that information before any text or images go on a web page. Information for your web site can be gathered using a number of techniques:

- **Personal interview:** If your project is based on a local club, business or organisation you can gather information by interviewing those involved.
- **Background knowledge:** You may already know a lot about the subject area through personal experience.
- **Library:** The library is a useful source of background information and research material.
- **Newspaper or magazine articles:** If your web site project is on a hobby or area of personal interest, you may have a wealth of information in the form of newspaper or magazine articles.
- **Internet search engines:** When all else fails, try a search engine. Always remember that the accuracy of information on the Internet is not guaranteed.

Generate Digital Images

During your research, you should generate as many digital images as possible, aiming to use the best images in your web site. A digital camera is very useful here. If you do not have access to a digital camera, you can use a standard camera and then create digital images by scanning the photos.

Evaluate Similar Web Sites

Choose two related web sites and evaluate them. Comment on:
• Use of colour and fonts
• Web page layout
• Use of images
• Ease of navigation.
You should also look at as many web sites as possible during this stage. Make a note of colour schemes, fonts, layouts and navigation structures that you like. This will help you to come up with your own web page design.

Phase 2 – Design and Layout (30%)

There are three stages in this phase of a web design project:
• Plan the web site structure.
• Design the navigation menu.
• Decide on the web page content and layout.

Web Site Structure

The site structure relates to how many web pages there are in your web site and how you can navigate from one web page to the next. How do you decide how many web pages to include in your web site? This is best approached in three steps.

• **Step 1:** Write down, in point form, everything that you want to include in your web site. Refer to the information you gathered during your research of the subject area.

• **Step 2:** Divide these points into sections. Each section should contain points that are related to each other.

• **Step 3:** The sections that you have identified are the web pages in your web site. You must now organise these web pages into a navigation structure, so people will be able to navigate through the web pages in your web site. The navigation structure determines which web pages are accessible from the home page. This may be indicated using an organisational chart.

Fig. 8.1 shows how four web pages: **u12team.htm, u16team.htm, minorteam.htm** and **seniorteam.htm** are accessible from the home page. Each of these web pages has two sub pages – a contacts web page and a league web page.

Once you have decided on a navigation structure, you must decide how web pages will be accessed. For example, in Fig. 8.1 the home page will have hyperlinks to the u12, u16, minor and senior web pages, but what if someone viewing the u12 web page wants to view the u16 web page? Will they have to go back to the home page before they can access the u16 web page or can they access the u16 web page directly from the u12 web page? A clear plan of how web pages are linked together will save you lots of editing later on.

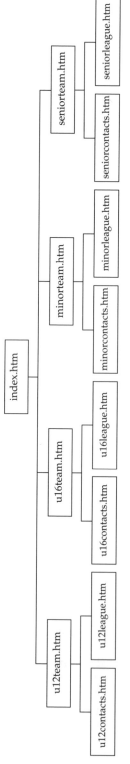

Fig. 8.1 Using an organisational chart to show the navigation structure

Navigation Menu

A navigation menu is a series of hyperlinks that allows someone to access pages in your web site. The hyperlinks may be buttons, icons or text. Navigation menus normally appear either vertically on the left of the web page or horizontally across the top of the web page. The navigation menu and site structure work together to allow people to move from one web page to another in your web site.

The most important thing about web site navigation is that it should be intuitive. In other words, the web site viewer should not have to learn from experience how to navigate through your web site. The navigation menu and site structure should make navigation easy. A well thought out site structure and navigation menu is much better than a navigation menu that looks fantastic but is very difficult to use.

You do not necessarily have to group all your hyperlinks together in a navigation menu. If you find another way of displaying hyperlinks in your web site that is easy for site visitors to understand, that's fine.

On long web pages, it is a good idea to include text versions of hyperlinks at the bottom of the web page, so that the web page viewer does not have to scroll to top of the page to access a hyperlink to another web page. Long web pages should also include bookmark hyperlinks, such as the Return to Top hyperlink, so that the web page viewer can easily move from one section of the web page to another.

Your web site should include at least two levels of navigation. In other words, at least one of the web pages accessible from the home page should have links to other web pages.

Web Page Content and Layout

Having decided on your web pages by grouping related points and thoughts together, you must decide how these points and thoughts will be presented on each web page. Each point could be represented using text, or an image or both. If you are including sound on a web page, how will the sounds be accessed? Having a clear idea of what text, images and sounds will be on each web page makes it much easier to decide on your web page layout.

The web page layout is the way in which the text, images and the navigation menu are positioned on the web page. There should be a consistency in the way each web page is structured. For example, the navigation menu should always appear in the same position.

Usually, a web site will have two main web page layouts – one for the home page and one for all the other pages in the web site. For each web page in your web site, show how text, images and the navigation menu will be positioned in relation to each other. Fig. 8.2 is an example of a web page layout.

Planning your web pages in advance like this makes it much easier to create your web pages and significantly reduces the amount of editing.

Having planned your web page layouts, you must now decide whether your page widths are specified in pixels or in percentages. If you use pixels, there will be unused space on your web pages at higher resolutions. If you use percentages, the web page will stretch to fill the horizontal space on the screen at higher resolutions.

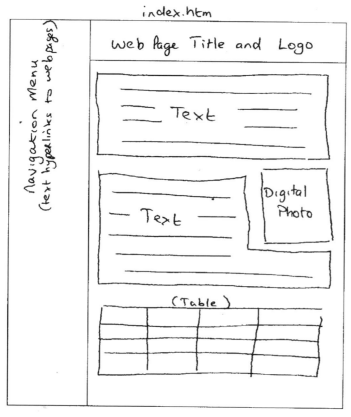

Fig. 8.2 A rough sketch of the layout of the home page

Fonts

List the fonts that you intend to use in your web site. Specify the font sizes and styles for headings and body text. It is best not to use unusual fonts. Remember, if someone views your web page and the font that you have used is not installed on their PC, the text will be displayed in the default font of their browser. The browser's default font is usually Times or Times New Roman.

Examples from Web Project 5:

Table 5.2 **Sample font specification for the home page**

HOME PAGE	
Web Page Text	**Font**
Main heading	Arial, 36px
Body text	Verdana, 12px, bold
Hyperlinks	Verdana, 12px, bold

Table 5.3   Sample font specification for all other web pages

ALL OTHER WEB PAGES	
Web Page Text	**Font**
Main heading	Arial, 36px
Paragraph and Table headings	Arial, 16px, bold
Emphasis	Verdana, 14px
Body text	Verdana, 12px
Hyperlinks	Verdana, 12px, bold

Colours

Although the issue of web safe colours is not as critical as it used to be, it is still important to realise that not everyone's PC is capable of displaying 16.7 million colours on a web page. It is possible to create an interesting colour scheme using the 216 web safe colours. Adopting this approach ensures that the colours that you choose can be seen by everyone who logs on to your web site. Specify the colours that you intend to use in your web site.

Example from Web Project 5:

Table 5.1   Sample web site colour scheme

Item	Colour	Hex Code
Page headings	Blue	#330066
Paragraph headings	Wine	#9900CC
Body text	Black	#000000
Hyperlink in link state	Red	#CC0000
Hyperlink in active state	Orange	#FF6600
Hyperlink in visited state	Black	#000000
Hyperlink in hover state	Green	#330099

File and Folder System

Decide on a folder structure to store your web pages, image files and sound files. Folder names and file names should not include spaces, should be as short as possible and should be lower case. You should regularly make a back-up of your folder as a safeguard against data loss. Fig. 8.3 shows a folder structure for a local club web site.

clubweb

   images

   sounds

Fig. 8.3   A folder system to store web pages, image files and sound files

Having set up your folder structure, make sure that you use it properly. In the case of the folder in Fig. 8.3:
- All web pages should be stored in the **clubweb** folder.
- All image files should be stored in the **images** folder.
- All sound files should be stored in the **sounds** folder.

If a red X or broken image icon appears instead of an image, it may be because you have stored the image in the wrong folder.

Phase 3 – Web Site Creation (50%)

1. Digital Image Creation and Editing

Digital Images: If you have already taken digital photos during your research and information-gathering stage, these should be downloaded from your digital camera to the images folder in your web site. All digital images should be resized so that they can be positioned on web pages together with text and other images.

Try to reduce the file size of each image as much as possible using optimisation. You will have to reach a compromise between file size and image quality. JPEG is the best file format for digital photographs.

Graphics, Symbols and Logos: If you create your own graphics and navigation buttons in Paint Shop Pro or other graphics package, these are normally saved using the GIF file format.

Make sure that all of your images are stored in the images folder.

2. Set up CSS Styles

During the design and layout stage you chose fonts for web page headings, paragraph headings, body text etc. You also specified font sizes, styles and colours for hyperlinks in link, active, visited and hover states. A separate CSS style must be set up for each set of formats. Once you have set up the CSS styles, they should be applied consistently across all web pages in your web site.

3. Navigation Menu

If you are using buttons or icons in your navigation menu, you will have already created them as separate image files. These buttons or icons are normally displayed vertically on the left of each web page or horizontally across the top of each web page. In the Southern Estate Agents web site (Web Project 3), the navigation menu was displayed horizontally across the top of the web page, as in Fig. 8.4.

Southern Estate Agents
Property Details   Financial Services   Property Valuation   Contact Details

Fig. 8.4   Navigation menu for the Southern Estate Agents web site

In the Online Database web site (Web Project 5), the navigation menu was displayed vertically on the left of the web page, as in Fig. 8.5.

Fig. 8.5   Navigation menu for the Online Database web site

The navigation menu does not necessarily have to appear on the left or at the top of your web pages. In the case of the Online Computer Tutorial (Web Project 4), the navigation menu was a series of buttons that appeared at the bottom of each lesson and test page (see Fig. 8.6).

Fig. 8.6   Navigation menu for the Online Computer Tutorial web site

The navigation menu appeared in all web pages in the Online Computer Tutorial web site except for the home page, which did not have a navigation menu. Navigation from the home page was facilitated by six text hyperlinks, each of which was a link to a specific web page. Whether you use navigation menus in some, all or none of your web pages, navigation through the web site should be easy and intuitive for your web site visitors.

It is important to note that if the navigation menu appears at the top or at the left of the web page, the web page viewer will see the menu as soon as they open the web page. One disadvantage of having the navigation menu at the bottom of the web page is that the viewer may have to scroll down before they see it. In addition, the top left of a web page is one of the few positions on a web page that you have absolute control over. If you display navigation buttons starting from the top left of a web page, they will always appear in that position whatever the screen resolution.

4. Create Web Pages by Entering Text and Positioning Images

This is the enjoyable part! Having put so much time into planning and preparation, you can finally create some web pages. It is always best to start by setting up the home page, because this is most important web page in your web site. Remember to set up the structure of each web page before you begin entering text and positioning images.

Tables are very useful for positioning elements on a web page. If all your web pages have the same structure, you can save yourself time by copying and editing existing web pages rather than setting up each new web page from scratch. Dreamweaver's site panel is very useful here. CSS Styles can also be copied from one web page to another in code view.

As you finish each web page, test it in both Internet Explorer and Netscape Navigator. If you notice something that does not work in both browsers, check for errors in the HTML code. If there are errors in the code, you may have to redesign that section of the web page so that it works in both browsers.

5. Create Site Map

A site map is a web page that contains hyperlinks to every page in a web site. Most site maps are simply a list of text hyperlinks, so they are relatively easy to create. For design ideas have a look through web sites that you visit regularly and check if they have site maps.

6. File Management

In any web site project, it is very important to keep on top of file management. The bigger the web site, the more files are generated and the more difficult it becomes to keep track of everything unless you have a structured approach to file storage and updating.

Here are the dos and don'ts of file management.

Do:
- Create and name a folder for your web pages.
- Use Dreamweaver's file management system to keep track of your files.
- Save **all** your web pages in the same folder.
- Store your image files in an images folder.
- Save images using the GIF or JPEG format.
- Store your sound files in a sounds folder.
- Assign meaningful names to your files.
- Regularly make a back-up of your web site.

Don't:
- Save a web page without first thinking **where** you are saving it.
- Include spaces, capital letters or unusual characters in file names. If you do, your hyperlinks may not work when you copy your web site to a server.
- Store image files outside the images folder. Using <img> tags to reference your images is much more difficult and prone to error if image files are in different folders. More than likely, you will see a couple of red Xs or broken image icons.
- Store sound files outside the sounds folder. If you create a hyperlink to a sound file using the incorrect folder name, the sound file will not play when the hyperlink is accessed.

Web Page Checklist

Photocopy the checklist in Table 8.1 and fill it out for every web page in your web site.

Table 8.1 Web page checklist

1. File System	Confirmed √
• Web page stored in correct folder	
• Images stored in correct folder	
• Web page and related files (images/sounds) correctly named	
• Sounds (if present) stored in correct folder	

2. Hyperlinks and HTML/XHTML Code	Confirmed √
• Hyperlinks working	
• Bookmarks working	
• HTML/XHTML code error-free	
• Unnecessary HTML/XHTML code removed	
• Code includes comments in correct places	
• Code properly structured and spaced	

3. Formatting	Confirmed √
• CSS styles applied correctly	

4. Images	Confirmed √
• Images correctly displayed	
• Alternative text for every image	

5. Browser Compatability	Confirmed √
• Web page displays correctly in Internet Explorer	
• Web page displays correctly in Netscape Navigator	

6. Monitor Resolution Web page displays correctly at the following resolutions:	Confirmed √
• 800×600	
• 1024×768	
• 1280×1024	

Phase 4 – Critical Evaluation (10%)

The aim of this section is to show that you have thought carefully about your web site and that you are aware of its strengths and weaknesses.

Strengths: List and explain what you consider to be the main strengths of your web site. Which sections of your web site are you especially pleased with?

Weaknesses: List and explain what you consider to be the main weaknesses of your web site. These may be specific features of your web site that were not completed to your satisfaction. Equally, you may have wished to include features in your web site only to discover that they were beyond the scope of the Web Authoring module.

Suggest at least three ways in which your web site could be improved if you had more time. Possible improvements should be illustrated using examples and diagrams where appropriate.

Possible Web Authoring Project Topics

- **Hobby Web Site**
  Create a web site about your hobby or a topic that you are interested in.
- **College Web Site**
  Create a web site for your college. This could be about the facilities of the college or could be a tutorial web site that gives help and assistance in certain subjects. You could also create a students union web site, which might include an online newsletter.
- **Club Web Site**
  If you are a member of a local sports club, you could create a web site for the club. This might include details of teams, leagues and upcoming fixtures.
- **Local Village Web Site**
  Many towns in villages now have their own web sites. Most of these sites give information about the local community together with forthcoming events.

For more ideas look through the examples and web projects in *Step by Step Web Design*. These are only suggestions. The list of possible web design projects is endless. What works best is if you can do your web design project on a topic that interests you.

The Web Designer's Golden Rules

To make sure that your web site looks good, is technically correct and is easy to maintain follow these rules while you are designing and creating your web site.

1. Design for the 800 × 600 web space

- It should be possible to display your web page at this resolution without any horizontal scrolling.

- All images created in a graphics package should fit in the 800×600 web space. The web page viewer should not have to scroll to see an entire image. Be aware of pixel size when you are creating your images.
- Decide how your web page will behave at higher resolutions. There are three techniques:

Technique 1: Specify widths in percentages. This means that the web page will stretch to fill the full width of the screen at higher resolutions.

Technique 2: Specify widths in pixels. If you adopt this design technique, there will be vertical blank space in your web page at higher resolutions. If your web page is aligned to the centre, the vertical blank space will be divided in two and will appear to the left and right of your web page content. If your web page is aligned to the left, all of the vertical blank space will appear to the right of your web page content.

Technique 3: Use a mixture of widths in percentages and pixels. For example, the width of a table used to position a vertical navigation menu together with text and images on a web page is set to 100%. The width of the first column of the table (containing the navigation menu) is specified in pixels. The widths of all the other columns are specified in percentages. This means that the navigation menu will always be in the same position but the rest of the web page will adjust at higher resolutions.

2. Use Fonts Sparingly and Consistently

Limit yourself to fonts that are guaranteed to work on every PC. Use fonts consistently across pages in your web site. For example, all web page headings should be formatted using the same font style, size and weight.

3. Use Web Safe Colours

When a PC's graphics card cannot display a colour used on a web page, the browser dithers that colour. This is where a close match to the colour is made by mixing other colours together. Older 8-bit graphics cards are only capable of displaying 256 colours, 216 of which are common to Netscape Navigator and Internet Explorer. These 216 colours are the web safe colours.

Limiting yourself to web safe colours prevents dithering and guarantees that everyone who views your web site will see the same colours. When you are creating GIF images, make sure you choose from a palette of web safe colours. The issue of web safe colours is not so important when creating digital photographs.

Use web safe colours and apply them consistently across web pages in your web site. For example, the colour of hyperlinks (link, visited, active and hover) should be the same in every web page. If you have used specific colours for the web page heading, paragraph headings and body text, make sure that the colour scheme is applied consistently across all pages in the web site.

4. Structure and Comment Your Code

Once a web site has been created and published on the World Wide Web, that is not the end of the story. The web site will have to be updated from time to time. Most of the updating can be done in design view, but sometimes you will find that you have to work in code view. Messy and unstructured code is very difficult to understand and edit. If you put a little effort into structuring your code at the time you create the web page, you will save yourself editing time later on. Including comments in your code will help you and others to understand what the function of the code is.

Example: Poorly structured uncommented code

```
<table>
<tr bgcolor="#FF6600">
 <td colspan="2<a href="lesson1.htm">Item
 1</a></td>
  <td colspan="2"><a href="lesson2.htm">Item
 2</a></td>
 <td colspan="2"><a href="lesson3.htm">Item
 3</a></td>
 </tr>
</table>
```

Example: Well-structured commented code

```
<!- Table with 1 row and 3 columns->
<!- Each cell contains a hyperlink to another web page ->
<table>
  <tr bgcolor="#FF6600">

    <td colspan="2">
    <a href="lesson1.htm">Item 1</a>
    </td>

    <td colspan="2">
    <a href="lesson2.htm">Item 2</a>
    </td>

    <td colspan="2">
    <a href="lesson3.htm">Item 3</a>
    </td>
  </tr>
</table>
```

5. Make Your Web Pages XHTML-Compliant

Although all browsers recognise HTML now, in the future they will only recognise XHTML. There are only a few minor differences between HTML and XHTML. For example, in XHTML the syntax of a break tag is <br /> whereas in HTML it is

. You can make your web pages XHTML-compliant by ticking the Make Document XHTML Compliant check box each time you create a new web page in Dreamweaver.

6. Less is More

Do not try to pack as much text and as many images as possible into a web page. You do not have to use up all the blank space on a web page. In fact, a web page often looks better when there is unused space. Remember, it is just as easy to split information across two web pages than to cram it into one web page.

7. Test Your Web Pages in Different Browsers

Although the majority of people use Internet Explorer, there is a significant number using Netscape Navigator. Opera is another browser to be aware of. Browsers can be downloaded free from www.microsoft.com, www.netscape.com or www.opera.com. The best approach is to test each web page as you create it to make sure that it works in all browsers. It is also a good idea to test your web pages in older versions of the browsers. This is because not all web surfers have the most up-to-date browser installed on their system. Features that work in the most up-to-date version of a browser may not work in earlier versions of that browser.

8. Keep Your Web Site Up To Date

Designing and creating a web site requires a lot of effort. Once the web site is live on the World Wide Web, it must be updated to keep it current. The kind of web site determines how often it should be updated. A news service web site would be updated a number of times every day, but a college web site would only need to be updated when a course changes or when a new course is being offered.

A lot of companies fall down in the area of web site maintenance. They simply do not keep their web site up to date! If someone accesses your web site and sees information is out of date, they may not access your web site again. If your web site includes links to other web sites, these should be checked regularly to make sure that they are all working correctly. As a web site designer, you should decide in advance how the process of web site updating will occur.

Once your web site is live, you should make sure that you know the answers to the following questions:

- Who will have responsibility for updating the web site?
- What resources should be made available to the person(s) responsible for updating the web site?
- When will the web site be updated?
- How regularly will the web site be updated?

HTML Tags Glossary

These are the HTML tags, special characters and CSS properties and values introduced in *Step by Step Web Design*.

HTML Tags

Tag Name	Description
ANCHOR	The Anchor tag is used to create a hyperlink to a web page, a bookmark an email address or another web site. The text or image enclosed in the opening and closing anchor tags becomes a hyperlink. *Examples:* 1. Hyperlink to a web page `<a href="index.htm">Home</a>` 2. Hyperlink to a bookmark `<a href="#top">Return to Top</a>` 3. Hyperlink to an email address `<a href="mailto:someone@somewhere.com">Email Us</a>` 4. Hyperlink to an external web site `<a href="http://www.gillmacmillan.ie">Publishing</a>`
AREA *Attributes* shape coords href	The Area tag is used to identify a hotspot in an image. • **shape** attribute can have a value of "rect", "circle" or "poly" • **coords** attribute indicates the position of the hotspot on the screen • **href** attribute identifies the web page that the hotspot is linked to *Example:* `<area shape="circle" coords="167,245,12" href="battery.htm" alt="CMOS Battery" />`
BLOCKQUOTE	Text enclosed in blockquote tags is indented from the left edge of the screen. *Example:* `<blockquote>` `Text in this paragraph will be indented from the left` `edge of the screen.` `</blockquote>`
BODY	The Body section of a HTML document contains text that appears on the web page when it is viewed in Internet Explorer. *Example:* `<body> </body>`
BOLD	Text enclosed in bold tags is displayed in bold print in the browser. *Example:* `<b>Month</b>`

Tag Name	Description
BREAK	The Break tag instructs HTML to go onto a new line in a web page. Each break tag is equivalent to pressing the Enter key once. *Example:* ` `
COMMENT	Allows you to insert descriptive comments in your HTML code. The beginning of a comment is indicated by <!-- and the end of a comment is indicated by -->. Anything typed between these symbols is not interpreted as HTML code by the browser. *Example:* `<!--Beginning of Table-->`

DESCRIPTION	If your web site is found by a search engine, the search engine may display text contained in the description meta tag in the search results.
	
	Example:
	`<meta name="Description" content="Access the Step by Step`
	`Databases online - all you need to start using`
	`databases"/>`

DIVISION *Attributes* **align** **id** **class**	Used to isolate sections of a web page. Divisions can be identified by adding the id or class attribute to the opening <div> tag. Styles can be applied to text contained between opening and closing <div> tags by adding the id or class attribute to the opening <div> tag. • **align** can be "left", "center" or "right" • **id** and **class** are used to link to CSS styles *Example:* `<div class="text"></div>`
FONT *Attributes* **face** **size** **color**	Text enclosed in opening and closing font tags will be displayed in the style, size and colour specified in the opening font tag. The font tag is being replaced by CSS Styles. Future versions of browsers may not recognise the font tag. • **face** can be any font installed on your PC • **size** ranges from 1 to 7 • **color** can be any RGB colour code *Example:* `<font face="Arial" size="1" color="#990000">Hello</font>`

Tag Name	Description
HEAD	The Head section of a HTML document contains the page title, meta tags and CSS styles. *Example:* `<head> </head>`
HEADING *Attributes* **align**	Text enclosed in <h1></h1> tags will be displayed in the Heading 1 style in the browser. <h2>, <h3>, <h4>, <h5> and <h6> tags can also be used. <h1> tags produce the largest text, with <h6> being the smallest. • **align** can be "left", "center" or "right" *Example:* `<h1 align= "center">Welcome To My Web Site</h1>`
HORIZONTAL RULE *Attributes* **size** **color** **width** **align**	Creates a horizontal line in a web page. • **size** refers to the thickness of the line and is specified in pixels • **color** can be any RGB code • **width** can be specified in pixels or percentage • **align** can be "left", "center" or "right" *Example:* `<hr size= "5" color= "#FF0000" width= "80%" align="center">`
HTML	Every web page begins with an opening HTML tag and ends with a closing HTML tag. *Example:* `<html> </html>`
IMAGE *Attributes* **alt** **vspace** **hspace**	Displays a photo or a graphic in a web page. • **alt** displays alternative text when the mouse pointer is positioned above the image • **vspace** inserts space above and below the image • **hspace** inserts space to the left and right of the image *Example:* `<img src="images/backdrop.jpg" alt="Dun Laoghaire Harbour" vspace="10" hspace="10" />`
ITALICS	Text enclosed in italic tags is displayed in italics in the browser. *Example:* `<i>January</i>`
KEYWORDS	If the search term entered in a search engine matches one of the keywords specified in the Keywords meta tag, the search engine will find your web site. *Example:* `<meta name= "Keywords" content=" database, Microsoft Access, data, data entry, sort, table, query, report, macro, module, data entry form" />`

Tag Name	Description

LIST ITEM	Each item in an ordered or unordered list must be enclosed in list item tags.
	
	Example:
	`<ol>`
	`<li>Hard Disk</li>`
	`<li>Floppy Disk</li>`
	`<li>Zip Disk</li>`
	`</ol>`

MARQUEE *Attributes* behavior width direction loop	Text enclosed in marquee tags moves horizontally across the computer screen. • **behavior** can be scroll, slide or alternate • **width** can be specified in pixels or percentage • **direction** can be left or right • **loop** can be any positive number or infinite *Example:* `<marquee behavior="alternate" width= "80%" loop= "infinite" />`

ORDERED LIST
Attributes
type
start
	Indicates the beginning and end of a numbered list.
	• **type** can be i, I, a, A or 1.
	i produces lower case roman numerals
	I produces upper case roman numerals
	a produces a lower case alphabetical list
	A produces an upper case alphabetical list
	1 produces a standard numbered list. The default is 1.
	
	• **start** can be used to specify a starting position other than 1, for example, start="5" or start="e"
	
	Example:
	`<ol type= "a">`
	`<li>Hard Disk</li>`
	`<li>Floppy Disk</li>`
	`<li>Zip Disk</li>`
	`</ol>`

PARAGRAPH *Attributes* align id class	Text enclosed in paragraph tags can be treated as one unit separate from other text on the page, for alignment and formatting purposes. Styles can be applied to text contained between opening and closing `<p>` tags by adding the id or class attribute to the opening `<p>` tag. • **align** can be "left", "center" or "right" • **id** and **class** are used to link to CSS styles *Example:* `<p class="text"> </p>`

Tag Name	Description
SPAN *Attributes* id class	Used to isolate sections of a web page. Specific parts of the web page can be identified by adding the id or class attribute to the opening <span> tag. Styles can be applied to text contained between opening and closing <span> tags. Unlike the <div> and <p> tags, the <span> tag does not include a line break, so it is very useful for isolating individual words or phrases. • **id** and **class** are used to link to CSS styles *Example:* `<span class="text"> </span>`
STYLE	Used in the Head section to indicate to the browser where the CSS styles are specified. *Example:* `<style> </style>`

TABLE
 	
Attributes
 	
width
 	
align
 	
border
 	
bordercolor
 	
cellspacing
 	
cellpadding
	Indicates the beginning and the end of a table.
	• **width** can be specified in pixels or percentage
	• **align** can be "left", "center" or "right"
	• **border** width is specified in pixels
	• **bordercolour** can be set to any RGB colour code
	• **cellspacing** is the amount of empty space around the borders of each table cell. Cellspacing is specified in pixels. Increasing the cellspacing pushes the table cells away from each other.
	• **cellpadding** is the amount of empty space between the cell contents and the borders of the cell. Cellpadding is specified in pixels. Increasing the cellpadding pushes the borders away from the cell contents
	
	Example:
	`<table width="80%" align="center" border="1"`
	`bordercolor= "#000000" cellspacing="10"`
	`cellpadding="5">`
	
	`</table>`

TABLE DATA *Attributes* align bgcolor rowspan colspan valign	Each cell in a table is specified with opening and closing <td> tags. • **align** can be "left", "center" or "right" • **bgcolor** can be any RGB colour code • **rowspan** merges cells vertically • **colspan** merges cells horizontally • **valign** aligns data in cells that have been merged with rowspan *Example:* `<td rowspan="3" valign="top" bgcolor="#FF0000"> </td>`

TABLE ROW
 	
Attributes
 	
bgcolor
	Each row in a table is specified with opening and closing <tr> tags.
	• **bgcolor** can be any RGB colour code
	
	Example:
	`<tr bgcolor="#990000">`
	`<td align="center"> </td>`
	`<td align="center"> </td>`
	`</tr>`

Tag Name	Description
TITLE	Text entered between the opening and closing title tags appears in the title bar of the browser window. Title tags are added to the Head section of the HTML code. *Example:* `<title>Welcome to My Web Site</title>`
UNDERLINE	Text enclosed in opening and closing underline tags is underlined when displayed in the browser. This tag should be used with care because underlined text may be mistaken for hyperlink text. *Example:* `<u>Web Design</u>`

UNORDERED LIST
 	
Attributes
 	
type
	Indicates the beginning and end of a bulleted list.
	• **type** can be disc, circle or square, each producing a different type of bullet symbol
	
	Example:
	`<ul type= "square">`
	`<li>Hard Disk</li>`
	`<li>Floppy Disk</li>`
	`<li>Zip Disk</li>`
	`</ul>`

HTML Special Characters

Name	Code	Effect
non-breaking space	` `	Each ` ` is equivalent to pressing the spacebar once.
euro sign	`&euro;`	Displays a euro sign.
less than sign	`&lt;`	Displays a less than sign>
greater than sign	`&gt;`	Displays a greater than sign<

CSS Properties and Values

Property	Associated Values	Example
font-family	any valid font name	`font-family: Arial,` `Helvetica,sans-serif;`
font-size	any size in pixels	`font-size: 12px;`
font-weight	normal, bold, bolder, lighter	`font-weight: bold;`
color	any hexidecimal colour code	`color: #330099;`
text-decoration	underline, none	`text-decoration: none;`